FAITH & FINANCES

The Dynamics of Monies and Ministries

Dr. Hong Yang & Dr. Esther Yang

All Scripture quotations are taken from the following Bible versions:

The *New King James Version.* Copyright © 1979, 1980, 1982, 1990, 1995, Thomas Nelson, Inc., Publishers. All rights reserved.

The *New International Version®. NIV®.* Copyright © 1973, 1978, 1984, 2011 by International Bible Society. Used by permission of Zondervan Publishing House. All rights reserved.

Cover Design: Dr. Esther Yang
Text Editing: Dr. Esther Yang
Text Layout: HGR Editorial Services

For further information, please contact: hongyang9264@gmail.com

ISBN: 978-1-64288-031-1

Copyright © 2018 by Dr. Hong Yang and Dr. Esther Yang

ALL RIGHTS RESERVED: No part of this publication may be reproduced, stored in a retrieval system, or transmitted in any form or by any means—electronic, mechanical, photocopy, recording, or any other—except for brief quotations in printed reviews, without the prior permission of Dr. Hong Yang and Dr. Esther Yang.

Published by Pathway Press
Cleveland, TN 37311

Printed in the United States of America

But remember the LORD your God, for it is he who gives you the ability to produce wealth, and so confirms his covenant, which he swore to your forefathers, as it is today (Deut 8:18).

Let them shout for joy, and be glad, that favor my righteous cause: yea, let them say continually, Let the Lord be magnified, which hath pleasure in the prosperity of his servant (Ps 35:27).

In the house of the wise are stores of choice food and oil, but a foolish man devours all he has (Pro 21:20).

Command those who are rich in this present world not to be arrogant nor to put their hope in wealth, which is so uncertain, but to put their hope in God... Command them to do good, to be rich in good deeds, and to be generous and willing to share. In this way they will lay up treasure for themselves as a firm foundation for the coming age, so that they may take hold of the life that is truly life (I Tim 6:17-19).

And without faith it is impossible to please God, because anyone who comes to Him must believe that He exists and that He rewards those who earnestly seek him (Heb 11:6).

For everyone born of God overcomes the world. This is the victory that has overcome the world, even our faith (I Jn 5:4).

Beloved, I pray that you may prosper in all things and be in health, just as your soul prospers (III Jn 2).

The wise does At Once what the fool does at last (Jewish Proverb).

Money isn't everything, but it ranks right up there with oxygen — Zig Ziglar

The final batter for Christian discipleship will be over the money problem: till this is solved, there can be no universal application of Christianity --- Balzac

Earn all you can, save all you can, and give all you can — John Wesley

Table of Contents

Introduction 7

Chapters:

1. Faith and Finances: Scriptural Stewardship as Spiritual Leadership --- Authoritative Approaches and Authentic Applications.. 11

2. Joseph and Spiritual Stewardship: An Excellent Example to Examine and Emulate.. 31

3. Jesus and the Parable of the Talents 41

4. Jesus and the Parable of the Unjust Steward 53

5. The Jewish Values, Views, Wisdom, Work, and Ways To Wealth.. 65

6. Faith and Finance: Puritan Ethic, Protestant Spirit, and Proverbial Wisdom on Work and Wealth.......................... 83

7. Money Matters: Erroneous Religious Folklores and Solid Biblical Principles on How to Make and Manage Money 107

8. Digging Your Way Out of Debt: The Causes, The Consequences, and The Cures of Indebtedness.............. 125

9. Budgeting Your Way to Balance and Bountifulness! 149

10. Put Your Money To Work for You: Savings and Investments 161

11. Caring and Sharing, Loving and Giving: The Gift of Generosity 175

12. Monies and Ministries: A Relational Approach to Fundraising for Kingdom Services 189

13. Effective Faith Strategies for Financial Vision, Vigor, And Victory 221

14. Faith and Finances: A Personal Theology with A Powerful Testimony 235

15. Living A Life That Really Matters: A Passion for the Kingdom 263

Conclusion 279

Bibliographic References 287

Introduction

Without any doubts whatsoever, the topics of the vitality of the Christian faith, the complexity of finances both personal and corporate, and the interesting, intriguing, intimate and integral connectedness of money sufficiency and the growth and expansion of Kingdom ministries, have been my long-term occupation and even mild obsession over the past 30 years in my (HY) humble and faithful service to our Savior and my Lord Jesus. The dynamics of their interdependence and interrelatedness has long excited me and fascinated me to the point of careful examination and profound exploration both academically and experientially. By God's grace and for God's glory as always, we have had the special honor and unusual privilege to travel and minister in over 100 countries. Having personally witnessed, met and visited with countless good peoples of numerous cultures, colors and creeds who for a variety of reasons, struggle with the scarcity and even extreme poverty of basic and bare daily necessities, I have been feeling in my soul an unusually strong and burning desire to not only practically and temporarily "give" out more fishes to them, but also to scripturally and systematically "teach" them how to fish strategically and skillfully to feed and fund themselves and those they love and serve. A world-famous, widely quoted Chinese proverb attributed to the greater philosopher Confucius 2500 years ago summarizes this vital and essential life lesson well by accurately declaring: Give a man a fish to eat, he will be hungry before the end of the day; but teach a man how to fish, he will be well fed the rest of his life! How true this principle has been in our ministries!

It is therefore, the central intention of this book to explore and examine sound and solid scriptural principles so as to encourage and equip God's people for daily life practices in theirs kingdom services! As one carefully and prayerfully studies the precious, powerful, peerless and piercing Word of God, the the inerrant and infallible Holy Bible, it becomes instantly obvious that so much has been taught in this area of faith and finances, monies and ministries, emphatically written to teach us children of Almighty God so that through the encouragement and the endurance of the Scriptures, we will be able to live enthusiastically with all joy, peace, and hope (Rom 15:4,13) and to succeed with more abundance of the blessings of the victorious life here and now with eager expectation for the eternal life there and then! Our very good, great, gracious, glorious and extremely generous God, who is the Maker and the Master of the heavens and the earth (Gen 1:1) and the Owner of everything in it (Ps 24:1, Hag 2:8), the Sustainer and Perpetuator of our lives, promises us who already have, that MORE will He give to us so that we will have abundance as a result of our obedience to Him and our diligence for Him (Matt 7:11, 25:29). The devil who is evil (he is also a dumb devil!) comes to try to steal our joy, kill our peace, and destroy our life, but our Lord Jesus Christ has come to give us life so that through our complete trust in Him, full dependence on Him, and our total obedience to Him and His divine instructions with our daily consistent applications, we shall live even more victoriously and more abundantly as a credible and compelling witness to His faithfulness and a convicting testimony for His eternal greater glory and majesty (John 10:10).

    This book has been written with Kingdom authority based on our daily intimacy, with special spiritual energy from consistently and constantly "eating" the Bread of Life, and with a serious sense of personal urgency (John 4:34-35) due to the dire necessity for the people of God needing to be thoroughly equipped and mightily empowered in both faith and finance to fund more mighty missions and multiple ministries. Fifteen chapters have been carefully developed based on vast research and strong conviction, along with key questions for personal application at the end of each chapter. They are succinctly presented from highly organized biblical, theological, historical, personal and practical perspectives with pointed priority! We truly believe and surely know that anyone

Introduction

reading these pages with an intelligent mind and prayerful heart will encounter challenging information in the head, experience inspirational formation in the heart, and engage in financial and ministerial life-transformation with persistent actions of the hand. Spiritually and financially healthy habits will be cultivated to help secure, by the grace of God, the desired victory and prosperity with our higher purpose for His greater glory (Col 3:23)! And our sincere prayer for you who read the book is according to III John 2, that the three-fold blessings of God will flow to you, fill you and even flood you as you flourish in, through and for the Lord Jesus! Amen!

Chapter 1

Faith and Finances: Scriptural Stewardship as Spiritual Leadership Authoritative Approaches & Authentic Applications

Heb 11:1, 3, 6 --- Now faith is the substance of things hoped for, the evidence of things not seen... By faith we understand that the worlds were framed by the Word of God, so that the things which are seen were not made of things which are visible... But without faith, it is impossible to please Him, for he who comes to God must believe that He is, and that He is a rewarder of those who diligently seek Him.

Faith pleases God, and God prospers the faithful! Always!
Your personal theology is your practical fiscalosophy that will definitely define and determine your future of either poverty or prosperity, just as your mentality decides your economic mobility.

Romans 1:17 For in the gospel a righteousness from God is revealed, a righteousness that is by faith from first to last, just as it is written: "The righteous will live by faith."

Faith increases finances, and finances increase faith
Proverbs 23:7 --- For as he thinks in his heart, so is he.

As the mind goes, the man follows. In other words, if you change your thoughts, you will change your life, for your life is the sum total of your thoughts. How you think will surely determine how you will live. What's in your head will decide what's going to be in your hand.

Matt 16:8-11 --- So the master commended the unjust steward because he had dwelt shrewdly. For the sons of this world are more shrewd in their generation than the sons of light. And I say to you, make friends for yourselves by unrighteous mammon, that when you fail, they may receive you into an everlasting home. He who is faithful in what is least is faithful also in much... Therefore, if you have not been faithful in the unrighteous mammon, who will commit to your trust the true riches?

The final battle for Christian discipleship will be the money problem: till that is solved, there can be no universal application of Christianity. --- Balzac

John 13:15, 17 --- For I have given you an example, that you should do as I have done to you. Now that you know these things, blessed are you if you do them --- Christ the Lord

I Corinthians 11:1 --- Follow my example as I follow the example of Christ --- Paul the Apostle

Faith Is It!

With no doubts whatsoever, faith, in the mighty living Jehovah God who revealed Himself by His Holy Spirit, through His Holy Scripture that became incarnated in Jesus the Christ, both the Son of God and God the Son, is the absolute foundation of our identity and industry – who we are and what we do as the children of the Lord. Like the ancient heroes of faith described vividly in Hebrews 11, we are also saved by faith, justified by faith, sanctified by faith, Spirit-baptized by faith and shall be eternally glorified by our unwavering faith in its Author and its Finisher the Lord Jesus Christ (Heb 12:1-3)! Faith is not a passive static state of the mind; but rather as a verb, faith is dynamic and transformative living. By faith, we live abundantly, and move victoriously and have our being fully in Christ Jesus (Acts 17:28). We daily function by faith as the redeemed and the righteous of God, regardless of our feelings, by fully focusing on our Founder. We are firmly fixed on the foundation of the Word of God, and we courageously fight the good fight of faith, knowing beyond the shadow of a doubt that the Lord Jesus has already won us the victory on the cross over the devil, demons, death, hell, and the grave (I Cor 15: 57-58). The Lord knows the way that we take, and "when He has tested me, I shall come forth as gold" (Job 23:10). In order to be proven genuine, we have to be tested and pass the test of the Lord (Gen 22, the test of faith for Father Abraham). I Pet 1:7 affirms the truth that our faith in Jesus Christ the Lord is proven to be genuine by the test of fire, and that this faith is much more precious than gold, for the praise, honor and glory of our God!

Faith and Fruit

The more we have deep faith and the more we courageously exercise this dynamic divine gift of faith, the more we will become faithful, fearless, forceful and fruitful for the Lord and for the cause of Christ. The more our heart is filled with the living faith in our Almighty God, the less fear we will experience in our lives. More faith, more focus; More faith, more fire; More faith, more freedom; More faith, more favors! The more of God's favor, the less will be your labor. More faith, more finances; more faith, more fruit. As the Lord emphatically teaches His disciples in John 15:2 and 8, "Every branch in Me that does not bear fruit, He takes away; and every branch that bears fruit, He prunes, that it may bear More fruit… By this My Father is glorified, that you bear much fruit, so you will be My disciples." Through His necessary disciplinary (pruning, purging and purifying) process, we as His disciples will become more and more responsible and mature spiritually, relationally, mentally, physically and especially financially to bear fruit, much fruit, more fruit and fruit that will remain lasting fruit. The Lord impressed upon me (HY) from early on in my Christian work when I was newly saved by the power of the Word of God and the conviction of the Spirit of God through dreams and visions from heaven, with this very verse --- John 15:16, that still impacts me every single day now as I go into all the world to preach the Gospel and teach the Word for more and more souls and disciples for Jesus, "You did not choose Me, but I chose you and appointed you that you should go and bear fruit, and that your fruit should remain." Move forward and look upward. Do not ever look back, for "No one, having put his hand to the plow, and looking back, is fit for the kingdom of God." (Lk 9:62). The Lord Jesus Himself urges us to always remember the life lesson from Lot's wife and the reason of her death so that we will be sufficiently warned not follow her path. The kingdom of God and the promises of God are all before us and not behind us. Looking back causes one to become backward both in hinting and in living, even to death-ward! The cross of Christ is before me, and the world of sins is behind me, no looking back and no turning back! Live a life that really matters with no regret, no retreat, no reserves and never ever retire! Re-fire and not retire! You are good before you are dead, then life gets much better, for the end of this earthly life is just the beginning of our eternal life in heaven with the Lords! Thus Philippians 1:21 the great Apostle Paul declares, For to me, to live is Christ and to die is gain!

Finances Are Essential and Vital

Money isn't everything, but it ranks right up there with oxygen — Zig Ziglar. This is our deep personal conviction both theologically and financially that faith increases finances, and in turn, finances increase faith for increase, growth and expansion. Faith pleases God and God prospers the faithful! If faith is foundational and fundamental for us true disciples and followers of Christ, then finances are critical, crucial, vital and essential for the furtherance of our faith. Both the Bible and the Lord Jesus talk much more about the issue of money than faith and prayer, heaven and hell combined! There are at least 2350 verses in the Bible that have to do with money and possessions while there are only about 500 verses on the subject of faith and prayers. As a matter of fact, most of the Jesus parables and Biblical proverbs (approximately two thirds) have an implicit and explicit connection with businesses and finances with both direct and indirect instructions with His clear command for our actions and applications. The number one item repeatedly but not redundantly stressed within the money matter is the gift of generosity, or the need for generous giving. And in order to be a generous giver to the Lord and the causes He is most concerned about, one must learn to be intelligent, diligent, and consistently disciplined to make money, save money and manage and multiply money with compounding interests of increases, as common sense wisdom informs us that we can not give what we do not have!

What is important is frequent and what is frequent has to be important. What is clear is important and what is important has to be made very clear. These are a few infallible hermeneutical principles we have learned both in seminaries and worldwide ministries over the past 30 years. Therefore the reason the Lord and the Bible speak so frequently and emphatically, and so clearly about money is because money is important to our life and ministries, just as finances are critical for our faith development! Through the thousands of verses in parables and proverbs, the Lord Jesus also wants us to learn and to know His divine and eternal perspective and priority in this vital and crucial area of life. Jesus dealt so much with money matters "because money does matter." (Dayton, 2011, P. 2). Money matters in life and ministry.

Jesus taught in the four gospels more about money than about any other single subject because "money is of first importance" when it comes to a man's real nature. No one can live without some measure or amount of money. Money is the exact index to a man's real character. All throughout the Holy Bible, there is clearly "an intimate correlation between the development of a man's character and how he handles his money." Through several powerful parables and real-life encounters and moving stories such as the parable of the rich fool (Lk 12), the touching transformation of Zacchaeus in Luke 19, and the rich young ruler in Matt 19), the Lord established for us this timeless truth and practical principle --- there is a powerful relationship between a person's true spiritual condition and his attitude and actions concerning money and possessions (Alcorn, PP. 15, 18). Undoubtedly, there exists a close correlation between faith and finances, between monies and ministries, and between loving and giving as will be dealt with in details in later chapters.

Stewardship According to the Scripture

"Let a man so consider us, as servants of Christ and stewards of the mysteries of God. Moreover, it is required in stewards that one be found faithful." (I Cor 4:1-2). A steward is a manager of the affairs and properties of another with the sacred trust from the owner. The word for stewardship in the New Testament comes from the Greek "oikonomia", from which we derive the word for "economy". Stewardship refers to the responsible and righteous management of another's property affairs, business or household. As an administrator for another, the steward must be proven unselfish and righteous, trustworthy and capable, as in the case of the good example of Joseph for Potiphar and Pharaoh. The steward himself is not the owner, but only the manager. He or she faithfully, wisely, proactively and productively directs the affairs, the finances and the keeping of records for the owner and master of the estates, large households or businesses. Spiritual stewardship according to the Holy Scriptures consists of the careful, prayerful, truthful, responsible and fruitful management of what has been entrusted to the steward and his care. According to the Word of God, we as faithful followers of the Lord, are all stewards by divine appointment and commission to take care of the Father's business on earth that He has graciously and generously entrusted to us. And we are to be integral and profitable in the details of our diligent stewardship, for we will have to give a detailed account to the Lord in the end (ROM 14:12). The very first requirement of being the manager of the Lord's ministries and mysteries is the character of faithfulness and loyalty. The managers are to respect and honor the wishes and desires of the Master, to obey God the Creator and the Owner faithfully and they are to serve the people wholeheartedly as onto God. They are to be held accountable in matters both small and big in their faithful service with that sacred trust (please carefully and prayerfully read and study such key scriptural verses as Matt 25:19,

Lk 16:1-2, Rom 14:12, and Heb 4:13, 13:17 as we will deal with the topic of accountability in much more details in later chapters.

As managers of God's world, properties, affairs, and monies, the stewards must be proven to be not only faithful, but also wise, just, decisive, effective, and fruitful in his ministries for the Lord! As in all things, there are always two sides to the same coin or for the same matter. In any of our studies of leadership, discipleship, and spiritual stewardship, two vital and essential parts must be taken into full consideration, namely, God's part and our part, for even the mighty operation of God in the affairs of the world requires the obedient cooperation of His children. As the late Rev. Myles Munroe of dominion theology often declared, that without God, man cannot; but without man, God will not. This is indeed a law of reciprocity in the Kingdom of God exemplified and illustrated with the "If" and the "Then" in II Chron 7:14, Deut 28, Lev 26, and Matt 24:14, and John 15:7. If we trust and obey the Lord, He then will be pleased to prosper us. Knowledge is necessary and very good for leadership as it is for stewardship, but knowledge by itself is never good enough. The Lord Jesus clearly teaches and challenges the disciples by precepts and by examples that now we know these things, we will be blessed only if we will do them (Jh 13:17). If we will do them, God will bless us. If we will faithfully apply what He teaches, He will fruitfully supply what we need, all our needs, abundantly and more than enough as the Lord promises us in Phil 4:19. The same is true in faith and finances in that if we will do our part according to His instruction, then the Lord will do His part in His bountiful provision to meet all our needs for His higher purpose and greater glory. We must be attentive and active as His stewards to fulfill our God-given premises before we can reasonably and confidently expect His promises. Let us take a careful look at His part and our part in this key area of faith and finances after gaining the following healthy and holistic perspective.

One of the great influential American pastors of both integrity and impact is undoubtedly the Rev. Bill Hybels (2014) who talks about developing ten practices to effectively unclutter the soul of the Christ follower. One of the areas is the money matter or clutter, as few things have the power to throw our lives into painful chaos like financial stress, with so many in the church overwhelmed with debts as a result of a dysfunctional relationship with money. Based on his vast experiential wisdom, Pastor Hybels offers five fundamental beliefs of financial reconciliation with both practical wisdom and eternal perspective (PP. 81-82):

1. All I have come from God (Jams 1:17). Our loving heavenly Father has given us everything we need and has invited us to steward our talents, time, and treasures for His purpose in the world.
2. I live joyfully within, and even intentionally beneath, God's current provision for my life (Phil 4:11-13). This implies that it's our responsibility to make the necessary adjustments in life, and not to want more than God's current provision for our lives (which would result in debts!).
3. I honor God by giving the first tenth of all my earnings to His purpose in the world (Prov 3:9-10, Mal 3:10).
4. I set aside a portion of my earnings into a saving account for emergencies, for giving opportunities and for my later years (Prov 6:6-8).
5. I live each day with an open ear toward heaven, eager to respond to any whisper from God regarding my resources. God did not set us free from sin so that we could live in bondage to debt. He wants us to be free to experience the privilege of watching our resources to help other people.

God's Part: Our Loving Creator, Owner and Sovereign Lord
The profound and powerful praise of King David (I Chro 29:10-12) makes it more than clear the sovereign ownership of God over all things everywhere. "Blessed are You, Lord God of Israel, our Father forever and ever. Yours, O Lord, is the greatness, the power and the glory. The victory and the majesty; For all that is in heaven and in earth is Yours; Yours is the kingdom, O Lord, and You are

exalted as head over all. Both riches and honor come from You, and You reign over all. In your hand is power and might. In Your hand is to make great and to give strength to all."

The Holy Scripture is our only final and absolute authority in all matters of the Christian faith, life and ministries. It offers us direction, correction and protection, as well as His sound instruction for our solid application. From the very first verse of the Bible we know that God is the Creator, Sustainer and Owner of all things both seen and unseen. The earth is the Lord's and the fullness thereof (Ps 24:1). He is the owner of every animal in the forest, and all the cattle on a thousand hills, including the hills themselves and all the filed and all the land (Ps 50:10-12, Lev 25:23). Not only the land God created is good, God also says that the gold in the land is good (Gen 2:12), and all "the silver is Mine and the gold is Mine" (Hag 2:8). God spoke all things into existence in that all things were made by Him and without Him nothing was made that was made (Jh 1:3). He maintains the position of authority and control over all His creation, and He has chosen and commissioned us to be the stewards with His sacred trust to manage His creation. God said in Gen 1:26, "Let us make man in our image, according to our likeness; let them have dominion over ..."! Wow, praise the Lord Almighty for such an honor, privilege and responsibility to magnify, testify and glorify His Holy name through our stewardship!

Our Part: "Be Good and Faithful" As His Entrusted Stewards

"Well done, good and faithful servant; you were faithful with a few things, I will put you in charge of many things; enter into the joy of your master." --- Jesus in the Parable of the Talents in Matt 25:21

The Bible teaches us clearly that our great and gracious God as the Creator, Owner and Master, has given us His servants and children, the awesome authority to be His stewards, to be in charge of managing everything that He created and always owns (Ps 8:6). As we will learn much more from the detailed studies of Luke 16 the parable of the unjust steward, and Matthew 25 the parable of the talents, God requires us to be always responsive to and responsible for His business, and we will be held accountable to, both the Source and the Resources of the Master. We are never to be selfish with any ulterior motives; we are not to be idle or lazy; and we are not to be fearful, critical, or accusatory. Rather we are to be vigilant, intelligent, diligent, perseverant, and thus excellent in all the things entrusted to us, be they small and big, as we faithfully and wisely watch out and carry out the affairs for the Lord, for His cause and by His missional prerogative.

And if we are faithful, we will become useful, forceful and very fruitful, for faith makes force, just as right makes might (even as haste makes waste!), and faith as an active verb of constant action, really does bring forth much lasting fruit and finances. Our faithfulness is a clear indication of our commitment to the cause of Christ and our faithfulness builds our Christ-like Character. Character counts the most in faith and finances! Faith and faithfulness are emphasized in both the list of the gift of the Spirit (I Cor 12) and the Fruit of the Spirit (Gal 5:22-23). Thus the meaning of Hebrews 11:6 becomes extremely obvious as a spiritual principle and a kingdom law: our faith pleases God and our God prospers the faithful! Since faith is a verb, let us exercise it daily and allow God to stretch and strengthen us through our consistent faith application and persistent faith practice so that we will be abundantly blessed to bless God and God's other children in needs. After His great exemplary object lesson of foot-washing in John 13, Jesus challenged the disciples with the same question He is using now to challenge us: "Do you understand what I have done for you?" I have set before you an example that you should do for each other as I have done for you... Not that you know these things, you will be blessed if you do them (VV 15, 17)! Always remember that we are really what we do, not what we say we will do. Faithful obedience to Jesus our Lord not only brings us material abundance, it also ensures us with spiritual confidence, personal guidance and eternal significance! And all this requires real spiritual leadership based on clear Scriptural commands. And no one can be more spiritual than he or she is scriptural. The Scriptures solidify the spirituality.

Faith and Finances:

Scriptural Stewardship as Spiritual Leadership

Abraham was the father of faith and the model of obedience in Gen 12 and 22 among his other life events. He was unmistakably a shining star with his compelling examples for us to emulate in our diligent studies of faith and finances. His trust and obedience to God brought him many bountiful blessings of riches, wealth, honor and praises from his God. Let us look at Gen 12:1-3 and learn how all this began from the humble beginning:

Now the Lord had said to Abram: "Get out of your country, from your family and from your father's house, to a land that I will show you. I will make you a great nation; I will bless you and make your name great; And you shall be a blessing. I will bless those who bless you, and I will curse him who curses you; And in you all the families of the earth shall be blessed."

What peerless, precious and powerful promises these are for Abraham and his descendants the nation of Israel and the God-fearing Jewish people forever and everywhere! Besides being divine promises that never fail, these are also visions and revelations from the Almighty Jehovah God for His chosen people, the Jews! This revelation, given by God thousands of years ago, has been and will always be crucial and critical not only for the Jewish people and nation to survive and thrive, but also for us the Christians as the people of the same gracious and generous God through adoption (I Pet 2:9). Visions as prophetic divine revelations are essential for the people of God, because where there is no vision (prophetic revelation), the people cast off restraint (go crazy, as everyone does what seems to be right in his own eyes!), but blessed is he who keeps the law. (Prov 29:18). The Word of the Lord is the root of our vision, and where there is vision, there is also clear direction and sufficient provision for the abundance and victory. His vision informs us of His will. And if it is His will, it is His bill, as the Lord does provide wherever He will guide.

As the promise and revelation of God, Gen 12:1-3 also contains the vital dynamic theology of premises (our part) and promises (God's part) in the following five levels:

1. To the level of His divine revelation, will be the level of our human responsibility;
2. To the level of our responsibility will be the level of our maturity, for only appropriate responsibility with intentionality can produce personal and spiritual maturity;
3. To the level of our maturity, will be the level of our accountability. One of the most essential elements of scriptural and spiritual stewardship is Accountability Factor that alone can ensure and ascertain faithfulness and fruitfulness. Several key verses emphatically instruct us the stewards of God the absolute necessity of accountability, and they are: Matt 25:19, Lk 16:1-2, Rom 14:12, and Heb 4:13 & 13;17); In stewardship accountability is not a luxury but an essential foundational necessity.
4. To the level of our accountability, will be the level of our integrity! No one is going to become integral if she or he refuses to be held accountable by proper leadership and authority, the ultimate being the Lord our Owner and Master Jesus known also as the Son of David. King David was deeply spiritual and thus highly successful because he manifested this stewardship quality in Ps 78:71-72. So David shepherded the people of God according to the integrity of his heart, and guided them by the skillfulness of his hands.
5. To the level of our integrity, will be the level of our impact and influence in life and ministries, as true leadership is measured in the final analysis by its influence, nothing more and nothing less, as the leadership guru Dr. John Maxwell often says! The first 3 verses of the first Psalm clearly illustrate the four key elements of Intimacy, Identity, Industry, and Influence, as stewardship and leadership must contain.

The 7 Purposes of Stewardship

Everything God has created for and given to us has a purpose to it. As stewards of the Lord, we must know what we need to do, and how we are to go about doing it. But even more importantly, we must know why we do what we do, as it has to do with our central motivational structure of the soul: the motive of the heart. Why would the Lord appoint us as His stewards over the economies of creation and redemption? According to the excellent NIV Stewardship Study Bible (P. xi), God desires to accomplish seven major purposes within each of us through our wise and faithful stewardship of His resources:

1. Unique calling --- a spiritual prompting inside of us towards fulfilling our unique role in the Body of Christ;
2. Unquestionable character --- a prompting toward who we are called to be as individuals;
3. Unquenchable compassion --- a prompting toward placing others' needs before our own;
4. Undying commitment --- a prompting towards obedience to God and His calling on our lives regardless of the cost;
5. Unending celebration --- stewardship is a constant expression of our worship to the benevolent Lord for His creation, redemption and sufficient provision for our need;
6. Unparalleled Commission --- a recognition of the privilege to share in the fulfilling of God's mission on earth;
7. Unwavering conformity --- a prompting toward conforming to God's will and desires over His creation and His resources, and in doing so, we become more and more like the Lord Jesus ((Rom 8:28-29).

The 13 Vital Aspects of the Steward Leadership

A close and prayerful survey of spiritual stewardship and Godly leadership in Scriptural instructions in general, and the dynamic and fruitful ministries of the Lord Jesus and Apostle Paul in particular, have helped us formulate the following personal convictions for a blessed life with bountiful ministries with our daily practical applications:

1. To lead is to heed (Acts 20:28). As leaders and stewards, we are responsible and will be held accountable for all our

words and deeds in the context of our relationships with others. One must take sufficient care of himself in all areas of life before he can effectively care for the flock the Lord entrusts him.

2. To lead is to read (II Tim 2:15). The steward must be diligent to apply himself to the Word of God and experientially know the truth of the Lord. She must also be well read in relevant areas of faith and finances with the Kingdom perspective and the King Jesus priority.

3. To lead is plead (II Cor 12:8). One must spend time in prayers and in intimacy with the Lord, seeking His will by studying His work before doing His work, on his knees. I am more convinced than ever before that the best theology is still the old-school kneeology that never becomes old fashioned! It is in our personal and private spiritual communion, we form a deeper and stronger union with the Lord!

4. To lead is to see the need (Jh 4). The Lord Jesus challenges us His faithful stewards to lift up our eyes and look onto the harvests for they are already white unto harvest. If we don't go quickly (Matt 28:7, Lk 14:21, Jh 9:4) to reap what's ripe, it will then be rotten and good for nothing! The needs are everywhere all over the world and are seemingly overwhelming and endless too. The harvest is truly plentiful, but the workers are few and quite idle (Matt 9 & 20). All I hear these days is the divine voice of urgency urging us to Go and Do likewise and much more (Lk 10:37 and Jh 15;2)! James 2:14-18 discusses the issue in vivid and real details. What good it is, if a man claims to have faith but has no deeds, Can such a faith save him? Suppose we see a brother or sister without clothes or daily foods. We who have plenty, just wish him or her well and yet do not do anything to meet the need with some relevant deed. What good is it? The sincere conviction and sound conclusion is that faith without deed is dead! It is hypocritical and deadly too, as such a "faith" negatively affect others around us, and is offensive to God!

5. To lead is to sow the seed (Jh 4). When there is a clear need, don't eat the seed; plant the seed that will multiply a harvest. This requires self-denial and major sacrifices that alone will cause successes. Unless a grain of wheat (rice or sorghum or corn) drops to the ground and dies, it will remain only one seed; but if it does, it will produce many more times (jh 12:24). Research studies tell us that a corn seed multiplies to the average of 400 seeds! 400 times more growth! No wonder the heart of the Great Commission is discipleship among all the nations! While conversion brings addition, discipleship makes multiplication! As 9 + 9 = 18, 9 x 9 = 81! Praise the Lord for the impact of discipleship with proper stewardship that exponentially grows the harvest! This infallible and universal Law of the Kingdom concerning sowing and reaping has been taught in several passages (II Cor 9 and Gal 6) of the Bible, especially Psalm 26 which assures us that if we sow with tears of hard work, then we will reap with great joy, bringing the sheaves with us! The promises of God never fail if we will faithfully and enthusiastically do our part.

6. To lead is to feed (Jh 13). Stewards must be responsible and of course resourceful in the critical areas of faith and finances so as to purchase more than enough foods (spiritual and physical both) to amply feed the family, the flock, an the followers before they are starved to death or instinctively run away to rich pastures for their survival.

7. To lead is to exemplify indeed (Jh 13). Albert Einstein was quoted for saying that there are only three ways to permanently influence people: example, example and example! No one can leave a worthy example for people to follow if he or she has not done anything, and has not lived the life of action and fruit. After demonstrating with the humble foot washing, the ultimate Servant Leader and the best Spiritual Model Jesus then declares, "I have set for you an example that you should do for each other as

I have done for you." (Jh 13:15). Apostle Paul urges the problematic Christians to seriously consider following his example of humility, hard work and sacrifices as they saw him following the example of the Lord (I Cor 11:1). Let us not love each other with words, but let us do so in deeds. As the ole saying goes, a friend is need is a friend in deed! Eventually, words become really cheap, meaningless and even hypocritical if they are not followed up with substantial actions. We are not what we say and declare; we are what we do and demonstrate! By our fruit, we shall be known, just as we know the trees by their fruit (Matt 7:15-20). And let us not just be wise in words only but wise in deeds also. "Do not merely listen to the Word, and so deceive yourself. Do what it says (James 1:22).

8. To lead is to weed (Acts 20:29). This is true both physically and spiritually if you have done any farming as small as a vegetable or flower garden, and have been involved in any church ministries. A whole chapter in II Peter 2 has been devoted by the Apostle Peter to dealing with the issues of weed apostles and thorny prophets who were false and fake, as did Paul in Acts 20 and II Tim 3:1-9. These "weeds" have to be exposed and uprooted before they negatively and destructively affect the whole Body of Christ.

9. To lead is to bleed (Is 53:5 & Christ on the Cross). In the necessary process of exposing and uprooting the wicked weeds, the enemy of our soul will directly attack us or arouse and deceive many others to even destroy us. The devil is evil and the devil is desperate as he knows that his days are numbered before the Second coming of the Lion of the Tribe of Judah! Spiritual stewards and leaders must be prepared to count the cost and pay the price of persecution and even martyrdom, as has happened and will continue to happen in these precarious and perilous end times.

10. To lead is to speed (Jh 9:4). Scriptural leadership concerning spiritual stewards is one of urgency, not idleness or laziness,

Faith and Finances:

hesitation, reservation, disruption, distraction, or other forms of procrastination and excuses. WE must carry our God-given responsibility with pure passion and personal urgency as the Master Himself said and did (Luke 14:15-24) in many places throughout the holy gospels. The faster we speed the light and spread the Word, the sooner will be then coming of the final end (Mt 24:14)!

11. To lead is to exceed (Matt 5:41). This famous verse from the Lord is known world wide as the Extra Mile Principle. When applied in real life and ministry, followers of Christ must never be satisfied with doing the bare minimum just to get by, but to do more and better than what's required and expected of us, with no concern for being noticed or getting paid for it, doing it wholeheartedly as onto the Lord (Col 3:23) who demands and deserves our uttermost best. Leading with intelligence, diligence, vigilance and perseverance in order to achieve the highest level of excellence! Service with a sunny smile is my only spiritual style!

12. To lead is to succeed (Josh 1: 8). God promised Joshua that if he would do his part in trusting and obeying the law of the Lord, then the Lord Himself would surely enable and empower him to prosper and succeed in whatever he did and wherever he went! This is the law of the Kingdom that obedience brings blessings while rebellion results in curses every single time.

13. To lead is to be on guard against all kinds of greed (Lk 12:15). While the Lord delights in the prosperity of His servants, He also is much more concerned about our heart attitude and our inner motives! Prosperity in all things (III Jh 2) is no problem as long as we seek first and maintain always His Kingdom perspective and uphold His priority in whose we are in Him and what we do for His purpose. With the help of God through His Word and Spirit, and with the assistance of accountability partners and the counsel of wise advisers, let us be vigilant against the deadly sin of covetousness (Ex

20:17) and let us work out our own salvation with fear and trembling (Phil 2:12). Let us strive always to be generous givers, and not greedy getters, for the Lord loves a cheerful giver and the heart of generosity defeats and destroys the spirit of greed!

Reflections and applications

Without any doubt, the authority of wealth creation and the wisdom of spiritual stewardship were granted and endowed by God the Creator since the very beginning of humanity. In Genesis 1:26-30, it's written:

Genesis1:26 Then God said, "Let us make man in our image, in our likeness, and let them rule over the fish of the sea and the birds of the air, over the livestock, over all the earth, and over all the creatures that move along the ground."1:27 So God created man in his own image, in the image of God he created him; male and female he created them.1:28 God blessed them and said to them, "Be fruitful and increase in number; fill the earth and subdue it. Rule over the fish of the sea and the birds of the air and over every living creature that moves on the ground."1:30 And to all the beasts of the earth and all the birds of the air and all the creatures that move on the ground-everything that has the breath of life in it-I give every green plant for food." And it was so.

Authorities are succinctly clarified and specified here in that our Creator God has graciously granted us the legitimacy and authority as His children to be like Him. Being made in the image of the creative God, we are not only to rule and manage His world with wisdom and gratitude, we are also to continue to be creative in everything we do for the glory of God, creating opportunities to grow and change, and creating wealth and riches for the good of man and the glory of God!

Creativity is a special divine gift to only the humanity among all of God's creations. Just as only humans bear the likeness of God, so only human being are given the capacity for all sorts of creativity and imagination. Because of this gift, humans have created all kinds of tools and technologies to make the toilsome life of pains and suffering much easier, more pleasant and more enjoyable. Praise the Lord. We have been given the creative capabilities to make money and accumulate wealth with a higher purpose:

Deuteronomy 8:18 — But remember the LORD your God, for it is he who gives you the ability to produce wealth, and so confirms his covenant, which he swore to your forefathers, as it is today.

Spiritual Stewardship is God's commandment to humanity. As with all things in life, along with the rights, come the responsibilities. One can not have one without the other. And they who cherish more of their rights than their responsibilities will soon lose both! The Bible clearly teaches us stewards in 1Corinthians 4:1 So then, men ought to regard us as servants of Christ and as those entrusted with the secret things of God.4:2 Now it is required that those who have been given a trust must prove faithful. And as we become proven wise and faithful and fruitful in small things, God the Owner will entrust us with more and bigger things to take care of for Him and His cause. Let us always be faithful (never foolish or wasteful) stewards of God's resources so that we will live and serve to truly please Him who will declare us His good and faithful servants to enter into the eternal glory and joy of the Lord (Matt 25)!

In order to make an impact in our own life, and positively and productively influence others, our thoughts and minds must be renewed first as Rom 12:2 instructs. The way that we can change our destiny or outcomes all begins with our faith or ideas. It is from our thinking that we begin to act upon it as ideas have consequences and lead to action. Proverbs 23:7 warns us that as a man thinks in his heart, so is he! Please know, remember and actively apply this famous formula of life or the law of sowing and reaping which the Word of God repeatedly emphasizes its importance:

Sow a thought, reap an action; sow an action, reap a habit; sow a habit, reap a character; and sow a character, reap a destiny!

Recently we were online chatting with our old school mates of college days in China and one of the stories we talked about was very intriguing as it was an ancient Chinese Confucius proverb with new financial nuances and implications. An old man sitting in the market place with a fishing pole and a basket of fish. A young man came by the side. The old man asked him, "Young man, would you like to learn to fish or would you like to receive a fish?" The young replied, "I'd like the whole basketful of fish!" Upon hearing, the wise old man sternly rebuked the young say, "have you never heard the old saying that it's better to teach someone to fish than to give Him a fish? For giving someone a fish he will be hungry before the end of the day, but teach him how to fish, he will be well fed the rest of his life." The young man smiled and answered, "Sir, you know only one part of request and you know not the part of my reason. I have observed in this place and studies the situation. There are a lot of senior citizens sitting on their little stools around the lake doing nothing. Therefore the reason I asked you for the whole basket of fish instead of of the one single fishing pole is that I am going to sell the fish and buy several fishing poles to start a fishing business right here by renting the poles to the idling seniors. This way they will be happy and I will develop my own business!" Upon hearing this rationale, the wise old man nodded at the young one with a smiling approval!

You may examine yourself by asking and answering these three questions:

1. What are the biblical implications and applications that this teaching has for me in my life right now?
2. What are the things that God has already put it in your hands?
3. What am I good at doing? Am I doing something with it or am I wasting my life?

Chapter 2

Joseph and Spiritual Stewardship: An Excellent Example to Examine and Emulate

With no doubt whatsoever, the biblical account of Joseph (Gen 37-50) is one of the most well-known and fascinating stories of all times! His life was as colorful as was his coat of many colors that got him into the deep pit. Joseph, a real hero of the faith by any measure, was, in many ways from spirituality, morality, through fidelity, ability, to integrity, affluence and influence, a prototype of our precious Lord Christ Jesus! As one of the most impactful stewards and influential leaders in the biblical and Hebrew history, Joseph was the perfect illustration of the law of the process, and an excellent example of the law of intuition for us all to admire, aspire, perspire and acquire so as to inspire others. Let us explore, examine and emulate Joseph now!

The law of the process teaches us that leaders, and in this case, Joseph the Steward, are developed daily, and not in a day. Stewardship as leadership develops over time and not overnight! The famous leadership guru Dr John C. Maxwell succinctly states it this way: "Becoming a leader is a lot like investing in the stock market. If you hope to make a fortune in a day, you are doomed. It's what you do day by day, over the long haul that matters most. If you continually develop your leadership, letting your "assets" compound over time, the inevitable result is growth." (P. 46).

To start out in Gen 37, Joseph was the favorite son of his father Jacob's old age. He was handsome, smart, but also cocky, arrogant and kind of carefree and thoughtless in revealing his dreams that caused rebuke from the father, and even worse, envy, jealousy, hate and attempted murder from the brothers who eventually sold him into Egyptian slavery and made twenty shekels of silver money for themselves (very Jewish with profit motive indeed, Gen 37: 26-28). Life is full of problems. But problems never paralyze real leaders. They propel them forward and eventually produce the results, for adversities are the best universities where great leaders are trained through the fury and fire of purging, pruning, and purifying! Throughout all his dark and difficult experiences of the pit, the prison and even the palace, Joseph never wavered in his trust relationship with God, never gave up the vision that the God of Abraham, Isaac and Jacob gave him, and never compromised his character of morality and integrity (Gen 39:9) even if he had to flee from (not flirt with!) temptation. Because of the blessings of God upon him through special spiritual gifts of dreams and interpretations, Joseph became very intelligent and intuitive. He was able to evaluate all situations from God's perspective. He learned to see and do things God's way, enjoying the special favors of the Lord upon him. The result was astounding, "because the Lord was with Joseph, he was a successful man; and whatever he did, the Lord made it prosper" (Gen 39:2, 3, 21, 23). What an excellent and awesome summary of a true success story to inspire and challenge us today!

    One more vital stewardship and leadership element at work in the successful and prosperous life of Joseph, besides the laws of intuition and process, has to be the Law of the Solid Ground (Maxwell, P. 49) which states the truth that "trust is the foundation of all leadership and stewardship." Trust is everything in any real meaningful and healthy relationship anywhere at any time, as there is no real connection or true relationship without sincere trust. Trust as the solid foundation for all human interaction, connection and collaboration can never be demanded or commanded. It has to be earned little by little and gained day by day over a long period of time. Joseph conscientiously did it, and it propelled him to great spiritual and successful stewardship for the whole Egyptian nation. This later also bountifully benefited Joseph's own household and the Hebrew race and nation! Joseph effectively utilized every human adversity as a divine opportunity not only to develop himself personally and spiritually, but also build trustworthy relationships with other people near him. He won the trust of others by demonstrating and displaying both his character of integrity and his competence in problem solving and special skills in his communicating, connecting and capacitating others to get the job done in the right way. As a result of his consistency through all his difficulties (deep pit, slavery, accused adultery, prison, palace, famine and brotherly confrontation), Joseph made one comeback after another and proved himself by his special spiritual intuition and deep divine discernments, extraordinary abilities, wisdom, patience and integrity, as a most trustworthy person for stewardship and leadership for the salvation of both the country of Egypt and his own people the Jews. What a marvelous story of supernatural success of diligence, intelligence and persistence!

    In order to be productive, the steward must be active and pro-active. This was obviously true of Joseph as the super spiritual steward in at least three specific ways, according to Blue and White (PP. 36-37). Based on his divine dreams and revelations, Joseph was authorized by the Egyptian Pharaoh to start his tenure as his COO (Chief Operating Officer) to do all the necessary preparations for the famine with immediate and decisive actions. (1). Joseph thoroughly surveyed all the territories to assess the state of the nation in terms of land, people, crop production, and considered all the alternatives for sufficient storage of the bumper harvests. This is none other than taking a serious and realistic financial physical to evaluate the fitness and determine what's to be done; (2). Joseph established a specific and long-term goal for the Egyptians to know where to go and how to go about storing up plenty to survive the 7 years of famine that lay ahead; (3). Joseph developed and implemented an effective plan of action to gather, out of the abundance, very much grain, as the sand on the sea until he stopped counting for it was immeasurable (Gen 41:49). This is the same effective strategy to move a person from point one to point two, by faithfully implementing the four time-tested and practice-proven principles of financial success after thorough studies and keen knowledge of your reality with accuracy:

1. Think long term with your financial goals and investment (Matt 24:13; Phil 4:13);
2. Learn to live within your means, your income: always spend less than you earn (Prov 13:11);
3. Become your own bank: build and increase your liquidity with sufficient emergency funds and plenty of savings (Prov 6:6-8);
4. Always avoid debt: get out and stay out of any debt (Prov 22:7).

III John 2 declares the intent of the Lord for us His children whom He loves deeply and gives liberally. He desires for us to prosper in all things, stay in good health, even as our soul prospers in the Lord! Let them shout for joy, therefore, and be glad. "Let the Lord be magnified, Who has pleasure in the prosperity of His servant." (Ps 35:27). What a fitting depiction of Joseph, and what a precious and powerful promise that the Lord has given to all of us who faithfully follow and sincerely serve Him! Let us study and apply these seven Joseph principles of spiritual stewardship for our financial prosperity and for the Lord's greater glory:

1. The visions to prosper. Where there is no vision, prophetic dreams and revelations, the people will cast off restraints and go every which way, as Proverbs 29:18 implies. The people without strong and visionary leadership would do what was right in their own eyes, as was the sad case in the book of Judges (21:25). What gave Joseph the supernatural stamina and strength, wisdom and boldness to achieve prosperity was doubtlessly his dreams of greatness and visions given by the Lord starting from the beginning of his life (Gen 37). These dreams sustained him in the worst of all the situations, and his divine ability of interpretation for others' dreams pushed him to connections of favors and positions of influence. Dream big for we serve a big God who will supply all we need as we wholehearted apply all that He instructs and commands us to go and do!

2. The preparation to prosper. Throughout the entire life of Joseph, we see everywhere the very presence and the hand of God upon him. Because the Lord was with him, guarding him every step of the way and guiding him every moment of the day, Joseph was granted divine presence and favors in his home, even in the pit and the prison and especially in the palace of the king. God was all the while training him with the character of caring kindness to people in the dungeon, sincere forgiveness to his brothers, true loyalty to the Pharaoh and fairness in dealing with the people. The Lord was building His Godly character so that Joseph could see and do everything from God's perspective. Dr. John C. Maxwell (P. 61) forcefully sums up Joseph's life, "How a leader deals with circumstances of life tells you many things about his character. Crisis doesn't necessarily make character, but it certainly does reveal it. Adversity is a crossroad that makes a person choose one of two paths: character or compromise. Every time he chooses character he becomes stronger, even if that choice brings negative consequences (remember why Joseph ended up in prison?). The development of character is at the heart of our development as leaders. If you want God's perspective on life, then make sure to develop your character. It's the only way as Joseph reminds us." Through all the ups and downs in Joseph's life and ministries, God indeed prepared him with such qualities as humility, patience, loving acceptance, true forgiveness, wisdom, competence, diligence, discipline, Biblical principles, integrity, and effective strategies to win and live the victories!

3. The connection to prosper. Without the right connectivity, it is impossible to win victory and reach prosperity, for no one is an island unto himself and no one can do all these things alone. Joseph's caring attitude and capable ability to read people and to interpret their puzzling dreams gained him trust and won his friends who would connect him to the right people in the right circumstances at the right time in the right place. This connection through vital human relationships is described vividly in both Gen 40:1-4 and Gen 41:1-14. There has to be a concentration on connections, communication and collaboration before once can expect any wealth creation, stewardship accumulation and generous and wise contribution. This is an infallible and timeless principle in stewardship and leadership, as the greatest asset and the number one resource of all organizations is none other than its people with special talents, abilities, calling, and trusted character traits of honesty, transparency and integrity.

4. The position to prosper. The dreams and interpretations with the prescription for specific plans of immediate and effective actions to adequately deal with the coming 7 years of famine given by Joseph to Pharaoh of Egypt centrally positioned him to prosper for the sake of the whole nation and even Joseph's own people. The detailed description of Joseph's rise to power is found in Gen 41:37-45. Upon receiving Joseph's advice and knowing Joseph's abilities as a wise and trusted steward, Pharaoh personally took his signet ring off his hand and put it on Joseph's hand along with royal garments, chariots and a gold chain on his neck, declaring that, "Inasmuch as God has shown you all this, there is no one as discerning and wise as you... You shall be over my house, and all my people shall be ruled according to your word; only in regard to the throne will I be greater than you... See, I have set you over all the land of Egypt." (Gen 41:39-41). Indeed, in order to get things done in an organization and nation, one must have the legitimate authority in order to exercise the wisdom and power with much courage. Praise the Lord for the earned legitimacy of authority and the position of power to exercise his wisdom and use his foresight and insight to make the difference.

5. The timing to prosper. There is a right time for everything under the sun. Even the will of God must be done in due time, in His "Kairos" --- divinely appointed hour of His favor. This requires patience and perseverance on the part of the steward. Joseph showed us how to gather in plenty during the times of abundance so as to survive the times of poverty and even thrive after the scarcity!

6. The ways to prosper. With his capable stewardship and wise leadership even at such a young age of only 30 years, Joseph went out and gathered through the land of abundance, all the food of the seven years and laid grain both in storages of the cities and in the fields of the country without number (Gen 41:46-49). Then the terrible famine did come (Gen 47:13-26) just as the Lord had shown him in the dream. Joseph never opened the barns and storages just to give people "free" food, or to develop some socialistic welfare system that ruins everyone in the end. He made the people work for their food and trade in order to eat. And all this was highly organized in a step-by-step systematic and orderly way.

Notice that he first sold people the needed grain for their money which he faithfully and fully brought into Pharaoh's house; then when their money was all spent, Joseph traded with them by giving them food for their livestock until they exchanged all their animals for food to eat; furthermore as the situation got worse, the people offered their land for food and sold their bodies for labor; finally Joseph said to the people, "Indeed I have bought you and your land for Pharaoh. Look, here is seed for you and you shall sow the land." (Gen 47:23). To lead is to see the need and to sow the seed in order to meet the need. This was exactly what Joseph did, with specific instructions, clear stipulations, and strict conditions as to how to fairly divide and wisely use the harvest brought about by the seed. Thus they people survived the famine for all the seven years and gratefully thanked Joseph for the favors of saving their lives!

One of the most fundamental ways to prosper is to learn from the ancient stewardship guru Joseph: establishing and implementing a realistic budget that is sustainable. In order to be fruitful, profitable and successful, one must be sustainable! A budget as a basic spending plan or a distribution of resources, is simply you telling your money where to go instead of you wondering where all your money went. Let us examine these two key verses 23-24 of Gen 47. "Look, here is the seed for you and you shall sow the land. And it shall come to pass in the harvest that you shall give one-fifth to Pharaoh. Four-fifth shall be your own, as seed for the field and for your food, for those of your households, and as food for your little ones." Joseph exercised his authority and made this national budget with special and strict stipulations (20% royal taxation basically) as the law of the land. The people were happy and thankful to Joseph for saving their lives and their families. Egypt as a nation sufficiently survived the long and hard famine, and greatly thrived under Joseph's wise and effective stewardship.

7. The purpose to prosper. Then the people said to Joseph, "You have saved our lives; let us find favor in the sight of my lord, and we will be Pharaoh's servants." (Gen 47:25). In addition, Joseph comforted his brothers and spoke to them kindly with such encouragement and truth, the same brothers who meant harm and evil against him, "Do not be afraid; I will provide for you…. But as for you, you meant evil against me; but God meant it for good, in order to bring it about as it is today, to save many people alive." (Gen 50: 19-21).   This higher purpose is even more clearly stated for our financial prosperity and successes in Deuteronomy 8:18, "And you shall remember the Lord your God, for it is He who gives you power to get wealth, that He may establish His covenant which He swore to your fathers, as it is this day." Praise the Lord for the higher purpose of prosperity so that we with the abundance of compelling evidences, can be more used of God to bring greater glory to Him and bigger blessings to others!

Reflections and applications

The story of Joseph is unquestionably one of the most intriguing and influential in all the world literature! He was one of the most courageous, wise and rich men ever lived and his story was one from rags to riches for a higher purpose! We can learn and apply so many practical and useful life lessons for our own ministries.

First of God, character counts the most, and the number one ingredient for influence is integrity. Joseph both declared and demonstrated throughout half of the book of Genesis that he was a man of his words and he was honorable in all his dealings. All of this was because Joseph knew God and knew that God was with him.

Secondly, don't be afraid of human adversity as it is often a divine university set up by God to train us, test us, mature us, stretch and strengthen us to be fit with force for the Master's purpose! Many a time, human setbacks are nothing more than a divine setup for us to progress and prosper later on. He who does not learn to endure short-term pains will not live long enough to enjoy long-term gains. This is true in all areas of life especially in faith and finance!

Third, Joseph teaches us through his life example how to triumph over your trials and tribulations! Life is full of insufficiencies, inadequacies, limitations and imperfections, But God (Gen 50:20) gives us wisdom and ways to be victorious and abundant in spite of them, and makes us spiritually stronger and relationally more mature and compassionate because of them! The key here is to always be faithful to God and to the call of God on our lives to the final finish and He will make us forceful and fruitful for His glory and for the good of others: family and friends. This is the most powerful conclusion on life for the Joseph and Kingdom perspective:

Genesis 50:19 But Joseph said to them, "Don't be afraid. Am I in the place of God? 50:20 You intended to harm me, but God intended it for good to accomplish what is now being done, the saving of many lives. 50:21 So then, don't be afraid. I will provide for you and your children." And he reassured them and spoke kindly to them.

Fourthly, never give up your dreams and never allow your past memories to become bigger than your future dreams. Hold fast to your God-given dreams and do not let them die, for when dreams die, they are like a broken winged bird that can't fly! May the same Lord who was with Joseph and helped Joseph touch and bless you with dreams, gifts, and passion like the apostles Peter and Paul so that you will be enthused and energetic to embrace the dreams and visions boldly and courageously, living a life of peace, abundance, generosity and prosperity for His pleasure and His glory.

Finally, let us learn from Joseph the most valuable relational lessons of love, forgiveness and acceptance! In order to get ahead in life spiritually and financially, one must learn and apply the art of getting along well with others. Being mistreated terribly with the jealousy and hatred by his own brothers and falsely accused and punished by many others, Joseph refused to be resent and revenge. There was absolutely no room for bitterness in his heart. In Matthew7:12Jesus our Lord gives us the Golden Rule and further commands us, "So in everything, do to others what you would have them do to you, for this sums up the Law and the Prophets." We have no control over how others will see others and treat us, but we are responsibly to God how we see others and how we will treat them. God's ways are always higher than our ways and His thoughts are not the same as our thoughts. And as we proactively treat others with kindness, generosity and favors, the funnel of divine favors will be flowing our way in increasingly greater measures (Lake 6:38) in all the vital aspects of our Being and our existence!

Here are some important questions for your consideration and application:

1. What is your dream in your life?
2. How do you see yourself when you are in the pit?
3. What are the opportunities that you can see and grasp to fulfill your dream?
4. What might the reason for your success?

Chapter 3

Jesus and The Parable of the Talents

The wise does at once what the fool does at last — Jewish Proverb

Compound interest is the eighth wonder of the world. He who understand sit earns it... he who does not, pays it. Co pound interest is the most powerful force I. The universe. Compound interest is the greatest mathematical discovery of all time — Albert Einstein

Kingdom Economics 101 --- Matthew 25:14-30 — Jesus Christ

Matthew25:14 "Again, it will be like a man going on a journey, who called his servants and entrusted his property to them.25:15 To one he gave five talents of money, to another two talents, and to another one talent, each according to his ability. Then he went on his journey.25:16 The man who had received the five talents went at once and put his money to work and gained five more.25:17 So also, the one with the two talents gained two more.25:18 But the man who had received the one talent went off, dug a hole in the ground and hid his master's money.25:19 "After a long time the master of those servants returned and settled accounts with them.25:20 The man who had received the five talents brought the other five. 'Master,' he said, 'you entrusted me with five talents. See, I have gained five more.'25:21 "His master replied, 'Well done, good and faithful servant! You have been faithful with a few things; I will put you in charge of many things. Come and share your master's happiness!'25:22 "The man with the two talents also came. 'Master,' he said, 'you entrusted me with two talents; see, I have gained two more.'25:23 "His master replied, 'Well done, good and faithful servant! You have been faithful with a few things; I will put you in charge of many things. Come and share your master's happiness!'25:24 "Then the man who had received the one talent came. 'Master,' he said, 'I knew that you are a hard man, harvesting where you have not sown and gathering where you have not scattered seed.25:25 So I was afraid and went out and hid your talent in the ground. See, here is what belongs to you.'25:26 "His master replied, 'You wicked, lazy servant! So you knew that I harvest where I have not sown and gather where I have not scattered seed?25:27 Well then, you should have put my money on deposit with the bankers, so that when I returned I would have received it back with interest.25:28 " 'Take the talent from him and give it to the one who has the ten talents.25:29 For everyone who has will be given more, and he will have an abundance. Whoever does not have, even what he has will be taken from him.25:30 And throw that worthless servant outside, into the darkness, where there will be weeping and gnashing of teeth.' — Jesus of Nazareth

Having prayerfully and carefully read this most important and significant passage of the Scripture first and on your own now, let us delve deeply in to the kingdom perspective, priority, principles and practices for the spiritual steward. And this process will be carried out, as the essence of the entire book, with BP: Biblical Principles with a Balanced Practicality! Now, let us also study and apply the lessons to be learned to our lives and ministries so that we can once and for all achieve a higher measure of financial fitness, a stronger sense of financial freedom and even a greater degree of financial force along with the proper process, peace of mind, and prosperity to achieve our spiritual stewardship purposes by the grace of God and for the glory of God!

"The Kingdom of heaven is like a man traveling to a far country, who called his own servants and delivered his good to them. And to one he gave five talents, to another two, and to another one, to each according to his ability." (VV.14-15). In these very two verses of crucial importance, there are major foundational principles of scriptural stewardship below that can be observed and applied to our lives with the right views and values as citizens of His kingdom.

1. The Lord, first and foremost, wants us to always and fully focus our undivided attention on the Kingdom of God and the perspective, priority and the purpose of His Kingdom, and how we must forever concentrate our total efforts and resources for the advancement and furtherance of His Kingdom and agenda on earth before the end comes. The final chapter of this book will deal in much greater details with the issues of faith and finances in light of the vision and the passion of the Kingdom of God. Jesus teaches over 200 times on the Kingdom of Heaven and of God, 56 times alone in the Gospel of Matthew. Why such high frequency? Because what is important is frequent, and what is frequent is important; likewise, what is important is clear, and what is clear is important! The Lord wants us to get His priority for our lives and stewardship ministries so that we will not waste our time or life in the trivial and the nonessentials. The wisdom of life consists in the elimination of all the non-essentials. Don't major in minors, our friends, or you will never graduate from the life university. We must seek first the Kingdom of God and His righteousness and then all that we need, be it physical, emotional, relational, psychological, educational, financial or spiritual, will be added unto us as He unfailingly promises us (Matt 6:33). His Kingdom comes not by our vain observation, but by our active participation and bold action as it comes forcefully. Not only are we to be faithful workers and stewards of His Kingdom, we are to enlist and recruit workers for His kingdom, the more the merrier, to cause Kingdom increases and accelerated its growth and advances all over the world. Of the increase of His Kingdom, there shall be no end. And this gospel of

the Kingdom shall be preached unto all the nations as a testimony onto all the peoples of the earth, and then the end shall come (Matthew 24:14)! Oh Lord, Thy Kingdom come and Thy will be done on earth, as it is already done in heaven. For Yours is the Kingdom, the power and the glory for ever and ever, Amen!

2. The Lord is the Owner and the Master of all the properties and talents and even the very lives of His servants and stewards. As it is common sense to all of us that there is no kingdom without a king. And Jesus Christ is the King of the Kingdom and King of all kings. We are stewards and managers of the Lord's monies, properties, and business. We are not in control or in charge of our lives or destinies, as some would like to assume only later to be disappointed and disillusioned by their own foolish presumptions. As stewards called, chosen and commissioned by the Lord for His purpose, we must be grateful and faithful, and never become critical, selfish, idle or lazy. The steward must pay full attention first of all to his or her own heart attitude as it will affect everything he/she does. The right attitude will elevate you to a high altitude.

3. As our Creator and Master, the Omniscient Lord Jesus knows our abilities much better than we know ourselves. He bestows His gifts and talents and treasures upon each of us according to His sovereign wisdom according to His will, and not ours. Instead of comparing with others that causes the carnality of envy, anger and jealousy, complaints and criticism, we as spiritual stewards are to be grateful and thankful for His gifts and trust that we have a part, any part, and even just a tiny small part, in the edification and the extension of His Kingdom on earth! What an honor and joy to be chosen and used of the Lord in some small way to bring Him glory and praises. What a privilege to be entrusted of the Lord for an eternal purpose! This verse 15 reminds us of the important passage in I Cor 12 about the Lord's distribution of the various spiritual gifts according to His will and for the common purpose of edifying the Body and exalting the Lord, saving the lost and advancing the Kingdom.

4. Matt 25:16 clearly states that the man who had received the five talents went AT ONCE and put his money to work and

gained five More. There are two vital concepts of conviction about kingdom economics here in one verse. First, investments must bring profits and returns (known as ROI meaning Returns On Investments, VV. 27, 30)), the more, the better; and in order to bring returns, the trustee or steward should immediately put the money to work. This is part of the Matthew effect with a powerful steward principle for personal financial practice that requires decisiveness and instant industry with discipline and intelligence. The Jewish proverb sums it well by saying that "The wise does at once what the fool does at last." This spiritual steward is decisive and active and not negative or passive. He is very active and proactive in order to be so productive and profitable. He did so with conviction and confidence, with passion and purpose, power and perseverance, and with no distraction, disruption, no hesitation or reservation, or any signs of procrastination. He was confidently concentrated on getting His Master's job done well, with indisputable results to show for it and prove it. Likewise did the second servant with his two talents. This reminds us of the same truth revealed to us in Ecclesiastes 11:4, "He who observes the wind will not sow, and he who regards the cloud will not reap"! Jesus our Owner and Master and Lord commands us in no uncertain terms, to "Go and do likewise" (Luke 10:37), and to go and bear fruit, much fruit, and more fruit, fruit that will last (John 15:16).

5. "After a long time, the Lord of the servants came and settled accounts with them". Matt 25:19 is a very significant verse as it lays out a spiritual foundation for trustworthy steward in that we are all to be tested and examined as emphasized in II Cor 13:5. The Lord will come back a second time, even if it takes a long time, and He is coming sooner than ever before. And He demands our faithfulness and integrity, and in order to live a life of integrity, we must live daily with His measures of accountability through the mirror of the Word, the prompting of the Spirit, legitimate structural authority and necessary polities and intentional accountability partners who love us and care for our soul. In Luke 16:2, the master demands and commands us to give an account of our stewardship. So then

each of us shall have to give an account of himself to God (Rom 14:12), with no exceptions or partiality or favoritism. And there is no creature hidden from His sight, but all things are naked and open to the eyes of Him "to whom we must give account" (Heb 4:13). This divine demand for accountability of His stewards is true of us all, but especially and more strictly true of the leaders of the church who are to be profitable and make the followers more faithful and fruitful (Heb 13:17).

    6. The Lord Rewards the faithful and fruitful stewards with high commendations and more leadership responsibilities (v. 21), while at the same time He severely rebukes and sternly disciplines the unfaithful and unprofitable servant who prepared many accusations and made excuses (VV. 26, 29, 30). God delights in the ministry of multiplication of His investments and blessings until they have reached all. He uses the vital matter such as finances to demonstrate His power and His love for us; and He uses money to also test our faithfulness and our trust in and obedience to Him. In this famous parable, the Lord also denounces the spirit of slothfulness and passive maintenance of His business (Burkett, 1993, P. 35). He has given us His talents and abilities so that we can urgently, vigilantly, intelligently and diligently go out and grow and multiply the assets entrusted to us. We are also convinced that the third steward was punished mainly because of his wrong belief about stewardship and bad psychology of fear, and poor attitude of passivity and negativity that propels zero altitude of passion, purpose, power or prosperity. The Master was just fair and firm, but this servant clearly did not know, respect and trust His master (Bentley, P. 90). This caused him to make bad decisions that led to his demise and destruction. Let us learn from the first two great stewards in stark contrast to the fearful and fruitless one. Let us not become idle and lazy and accusatory. We as His responsible stewards must get rid of the mentality of excuses of Moses (Exodus 3-4), of Jesus' disciples (Lk 9, 14) and of this worthless and wicked servant, as excuses are even worse than idleness and laziness put together (Prov 19:15). Why? because excuses prevents the person

from making the slightest possible efforts of even just giving it a try. Try and fail is much better than not trying at all because one can learn valuable lessons from his failures which become the mother of his future successes. As Ben Franklin once correctly lamented, "He who is good at making excuses is seldom good at making anything else." As we all know by numerous previous personal experiences and encounters, that our attitude is everything and without the right spiritual attitude, we will never mount up with wings to reach the eagle altitude, the God-given potential intended for us. Therefore, Get rid of this passive and negative attitude before it will affect us and even ruin us. And if you don't get rid of it, sooner or later it will get rid of you! Remember that passivity produces pitiful poverty, and negativity navigates you nowhere.

    7. He who is fearful is not faithful and cannot be forceful or fruitful either (VV. 25. 30). Don't be a fearful steward. Fears are the Number One natural human emotions due to numerous and various circumstances and conditions, real, perceived or just imaginary. Fear of failure, fear of the future, fear of others' opinions and fears of uncertainty, of scarcity and poverty, are among many others in this fallen world of imperfections. As the acronym says it pretty accurately that most of our fears don't eve actually exist and thus never come to pass, for FEAR means False Expectations Appearing Real! Fear and faith do not mix very well when they are put together. Fear knocks at the door and Faith goes and opens it and finds nothing there! Get rid of, as soon and as early as possible, this erroneous and illogical notion that "I must always play it safe." Rich rewards come only from taking careful, calculated and bold risks at times. Face your fear by faith in the promises of the Lord and by the power of the Holy Spirit. Move against the very thing that has or is causing you fear, by faith go and do exactly the very thing that you have been afraid of doing, knowing that greater is He who lives in you and who empowers you with faith, than he who is of the world to cause you the fear. No wonder the Bible declares 365 times "Don't be afraid" or "Fear not" as most of us have to deal with the issue on a daily basis. By the grace of God,

which is both the unmerited favor of God and the overcoming power from God, we shall make up our mind to live a life that really matters for eternity: be faithful, fearless, forceful, fruitful to the final fabulous Finish! Jesus declared His mission was to do the Father's will and finish His work (Jh 4:34), and on that bloody cross with excruciatingly painful suffering and sacrifices, "It Is Finished" with spectacular successes. Fear does put a lot of limits on us and prevents us from reaching and realizing our God-given potential in Christ Jesus. It is of the devil indeed for the Lord hasn't given us and never doesn't give us the spirit of timidity or fear, but He gives us the spirit of love, power and sound mind! (II Tim 1:7). When our faith in Jesus makes us more and more fearless, then our life and ministry, stewardship and leadership will become limitless! We can and we must do likewise with His help: to work closely together and make the Great Commission a Great Completion for the glory of the Lord of the soon coming King of kings!

8. The Matthew Effect: How accumulative advantages keep on accumulating and advancing with much more abundance from compound interests

"For to everyone who has, more will be given, and he will have abundance. But from him who does not have, even what he has will be taken away." --- Jesus in Matt 25:29

The term "The Matthew Effect" is the name of a rich-poor dichotomy in the studies of education and economics. It originates from the famous sayings of the Lord Jesus in His well-known Parable of the Talents under our consideration, ending with the above-quoted verse 29. The Matthew Effect is a social economic and educational phenomenon discussed in details by Malcolm Gladwell (see bibliography at the back of the book). It refers to the idea and the reality that the rich get richer and the poor get poorer due invariably to certain hidden advantages such as patronage and parentage, extraordinary opportunities and relational connections not readily available to most, and due to one's cultural identities and legacies (Gladwell, P. 19). This concept also refers to those who "already have", and yet they are put in a situation where they are given even more. On the other hand, those who have little are constantly struggle with a meager standard of living just to survive, trying to make ends meet by living from paycheck to paycheck (7 out 10 Americans), suffering from the hand-to-mouth disease of constant pressurized scarcity and even extreme poverty. This indeed does not seem to be "fair" from a typical leftist liberal and the so-called "progressive socialist" view of income equality and equal distribution that leads only to "equal" destruction, but the Lord of the Bible is, while being very generous and compassionate, more concerned about His righteousness than our self-perceived or self-imposed standard of "fairness", just as He is more concerned about His holiness in His children than the fluid measure of our "happiness".

The clear manifestation of this Matthew Effect has been easily observable everywhere regardless of times, cultures, ethnicities, races or religions. Those who have more have the accumulated advantage of acquire much more while the poor suffer lacks and wants due to different reasons. It suggests that the wealthy tend to acquire more wealth because of their increased educational opportunities, increased abilities and thus wider accessibilities to jobs and investments while the poor fall further behind into deeper poverty due to their loss of personal drives and or lack of academic and financial opportunities for potentially higher profitability. Karl Marx's conflict theory of social classes was a strong example and reaction to the effect and reality that has caused the disasters and the horrors of the deaths of over 100 million lives the world over with the false promise of a classless society of socialist equality and superiority, with China being the worst under Chairman Mao as we personally experienced for over twenty long years of absolute misery with abject poverty and modern-day slavery with no human freedom or dignity whatsoever, never having the chance of even hear the name of Jesus or the existence of the Bible for the first 20 long years of both of our lives.

The more decisively, actively and wisely you use the available resources the Lord has entrusted to you, the more He will enable you to produce, and empower you with His favors of more abundance. "The devil comes to steal, kill and destroy; but I have come that you might have life and have it more abundantly." (Jesus in John 10:10). On the other hand, however, if one, for whatever reasons such as idleness, laziness, indulgence or fears, does not use it, she or he will surely lose it. This may not be "fair" to the individual, but it is valid and true both spiritually and materially in the real world and in any given society, for it is how the real world really works, and Utopia is just that, a utopia that does not even exist! According to the reliable Hebrew scholars and rabbis, the words such as "fair" "retire" do not even appear in the Hebrew Bible. And since a word for the concept does not exist in the Word of God, it is not a concept from God for us either.

9. This parable is quite prophetic in nature in that it alludes to the most exciting event of the Second King of the Lord Jesus Christ. As much as this famous parable of the talents is about the financial and material, it is deeply and urgently spiritual in nature. This is so because Christian stewardship is profoundly spiritual! Maranatha: "Even so come quickly, O Lord." as the Revelator and Apostle John cries out from the heart! Although it has been a very long while (2000 years) now since the ascension of Christ to heaven after His earthly ministries were finished, yet we are not discouraged at all for we know that one day to the Lord is like a 1000 years and a 1000 years to Him is just like one day (II Pet 3:8-9)! He is always faithful to His promises as we fulfill our obligation and carry our God-given responsibilities described in Matthew 24:14. And this gospel of the Kingdom shall be preached unto all the nations as a testimony unto all the peoples (our part), and then (God's part) the end shall come! The Lord is not slack concerning His promised second coming; He is simply allowing us a little extra time to do His will and to Finish His work, as soon as possible. The faster we spread the Word and speed the Light, the sooner will be the Second Coming of our Lord! In light of this prophetic significance, Let us never become disheartened to give up, knowing that the Lord has intentionally, out of His mercies, patience and compassion, given us

just a reprieve for more soul winning and more disciple making all over the world before the final dreadful Judgment Day. Therefore, let us fearlessly and passionately go all out while it is still day, to do His will and finish His mission, the Great Commission, with absolute Kingdom authority, supernatural spiritual energy, and a stronger sense of personal urgency, as Jesus Himself exemplified to us in both words and deeds and by both precepts and examples (John 9:4), John 4: 31-38). We must work enthusiastically for the Lord while it's still day time, for when night comes, no one can work

He who has ears, let his hear what the Lord Jesus is emphatically instructing us on Biblical leadership as spiritual stewardship. Let the Word of Christ dwell deeply in our heart to challenge and inspire us, stirring us and spurring us onto His call and His cause. And now that we have known these things, we will be greatly blessed if we will confidently go ahead and courageously do them (Jh 13:17), the more the better for the fulfillment of the Great Commission of Christ on earth.

Reflections and Applications

There is a Chinese proverb that says that by collecting the small, one will become big; and by the daily piling up the dirt and stones , one can form mountains. In our wonderful Hiwassee river pointe community here in Charleston TN USA, there is a beautiful-man made lake. In forming this lake, there are a few things that one needs to keep in mind:

1. The proper location — there must be a low land or deep valley area.
2. The incoming stream — there has to be a feeding creak or stream.
3. The overflowing outlet — there has to be a flood prevention system.
4. The timing of collecting the water resources — when water is scare, accumulate; and when there is too much water due to rain, release. There must be time to properly regulate the water level and quantity.

Faith and Finances

As is the case with our community lake, so it is with our individual financial well-being! If you want to build a solid financial reservoir of lake of abundance (my cup runneth over, as the Psalmist joyfully proclaims), you too, need to apply these principles to your personal financial satiation by making wise and timely monetary decisions that will generate long term results. Know your own situation clearly and objectively; develop and follow a budget which allows you to tell your money where to go instead of you wondering g whereas your money went. Live always within the budget and even intentionally below your means so that you can accumulate plenty in a long run to live in prosperity with great abundance. Don't forget the overflow and the time to give, as the Lord has blessed you with prosperity so that you may exercise liberality and practice generosity wisely!

You might ask yourself these following questions:

1. What are the current financial incoming streams in my life?
2. In which suitable location could I build a financial pool, pond or lake?
3. How long will it realistically take me to get it done for long term results?
4. What are 3 proven-effective means for me to get started now?

Chapter 4

Jesus and the Unjust Steward

Luke 12:15 --- Watch out! Be on your guard against all kinds of greed; a man's life does not consist in the abundance of his possessions.

Luke 16:8, 10 --- The master COMMENDED the dishonest manager because he had acted SHREWDLY. For the people of this world are More Shrewd in dealing with their own kind than are the people of the light... Whoever can be trusted with very little can also be trusted with much.

The Jewish shrewdness with money is the stuff of legend. And this does not happen by chance, but by choice; not by default, but by design.

Let the temporal things serve your use, but the eternal be the object of your desire --- Thomas A. Kempis.

Luke16:1 Jesus told his disciples: "There was a rich man whose manager was accused of wasting his possessions.16:2 So he called him in and asked him, 'What is this I hear about you? Give an account of your management, because you cannot be manager any longer.'16:3 "The manager said to himself, 'What shall I do now? My master is taking away my job. I'm not strong enough to dig, and I'm ashamed to beg--16:4 I know what I'll do so that, when I lose my job here, people will welcome me into their houses.' 16:5 "So he called in each one of his master's debtors. He asked the first, 'How much do you owe my master?' 16:6 " 'Eight hundred gallons of olive oil,' he replied. "The manager told him, 'Take your bill, sit down quickly, and make it four hundred.' 16:7 "Then he asked the second, 'And how much do you owe?' " 'A thousand bushels of wheat,' he replied. "He told him, 'Take your bill and make it eight hundred.' 16:8 "The master commended the dishonest manager because he had acted shrewdly. For the people of this world are more shrewd in dealing with their own kind than are the people of the light. 16:9 I tell you, use worldly wealth to gain friends for yourselves, so that when it is gone, you will be welcomed into eternal dwellings. 16:10 "Whoever can be trusted with very little can also be trusted with much, and whoever is dishonest with very little will also be dishonest with much. 16:11 So if you have not been trustworthy in handling worldly wealth, who will trust you with true riches? 16:12 And if you have not been trustworthy with someone else's property, who will give you property of your own? 16:13 "No servant can serve two masters. Either he will hate the one and love the other, or he will be devoted to the one and despise the other. You cannot serve both God and Money."

Before we embark upon a study of the life lessons of Christian leadership as faithful and fruitful stewardship, please carefully study the Gospel of Luke and read Chapter 16:1-13 above quoted for you very carefully and prayerfully as we prepare our hearts and heads with biblical principles for balanced practices. As you read this famous and yet also known as the most puzzling and the most controversial parable (mostly due to our shallowness or ignorance in understanding the ancient Jewish context), with these 13 verses, you will understand with deeper insights the Lord's teaching on the value of wealth, the Kingdom of God, and how we are to go about carrying out our stewardship duties with Him as the Source and with His resources to reach His objectives and accomplish His mission. There are basically two parts in this parable. Verses 1-8 are the basic spiritual instructions, and verses 9-13 are the practical applications for each of us today. This is so typical of the Lord's parable in that we must know the truth, and His truth shall set us free only as we seriously apply it to our life. It is important that we know these things (sound biblical instructions), but it is more important that we go ahead and routinely practice them (solid personal applications) in order to really get the abundant blessings promised to us (John 13:17).

The Essential Stewardship Principles

Here are some of the essential stewardship principles we can learn from the parable:

1. More than our intellectual capacity of the head and the powerful ability of the hand, the Lord looks first and foremost at the conditions of our heart: the motives and the intents of the heart. This central and crucial truth of Scripture has been made very clear in Hebrew 4:12, Proverbs 4:23, and I Sam 16:7. Please go ahead and check them out now. Study and memorize them as a mirror in front of you. The heart of all issues is the issue of the heart, and the heart of all matters is the matter of the heart. Here lies the essence of the spiritual stewardship in biblical leadership that this "unjust" "unrighteous" and very ungodly steward has utterly violated. He violated rule number one: stewards are not in it selfishly, for themselves, self-serving to enrich themselves with the Master's property and wealth, for their self-preservation and self-promotion. Leadership is not to be used for personal benefits (VV. 1-2). This unjust steward seems to have forgotten or has willfully chosen to ignored this most essential of all stewardship and leadership truths, due to his selfishness and self-serving heart, that leadership is not about getting, but about giving, and true leaders lose their right to be selfish. We must learn that the Lord is the Owner and Master and we are just appointed and trusted stewards managing His properties, for a steward cannot hide his heart from His Master, and to his own Master, he shall stand or fall. "I, The

Lord also search the heart, I test the mind, even to give everyone according to his ways, according to the fruit of his doings." (Jer 17:10). The leader as the steward, while powerful and resourceful, is also always vulnerable in that he rises or falls to the level of the leader's personal and spiritual integrity (Maxwell, P. 1285).

 2. While the world may applaud their own leaders for their great successes, God highly honors faithfulness, and prospers those who exercise their faith to please Him. Our faith in the Lord enables us to be faithful to the Lord, and in turn the gracious and generous Lord makes us fruitful for the Master's use and purpose. And this principle is clearly shown in this somewhat controversial parable in that if one is faithful in managing the small things for the Lord, He will entrust the steward with many big things as the steward is proven over time to be trustworthy (V. 16:10). Trust is central in all reliable relationships, and she or he who has not been tested should not be trusted, for trust is the only reliable foundation of spiritual stewardship and it is the law of the solid ground. Trust can never be demanded or commanded over night. It has to be earned over time!

 3. In order to ensure and achieve a life of authentic integrity, the spiritual steward must be willing to go through the necessary checks and balances of accountability of his stewardship responsibilities, for there is no real integrity without serious accountability, just as there is no real maturity without intentional responsibility. This is so because no one is immune to temptation and no one is fully exempt from the devilish deception in this secularized, sensualized and satanized society with our sinful fleshly nature in its fallen condition and shaken structure (Jer 2:13). The weeping prophet Jeremiah (17:9) declares under the divine anointing the ugly truth that "the heart is deceitful above all things, and desperately wicked; Who can know it?" But the Lord knows and uses our earthly authorities such as the masters and mentors, parents and leaders, to challenge and check on us to ascertain integrity. "What is this I hear about you? Give an account of your stewardship, for you can no longer be steward." (Lk 16:2). This hard and even

somewhat harsh confrontation and decision make me think of a famous Chinese proverb that in essence declares the same principle of leadership and truth on stewardship: Don't use those you suspect; and don't suspect those you use! Once trust is fractured or lost, then the relationship becomes nonexistent, for all real and meaningful relationship and partnership and friendship are built on the cornerstone of trust. True trust has to be tested (Gen 22:1 and John 6:6). He who is not tested should not be trusted or used of men, let alone be used of the Lord. And he who has failed the test of faithfulness and obedience, as in the case of the disobedient King Saul, no matter how good looking or charismatic, can never be used for God's glory and purpose in the same way as before, in spite of confession and repentance. Based on our 30 plus years of full-time faithful and fruitful ministries and humble servant leadership, we can assure you that this is how the real world really works, even in the church world. Please also turn now to Heb 4:13 and 13:17, Matt 25:19, and Rom 14:12 to read and reflect on the divine command and demand of human accountability to the proper authority for our own formation of integrity and transformation of Christian life and stewardship ministries.

    4. This man was wasting His goods (Lk 16:2). A spiritual steward is never to be lazy, lavish and thus wasteful; rather he is to be faithful and frugal as frugality is the foundation of much more lasting financial fruit and future prosperity. King Solomon wisely concludes in Proverbs 13:11, that he who gathers little by little makes it grow. Do you know the three key words that profile the affluent based on numerous serious studies? In case you don't, they are: frugal, frugal and frugal. Being frugal is the cornerstone of wealth building (Blue & White, P. 56.). The individual's industry and frugality will bring him or her much prosperity because as industry makes and earns the money, it takes the spirit of frugality to really save and conserve what's made and earned. But if he is lavish and wasteful, as the accusation was against the unrighteous manager, then the steward will not have much left for the master. Let us never become wasteful consumers but work hard with the divine

favors to become frugal conservers and cheerful givers for wealth creation with the higher purpose of pleasing our Lord when we wisely and generously do the contribution and distribution, so that His name can be highly exalted above all gods, and His mission can be extended unto all the earth! Just as the water covers the sea, may the glory of the knowledge of God cover the entire world (Hab 2:14).

5. The Lord does commend the steward for his shrewdness and does declare the sad fact, unfortunately that even the children of the world are more shrewd than us the children of light. In spite of the major problems above listed, of this lousy leader and selfish steward, the Lord Jesus does use this parable to teach us some vital life lessons and subtle Kingdom truths through shrewd and fruitful business practices with the right motives that bring much more eternal profits for His cause:

- A. A spiritual steward is to be smart and successful, not slow and stupid;
- B. A spiritual steward is to be decisive and active, not hesitant and passive;
- C. A spiritual steward is not only to be cleared from any illusion, delusion, confusion and consternation, but also be filled with divine wisdom, Spirit's power and personal courage to make smart decisions followed up by immediate actions (Lk 16:3-7) based on an accurate assessment of the real condition and situation.
- D. A spiritual steward is to be always passionate and proactive, and never become filled with apathy or passive, for pro-activity propels productivity and prosperity, while idle and lazy passivity only produces powerless and pitiful poverty! Apathy is a terrible thing that leads to lethargy. Remember that the opposite of love is not hate, but apathy, the spirit or attitude of indifference and lukewarmness that seriously hinder progress.
- E. A spiritual steward is not to be negative in his attitude, but always positive and thus promising about the future as he

is rooted deeply and based firmly on the Promises of God. Positivity propels passion and perseverance while negativity navigates one to nowhere!

F. A spiritual steward is hopeful and optimistic, and not pessimistic, for while a poor pessimist sees only the obstacles in any given opportunity, the optimist sees clearly and seizes quickly all the opportunities in spite of the obstacles and oppositions. The Chinese character for the English word "crisis" is a compound word composed of two separated but related parts: "Wei-Ji", meaning "dangers and opportunities". This is an optimistic life philosophy with the conviction that in the middle of dangers in life, there are always opportunities. The great Christian leader who was also a powerful and profitable spiritual steward, Apostle Paul declares in Ephesus essentially the same truth and theology in I Cor 16:9. "For a great and effective door has opened for me, and there are many adversaries" and many oppositions to the ministries even to the anointed apostle. The Lord intends to teach us His stewards through Luke 16 and the apostle Paul that no matter what the circumstances and situations, be firm, be stable, be strong, be immovable, and never ever give up! Your obstacles and oppositions are your God-given opportunities to prove your fidelity and manifest His glory, and your Adversity is the available best University for you to attend and get your degrees free of charge! This precious, powerful, peerless and piercing verse (I Cor 16:9) illustrates also my thoughts on doors with three D.O's --- (1) Divine Opportunities (D.O) are always available to those who desire to do His will and to finish His work as open Doors normally represent; (2). Devilish Oppositions (D.O) will also be present there to attack you when you seriously endeavor to embrace the divine opportunities; (3). Great blessings and rewards will be gloriously bestowed in the end only upon the Dedicated Overcomers (D.O) who are faithful, fearless, forceful and fruitful to the final fabulous finish!

G. A spiritual steward is to be always content in and grateful to the Lord his Master and Owner, and never to be covetous and greedy for selfish gains or personal preservations (Lk 12:15). We must be always on our guard against any greedy intention or greedy action as it is truly ubiquitous and rampant in all the nations. Carefully study James 4:1-3 and take heed to lead with righteous motivation and pure passion for the Lord, doing everything from the heart as unto the Lord, not for our selfish gains or for others to see, for it is from the Lord that we shall receive our reward and commendations in the last days (Col 3:23).

H. A spiritual steward is BP: a good and proper combination of Biblical Principles with Balanced Practicality; His spirituality is to be based on both the timeless truths of God's Word and the objective and even brutal reality and authentic actuality, operating out of faith and courage, and not fear and cowardice!

I. A spiritual steward clearly understands and effectively utilizes the value of human relationship to produce influence, which is what true leadership is. The steward should take the initiative to use the temporal and material things in order to accomplish the spiritual and the eternal, and use debt reduction as an effective incentive to encourage and motivate people to follow the Jesus call and fulfill the Jesus missions! Initiatives, incentives and objectives are all integral components of stewardship.

J. A spiritual steward motivates and mobilizes others by making friends to maximize and multiply the desirable results: using the temporary tangible means such as the "unrighteous mammon" to obtain the unshakable eternal and invisible kingdom. A true leader produces effective results which speak for itself and for all to see and believe.

K. A spiritual steward is to be extremely shrewd in sharing His life, showing His love and shining His light in this shaky and shady world! Remember the Owner and

Master, while exposing, denouncing and clearly condemning this dishonest steward for his unfaithfulness and his unrighteousness, did also commend and praise him for his "shrewdness" ---astute intelligence, smart and sound judgment, and a well-thought-out planning, as the central controlling idea of the parable is Jesus instruction of the issue of shrewdness. "For the sons of this world are more shrewd in their generation the sons of light." What a gentle and loving indictment and a soft rebuke with a spiritual remedy! What a wake-up call to us all.

L. Together with all the positive and powerful and productive instructions, Jesus gives us the practical applications of spiritual stewardship in verses 9-13. Practice generosity with the available wealth because it blesses and empowers people, and makes friends who can be used for the spiritual purpose of advancing the Kingdom of God! Be faithful to God in small earthly things, and He will commit to your trust and reward you with much more true riches of eternal kingdom values and treasures. Most important of all, the spiritual steward must know once and for all, that material wealth is not the end in and of itself. It is only a mean, an effective and indispensable mean to the end.

M. No one can serve two masters... You cannot serve both God and money (V. 13). What a timely and serious warning for all of us in all places at all times as stewards of the Lord. God demands and deserves our complete loyalty and full faithfulness. One must daily align himself to be totally focused on serving the Lord alone, with undivided attention and with the perspective of eternity! The Lord promises you perfect peace and power for your life if your mind is stayed on Him and if your heart deeply trust in Him (Isa 26:3-4).

Reflections and Observations

When I was visiting in the Holy land of Israel, I was greatly amused to see many wonders 5ere, and to be in the places where

Jesus walked and taught over two thousand years ago. The Bible really became alive! And through the teachings and guidance of our excellent Messianic Jewish pastor/teacher and tour guide Arie Bar David, I have gained much deeper understanding and apprehension on the teachings of Jesus. Especially on the methodology of the teachings of the Lord Jesus who is the master of all masters, and teacher of all teachers. He is the master of "point and teach" with parables in which He uses the visible things to reveal the invisible, to use the temporal to the eternal, to use the material to reveal the spiritual.

In the Parable of the Unjust Steward, Jesus the Lord surprisingly praised the manager for his shrewdness in terms of his adequate and timely preparation for the impending future existential crisis, and his shrewdness in using the temporal materials to gain favors from others, which would position him to secure a higher and bigger return in terms of Human Resources way beyond monetary gains.

In reflecting on the parable, we must go beyond just serving the present daily necessities of life. We need to be thinking long term and not merely existing and serving from paycheck to paycheck (known as the "hand to mouth" disease) every month. Therefore be sufficiently Prepared for time of crisis way ahead of the possible crisis, with preparations of emergency funds and accumulation of other relational and spiritual assets and resources.

If we want to increase ourselves and influence others in our lives and ministries, it will be very advantageous for us to learn from this Chinese proverbs depending on the specific individual situations of short-term objectives and long-term goals. "If you want crops, plan and plant for a season; if you want trees, plan and plant for a decade; but if you want people, plan and plant for a century!"

Some questions you may ask yourself for your personal and organizational situation:

1. If I am out of a job, how long can I sustain with my financial situation?

2. What are the available Human Resources that I can rely on in time of crisis?   And how long can I count on them?
3. How can I develop trusting relationships with others and become more shrewd myself?

Chapter 5

Jewish Values, Views, Wisdom, and Ways to Wealth

He who walks with the wise grows wise, but a companion of fools suffers harm (Prov 13:20).

The crown of the wise is their riches, but the foolishness of fools yields folly (Prov 14:24).

Proverbs 12:24 Diligent hands will rule (bring wealth), but laziness ends in (poverty) slave labor.

Proverbs 20:4 A sluggard does not plow in season; so at harvest time he looks but finds nothing. 20:13 Do not love sleep or you will grow poor; stay awake and you will have food to spare.

There is a close correlation between wisdom and wealth in that the greater the wisdom, the more the wealth.

My people are destroyed for lack of knowledge (Hosea 4:6).

It is in the nature of man to long for wealth — Jewish Proverb.

If you have money, men think you wise, handsome, and able to sing like birds (Jewish Proverb).

Faith and Finances

Sad is the man who has nothing but money (Jewish Proverb).

A heavy purse is light to carry. A heavy purse makes a light heart. A golden key (money) opens all doors (Jewish Proverb).

The world rests on three things: Money, money and money (Jewish Proverb).

A good income cures most ills. To be without money is a great mistake (Jewish Proverb).

It's easier to make money than to keep it (Jewish Proverb).

Better a steady dime than a rare dollar (Jewish Proverb).

It's not that money makes everything good; it's that no money makes everything rotten (Jewish Proverb).

If you want to earn, you must first learn. He who refuses to learn deserves extinction --- (Jewish Proverb).

An "illiterate" Jew is a contradiction in terms – Jewish Proverb.

Even a learned bastard stands higher than an ignorant high priest ---Jewish Proverb

Who is wise? The one who learns from everyone ... who is powerful? The one who subdues his own ego (inclinations)... who is rich? The one who is content (satisfied) with his lot... who is honorable? The one who honors others --- Ben Zoma, Ethics of the Fathers.

By your wisdom and understanding, you have gained wealth for yourself and amassed gold and silver in your treasuries. By your great skill in trading you have increased wealth, and because of your wealth your heart has grown proud (Eze 28:4-5).

Therefore, keep the words of this covenant, and do them, that you may prosper in all that you do (Deut 29:9).

What must a man do that he may become wise? Let him engage much in study (The Talmud, Niddah 70b).

Everyone complains about the lack of money, but none complain about a lack of brains. You must first learn and then you will earn. --- Jewish proverb.

Not to teach your son to work is to teach him to steal --- Jewish Proverb.

Jerusalem was destroyed because its children did not attend school. One lesson we have learned from history is that people don't learn lessons from history.

You are not living in poverty when you have no butter for your bread!

Brains to the lazy are like a torch to the blind --- a useless burden!

Matthew 25:16 The man who had received the five talents went At Once and put his money to work and gained five More — Jesus of Nazareth

Ecclesiastes 11:4 Whoever watches the wind will not plant; whoever looks at the clouds will not reap.

The wise does at once what the fool does at last — Jewish Proverb

The chief source of man's misery is his obsession to add to his wealth and honor.

It is an open secret that Jews do not work, but rather let others work for them... No other ethnic group has even come close to matching the abilities and accomplishments of Jews --- H. W. Charles.

Man's best companion is intellect, and his worst enemy, lust --- Jewish Proverb.

The man who thinks that anything can be accomplished by money is likeLy to do anything for money — Jewish Proverb.

Proverbs 11:24 One man gives freely, yet gains even more; another withholds unduly, but comes to poverty.11:25 A generous man will prosper; he who refreshes others will himself be refreshed.The love of money leads to idolatry, and causes those who have it to fall into madness.

When death summons a man to appear before his Maker, his money can not go with him. Gold, silver, precious jewels and pearls are left behind when God calls you.

The Torah spreads light, but it is the money that gives warmth --- Jewish Proverb.

Prosperity is power; and nothing is more painful than poverty – Jewish Proverb.

When a habit begins to cost money, it's called a hobby (Jewish Proverb).

While many ethnic and religious groups are mainly focused on the afterlife and downplaying this world, Jews view wealth and success as a blessing and gift of God... Jews believe that people are creators, not consumers. The role of humans is to improve and perfect God's creation through work, creation and innovation... It is the Jewish religious texts such as the Hebrew Scriptures that contain valuable information on acquiring wealth --- H.W. Charles

The Jews are known for their perseverance, and this is what helps them achieve their goals. Perseverance means continuous persistence in a course of action, a purpose, in spite of difficulties, obstacles, or discouragement --- H.W. Charles.

In Jewish history, there are no coincidences --- Elie Wiesel

Some people like the Jews, and some don't. But no thoughtful man can deny the fact that they are, beyond any question, the most formidable and the most remarkable race which has ever appeared in the world --- Sir Winston Churchill

The 5 Key Factors of Jewish Success

Having done extensive studies over many years along with personal observations of and participation with the precious Jewish people around the world, especially with the Messianic Jews of Israel, I have summarized five central and crucial factors that have contributed to their enormous and extraordinary successes in many numerous fields of endeavors. Of the many areas, we will examine and explore in relation to faith and finances the Jewish way:

1. Faith. To be a Jew means to be ready to be a martyr. Certainly the heroism of the defenders of every other creed fades into insignificance before this martyr people, the Jews, who confronted all the evils and endured the most hideous sufferings, rather than abandoning their faith (Rosten, 1972). The Jewish faith believes and emphasizes wealth and riches as a gift and blessing from God their Creator.
2. Family. Family is everything to the Jewish people. They are strongly united in faith and unselfishly support each other in finances to ensure successes and victories for their members. Parents are disciplined to teach their children with both precepts and examples. One is worse than an infidel if she or he does not take care of the family first. It

has been the cultural norm for the Jewish parents to bring up their children to value education and wealth creation within the family, communal and social contexts. Jewish families strongly encourage the pursuit of wealth accumulation, high-income careers, and investing long term.
3. Friends. In order to prosper and succeed in faith and finances, one must make steady and constant efforts to build a network of trusted friends and associates. In order to really get ahead in life, one must learn to effectively and efficiently get along with others!
4. Fortification through extreme emphasis on education. Even a learned bastard stands higher than an ignorant high priest (Jewish Proverb). The Jews are bibliomaniacs unparalleled to all the other sections of humanity, because they know that one must constantly learn in order to earn! They understand the close correlation between learning and earning..
5. Finances. He who increases books, increases wisdom and wealth, for your books are your true treasures, thus accurately says another Jewish proverb. Nothing can replace the central role of education as the foundation for wealth creation. The Jewish culture is high on giving charity. And philanthropy necessitates finances. Everyone would have become a philanthropist if it did not cost money.

In order to succeed and prosper with both spiritual victory and financial abundance, it is also of absolute necessity, for us to seriously develop and efficiently utilize the combination of these five crucial concentrations, because the five key factors (what to do) are put into real life practice though the following methodology (How to do it) of communication, connection, collaboration, creation, and contribution. Let us take a careful look at them:

1. Communication. If something is to be sold, it has to be first told, as an old saying goes. This takes both the desires for and skills of, effective communication. In order to succeed in

life, one must be constantly communicating with a variety of people so as to be "in the know" and on the cutting edge of what's happening (ignorance is not a bliss). Communicating with others not only keeps you well informed with news, but also opens many doors of opportunities for your future. It stimulates your mind and heart with admiration, inspiration and aspiration.

2. Connection. Belonging to a group is a powerful thing. This inter-connectedness with the group, be it religious, financial, cultural or political, will bring you the encouragement to lift each other up, the wisdom to sharpen each other's saws, and the accountability in that you will be held accountable by the most virtuous people in the group. Making and maintaining connections with other people is absolutely crucial to your career and the health of the overall economy.

3. Collaboration. No one, no matter how smart and strong, can ever succeed in life on his or her own. It really takes a village. You need a team. We see this principle at work in Luke 5 as Peter was actively recruiting workers to expand his network with bigger net worth of fishes. Without a doubt, your current network determines your future net worth, and the kingdom of God is vivdly likened unto a dragnet, according to Jesus teaching. No one can get ahead spiritually or financially without making serious efforts in getting along with other people.

4. Creation. Where there is a harmonious cooperation with synergistic passion, there will inevitably be new innovations and new creations of better products and more services, which when put into the market, will in turn reap a huge harvest of wealth and prosperity for everyone involved. The unleashing of the collective force with purpose and passion will result in much wealth creation. But remember that a man's drive for profits should be prompted equally by his desire to give to charity, in order to live a life of healthy and beautiful balances.

5. Contribution. The more wealth created and becomes available, the more there is to give. Giving to charity with generosity is spiritual, moral, honorable, and healthy for us all, as Jewish wisdom emphatically teaches. Remember the close correlation between giving and loving. Love life and life will love you back. The more we love others, the more we will be loved by others. We must first give before we can expect to get, although the motive of giving should never be getting. As you invest wisely, actively, and generously, your returns will automatically take care of themselves. The secret of living is in giving and not in getting, thus says a Jewish proverb. This is made super clear by the key principle laid out by the Lord Jesus in Luke 6:38 as a law of the kingdom.

In an interesting and insightful online article I read at **www.smartmoneytoday.com**, entitles, "Do you Want t Be Rich? Think Like A Jew", Rudy asserts that there is no doubt that Jews are disproportionately successful and wealthy. They are the smartest and the most educated people group in the world, and as a result they are the most successful businessmen and women out there. While the Jews are only 0.02% of the world population, yet 25% of the all billionaires and 35% of the all Nobel Prize laureates are Jewish! This Jewish phenomenon has been rooted, for thousands of years now in their unshakable and unstoppable faith Judaism in the Jehovah God who gives them the wisdom and the ability to prosper by acquiring enormous wealth! Their religious teachings through the Tanakh, the Torah, the Talmud, the Mishnah and other authoritative texts are deeply ingrained into their cultural psyche that provide the secrets to their success, especially in the educational and financial arenas. They together help form a special and unique Jewish mindset, if you will, with practical principles and personal disciplines for successes in life and in business with abundance. Faith is foundation, and the best education for themselves and their children is absolutely crucial to the Jews and their prosperity. Ever since the time of Moses over 3000 years ago, the Jewish people were commanded to teach their children and their children's children to become an educated people. The Talmud repeatedly teaches, "A community that has no school teachers shall be excommunicated."

The Judaist faith holds a very high value and a positive view on wealth and money. Money is not evil, not neutral and not just essential for the abundant life, success and prosperity. Rather money is consistently viewed as spiritual, and moral and a great blessing and a visible and tangible favor of the Almighty. Making money is a spiritual activity that has inherent value, morality and dignity when business transactions provide good customer satisfaction with services of excellence and products of high quality (Lapin, 2014,28-34). Riches and honors are praised along with godliness and righteousness. They as a culture really look down on poverty because those who live in poverty cannot help anyone else when they cannot even take care of themselves. The poor instead become a burden and a liability to society and to all that are around them. The only virtue for the existence of poverty is that the rich can have a chance to practice a little bit of their charity, thus says the sage in a Jewish proverb. They strongly believe and heavily invest in themselves and their children's education that in turn equip them to make smart decisions and wise choices for their lifestyle over a long haul. The most important investment one can ever make is investing in himself, and his education, an appreciative asset of high values or life that will pay you back many times over. An old saying goes like this: "If you think education is expensive, you should know that ignorance is much more expensive!" If one wants to earn, he must be willing, eager and ready to learn. More learning when properly applied results in more earning, as a good education is indispensably a most effective key to wealth creation.

H.W. Charles strongly asserts a central truth for religious Jews throughout his excellent Little book (2016). The Jews understand that the divine blessings of wealth and riches upon them are dependent upon their obedience to the laws and covenant of God.

The laws in the Torah, if faithfully followed, will doubtlessly brings the divine favors of much blessings for each generation. If they listen to and obey God, they will be blessed with prosperity throughout their lives (Job 36:11). And they who fear the Lord and finds great delight in His commandments, will be mighty and be blessed with wealth and riches in their houses along with righteousness (Ps 112:1-3). We must do our part with trust and obedience before God will do His part for us with rich abundance. What an unfailing promise for us if we heed the Word!

According to countless studies of the Jewry, the Jewish way of educating the children has been far more advanced than any other racial or ethnic group from centuries back in that it demands not just mental memorization of key concepts and principles, but develops critical-thinking skills, team work, and encourages questions and answers. The definition of a "good student" is one who asks great questions that make the teacher wiser! The emphasis in Jewish tradition has always been the education of the whole child, with rich spiritual foundation, in the context of a closely-knit family and community relations with strong and distinct ethnic identity, with tough reasoning skills for making smart choices in all areas of life, especially in money making and money management. Choices are indeed the most powerful influence in life. Poverty is a result of poor choices, not of poor luck. On the other hand, riches and prosperity become a reality, not by random lucky chance, but by prayerful and careful choices, not by default, but by design. And this design is both human and divine, as it, of necessity, always consists in the two parts harmoniously and effectively working together: God's part and our part.

The Jar System of Jewish Money Management: The Five Principles

For the Jews, financial education starts at a very young age, teaching and training the kids about money matters with financial disciplines as early as only 2 years old. Children are taught by precepts and examples with a jar system to develop a real and visual understanding of money and how it is to be made and used. Money is segregated into five separate jars, and one is not allowed to move the money from one jar to another (known as the misappropriation of funds!). Here goes the Jewish Jar System of personal finance with these following five principles:

1. **Tithe**: The paying of the tithes (10% of one's earning) is an important part of Jewish religious worship and spiritual life, as one's sacred visible and tangible commitment to God. The Talmud (Shabbath 119a) commands all Jews to tithe with a clear promise: "Give tithes so that you may become wealthy." According to America's rabbi Daniel Lapin (2014, P. 234), the Hebrew word for "tithing" is "ashar" which is also the word for "wealth". There is no coincident for there is no such a word as "coincident" in the Lord's language of Hebrew. If a word in Hebrew like "ashar" has more than one meaning, it means that the Lord wants to let us know the inter-connectedness of the meanings. The two concepts of tithes and wealth as expressed by "ashar" are inextricably linked with each other although the concepts may seem counter-intuitive. Wealth is all about making money, and tithing is all about giving money. Yet as we give our tithes and other offerings, God will give wealth back to us in abundance. We must remember and learn to give first before we will get. There is great morality in generous charity. This is why charity is one of the greatest tools for making money!

2. **Giving**: 10% is giving or offering for your neighborhood in need through charity: care and share. Charity is the spice of riches. For every action, there is always a reaction. This is the law of cause and effect. One is taught to first give before he or she gets. The more you give away, the more it comes back to you. Giving money makes you a desirable person and others will want to be around you. Charity is a powerful act because it makes you feel better about yourself;

it also makes other people view you more favorably, which is always good for connections for future businesses and finances. Giving provides the human interaction that is the foundation for wealth creation. It is a virtuous cycle with many blessings for everyone.
3. **Saving**: 10% is to be kept away for emergency. One must always be reasonably prepared for the rainy days ahead with an emergency fund.
4. **Investing**: 20% is to invest, as early as possible, with a long-term strategy of growth and multiplication with the compounding power to create and increase wealth! A slow but steady strategy always succeeds.
5. **Spending**: 50% of the income is the budgeted spending for daily needs

Religion, Education, Wealth Creation and Generous Contribution

From the studies of the numerous successful Jews who annually top the Forbes' fortune list (the top 139 of the 400 richest people in the world were Jewish in 2009, for example and annually about the same, varies little!), one clearly convincing and completely compelling conclusion is that their deeply imbedded Judaist religion directly influences the wealth creation and accumulation and thus the levels of contribution and distribution. This is so because religion shapes one's values, sets one's priorities, and greatly contributes to the set of competencies from which action is constructed. The religious context also provides the necessary spiritual, financial and relational contacts that are conducive to one's inspiration, mentorship, prosperity and success. There is solid evidence beyond any disputes, that being raised Jewish and practicing Judaism leads to wealth with all the environmentally available, timeless, and practice-proven strategies and tools at their disposal to acquire prosperity, so much so that leading authority in the area declares that "Judaism is the most important intellectual development in human history." (Charles, P. 9).

However, one does not have to become a Jew or convert to their religion Judaism to become wealthy. What is needed for one to accumulate massive wealth is to forsake the lies they are constantly told and stay out of the self-destructive path (Jer 8:4-5). One must be willing to carefully examine and radically change his ways of thinking (your mentality determines your economy!) and doing things (as the mind goes, the man follows!) in order to generate a different life, for the gracious and impartial God has also promised us all the righteous Gentiles that He will also bless the foreigners who commit themselves to trust and serve the Lord and do what pleases Him (Isa 56:6-8). This is the heart of the Good News of Jesus Christ to all peoples on earth regardless of their cultures or colors, races or ethnicities! And His promises of peace, purpose, power and prosperity in all things never change and never fail, and they are ours to embrace, inherit and enjoy if we will trust and obey and follow His prescribed premises. Remember no premises, no promises! And as we diligently do our part, God will surely do His part with fabulous favors to bless us.

The famous Jewish rabbi in the USA, Daniel Lapin (2002), wrote a marvelous book on Jewish prosperity whose principles and commands are readily available and applicable to all of us who are not Jewish. This book *Thou Shall Prosper: Ten Commandments for Making Money,* leads you to the deep fundamentals and the bare essentials of the Jewish core values and views that have given them the vision and empowered them with faith and financial victories over many centuries. It contains what he calls "the ten commandments" for making money. They are full of life-transforming and life-giving principles that have greatly encouraged, empowered and equipped us over the years. Here is a succinct summary of the book I highly recommend Thou Shall Prosper:

1. You must believe in the dignity and morality of business. You and all of us are actually in business. What you do for a living is your business to serve other people, "God's other children". When you do your job with professionalism and excellence, you are a benefit to yourself and many others, and you will be amply rewarded as a result! Each of the

dollar bills you receive is a literal your certificate of excellent service that your satisfied customers give you as tokens of their appreciation.
2. You must extend the network of your connectedness to many people. Actively, genuinely, joyfully interact with other people with the purpose of cultivating real trusting relationships, for human interaction is a foundation of wealth creation, and people do business with those they like, know, and most importantly, they trust. Improve your network and it will enhance your net-worth, and there is zero doubt about it.
3. You must get to know yourself. Know both your weaknesses and strengths. Eliminate the unhealthy habits and undesirable human traits in you that get in your way of growth. Build and develop good character and healthy and attractive habits that people will admire and trust to do business with. The law of attraction applies here. Character always counts the most. You habits can make you or break you, all depending on what they are. Be careful with your daily habits and be cognizant of their effects on your life, especially on your spiritual, relational and financial life. A wise Jewish proverb says it well that "habits become a hobby when it begins to cost money."
4. Don't pursue perfection. Perfection is an infection and is indeed a delusion and unhealthy and unproductive distraction, for nothing in this imperfect world will ever be perfect. Don't insist on "fairness" either in this unfair world with all kinds of problems (no such a word as "fair" in Hebrew). Don't blame the world or others for your own problems, and don't make any excuses. Instead, take serious responsibilities for your personal growth and progress regardless of the world and others, for only responsibility produces in all of us the measure of maturity.
5. Lead consistently and constantly. Leadership is all about influence. We are all leaders in one way or another because

we all have influence on others. Tirelessly develop the character, the will and the skill within you so others will be attracted to you and naturally want to follow you.
6. Constantly change the changeable while steadfastly clinging to the unchangeable. The more things change, the more we must depend on the things that never change. Make sure you know the differences between the unchanging values and principles, and the flexible strategies and methodologies. Never violate the moral and spiritual truths of God. Keep the balance with the proper priority and perseverance, and you will prosper.
7. Learn to foretell the future by learning historical lessons and observing certain consistent patterns so as to be prepared to predict the trends reasonably and face the future with confidence and appropriate plans to prosper. The more you do it, the better you will get, and the more money you will make as you plan ahead of time. Be prepared to prosper.
8. Know your money. This requires serious diligence in gaining financial information and knowledge (20% of your success), and more essentially in your disciplined long-term and lifestyle applications (80% of your success). Learn the principles of how to make and manage your money well, especially on how to properly budget your finances so you will always avoid debt, stay out of debt, you will aggressively save, generously give, wisely invest to make your money work for your prosperity and your posterity.
9. You must act rich! Don't live beyond your means; instead give beyond your means! Giving charity jump-starts wealth creation. Giving meets a need and makes one feel virtuous! Charity focuses you outside yourself. Donation is like investment that opens new doors with new friends to partner with in life and business. Giving to charity really does enhance your own money-making ability! Be an active creator of wealth, and not a passive consumer. Be a generous giver and not a selfish getter or taker! What goes around will

eventually come around with more blessings. This has been tested and proven true over and over again in both Jewish and Christian traditions.
10. You should never retire! There is no such a thing as "retirement" in the Hebrew language and in a biblical sense. Retirement is not healthy for you but selfish of you. Staying useful in some ways in the work you deeply care for and are passionate about helps others, and it helps you to live happier and longer and more productive life with rich meanings and a higher purpose when connected to God above and people around.

In his more recent and also excellent book (2014), *Business Secrets from the Bible,* Spiritual Success Strategies for Financial Abundance, Rabbi Daniel Lapin reveals to us, in much further details with practical applications, 40 biblically "secret" spiritual success strategies for us to achieve financial prosperity. They are extremely helpful and truthful Jewish wisdom and ways for us to read, study, apply and share with others so as to be blessed together to bless others more and more. These success secrets are deeply rooted and grounded in the Word of God, the basis of our faith and core value system. Among the most important instructions for immediate personal application and profitable practices are:

1. Our infinite Creator God created us in His image with the potential for infinite imagination, connection, wealth creation and life transformation.
2. God wants us to be obsessively preoccupied with the needs and desires of His other children. He desires for us to get before we get.
3. When we focus on serving others' needs and desires, we will never ever be short of what we desire and need.
4. Become a people person in genuine relationship and partnership with others to serve them faithfully, professionally, effectively and joyfully.

5. Life is not about what you know, but rather it is about who you are! Therefore, focus on building your self-discipline, integrity and character in order to achieve abundant success and prosperity.
6. You must strike a balance and live a well-balanced life, simultaneously developing all the dimensions of your life, spiritual, physical, relational, psychological and financial, in order to achieve the real Shalom: totality, completion, peace and harmony.
7. In order to lead others, we must learn to follow, for you cannot lead if you cannot follow. Trust, obey and follow the solid Biblical instructions with daily, diligent and disciplined applications.
8. Know how the world and especially the business world really work through courage, vision, specialization and cooperation. One must first be willing and eager to learn before he or she can earn. More learning more earning.
9. Know the nature of money: the spirituality, morality and dignity of making money and managing money with a higher purpose.
10. How you feel about yourself is how others will see you. Respect can not be demanded. It has to be earned, like trust. In order to earn others' respect, you must have self respect and always respect others. Then respect from others will come naturally your way.

Reflections and Observations

Once I watched a movie which made a big impression on me. In it there was a chauffeur for a rich business family. The family had various investment businesses. As the chauffeur drove them around, he overheard them day in and day as to what they were investing in to get wealth, he began to learn from the, and followed their examples. Whatever they invested in, he would invested in the same thing also; and whenever they cashed out, he'd also cash out. As time went by little by little, the chauffeur himself become a millionaire!

Sometimes we may lack the wisdom to make money or are not as smart as other people such as the Jews in this chapter, but if we can humbly and actively learn from the rich and successful and emulate their examples for our lives, before we know it, we will become successful and prosperous ourselves. The ancient Chinese proverb pinpoints it well that, the one who stays near vermillion gets stained red; and the one who stays near ink gets stained blacks. One does take the attributes of his or her associates without realizing it sometimes. Therefore, choose your close associates very prayerfully and carefully as they will have an effect and an influence on you for better or for worse. Remember that stuff really rubs off on you!

Questions to ponder upon:

1. Who among my friends are very wise and successful in financial matters?
2. How can I pattern after them financially to be successful?
3. What are the vital principles I have learned from the Jewish wisdom and wealth that I can directly apply to my life here and now?

Chapter 6

Faith and Finances
Puritan Spirit, Protestant Ethics,
And Proverbial Wisdom on Work and Wealth

Proverbs 22:29 --- Do you see a man skilled at his work? He will serve before kings; he will not serve before obscure men.

II Thess 3:7-10 --- For you yourselves know how to follow our example. We were not idle when we were with you, nor did we eat anyone's food without paying for it. On the contrary, we worked night and day, laboring and toiling so that we would not be a burden to any of you. We did this, not because we do not have a right to such help, but in order to make ourselves a model for you to follow... If anyone will not work, he shall not eat.

Thomas Jefferson — Never spend money before you have earned it.

Benjamin Franklin --- An investment in knowledge pays the best interest.

Benjamin Franklin --- Tell me and I forget. Teach me and I remember. Involve me and I learn.

Benjamin Franklin --- A plowman on his feet is taller than a gentleman on his knees.

Faith and Finances

Benjamin Franklin --- He that is of the opinion money will do everything may well be suspected of doing everything for money.

Benjamin Franklin --- It's better to go to bed without dinner than to rise in debt.

Benjamin Franklin — If would be wealthy, think of saving as well as getting.

T. T. Munger — The habit of saving is itself an education; it fosters very virtue, teaches self-denial, cultivates the sense of order, trains to forethought, and so broadens the mind.

Jonathan Swift — Wise persons should have money in their heads, but not in their hearts.

Martin Luther --- There are three conversions necessary, the conversions of the heart, the mind and the purse. Of the three conversions, the last one is the hardest one.

John Wesley --- Earn all you can (industry); save all you can (frugality); and Give all you can (generosity).

John Calvin --- There is no work, however vile or sordid, that does not glisten before God... All the blessings we enjoy are divine deposits, committed to our trust on this condition, that they should be dispensed for the benefits of our neighbors.

Honor your Lord with your work, for work is your solemn and noble Christian duty for the glory of God and the good of man.

Thomas Edison — Opportunity is missed by most people because it is dressed in overalls and looks like work!

Jim Rohn —Money is usually attracted, not pursed (the law of attraction).

P. T. Barnum — Money is a terrible Master but n excellent servant.

Dave Ramsey — You must gain control over your money or the lack of it will forever control you!

S Truett Cathy --- Wealth is worth it if you earn it honestly, if you spend it wisely and save reasonably, and if you give generously.

In our studies of faith and finances, and the economics of Christian stewardship, a serious student must face the reality of both the psychological and economic issues of scarcity and poverty, and people's search for the needed sense of security. Faith and Stewardship are intricately and inseparably related in that our Christian faith must be deeply rooted and solidly grounded in the living Word and guided by knowledge (Klay, P.34). As stewards of God, we are called by Jesus to bold action based on wise choices. Economic scarcity forces us to choose, and God has called us to make well-intentioned and well-informed choices because of our love for Him and His creation. Making wise and spiritual choices is for us an exercise of faithfulness, when it is based on both faith and knowledge. Let us have a brief historical overview of the Puritans, Protestants, and the many resulting Proverbs on prosperity with a higher divine perspective and the Christ priority.

Without any doubt, the most well known literature on the close correlation between the Christian religion and wealth creation has to be the one done by the German sociologist of religion Dr. Max Weber, entitled, *The Protestant Ethic and the Spirit of Capitalism*, translated into English and published in America 1958. It was a most fascinating and comprehensive study on the nature of the Protestant life theology and work ethic, which in turn have resulted in a massive amount of wealth and capital for the higher purpose and the greater glory of God!

The puritans and the Protestants lifted out and raised up such virtues as their core values and visions from the teachings of the Holy Bible: the virtues of honesty, industry, diligence, frugality, trustworthiness, and punctuality. They both strongly held that view that their work was their direct calling from God and thus a solemn duty to God. They did their work with absolute trustworthiness that assured them with more and larger credits for growth and expansion of their businesses. To them, credit was money. Time is also money in that quality products must be delivered and payment must be made in a timely fashion with punctuality: on time and every time. "The good paymaster is the Lord of another man's purse", meaning that he who was known for paying exactly and punctually to the time he promises, may at any time and on any occasion, raise the money his friends can spare (Weber, PP.48-50). Trust-worthiness is the cornerstone and foundation in business success and expansion, as trust is the law of the solid ground for all real human relations and interactions.

In addition, they emphasized the strict avoidance of all spontaneous enjoyment of life, especially with any hedonistic admixtures as is described in Proverbs 23:20-21 (Weber, P.53). To achieve any success in life, one must work, and work very hard with both discipline and diligence. Discipline was to work hard every day and diligence was to work hard daily to reach excellence, to excel in what one does. Do you see a man who excels in his work? He will stand before kings; He will not stand before unknown men! (Prov 22:29). A person of excellence in his work will be highly exalted, but he who does shoddy work will be, sooner or later, out of business and becomes bankrupt! One's work, no matter what type or kind it might be, was viewed as a sacred calling from above, a divine duty. It was considered a solemn obligation to God for someone to do his job with quality and excellence! Puritan people were taught that no unrestrained, ruthless and unethical acquisition of wealth was to be tolerated as they fulfilled their call from, and duty to their Creator God!

Martin Luther, the Protestant Reformer, had much to teach on work as a calling. According to him (Weber, PP. 80-81), the valuation of the fulfillment of duty in worldly affairs as the highest form an individual can morally assume with religious significance. The only way of living acceptable by God, not by monastic asceticism, but solely through the fulfillment of his obligation imposed upon the individual by his position in the world, for that was his calling. The labor as a calling is an outward expression of brotherly love. This is the will of God. Hence every legitimate calling has exactly the same worth and value in the sight of God. This is the moral and religious justification of worldly activities. Labor was no longer viewed as a curse, or just a thing of the flesh without an end in and of itself. Work as a service to fellowmen as an expression of brotherly love was to be carried out in practice to promote the glory of God, and hence it was willed by God Himself! This doctrine was one of the most important results of Protestant reformation, and it was true not only of Luther, but also of George Fox, John Wesley, and John Calvin of reformed Protestantism.

The principal representative of the Calvinistic ethic was individual and personal responsibility (Weber, P. 115). One must get rid of the fear of the damnation of hell, and start to be become responsible for his life, for "God helps those who help themselves"! A man can know himself, not by mere observation, but only through action, by doing his duties, performing his daily tasks, and carrying out his obligations.

There was, furthermore, a direct instruction on and relationship between religious asceticism (no worldly pleasure) and the spirit of capitalism. Idleness, the waste of time, was the first deadliest of all sins. Relaxation in the security of one's possession was a real moral objection! One was to be on guard against distraction from the pursuit of a righteous life. The person was to work with urgency while it was still "day" (John 9:4), for when night came, no one would be able to work. Saints were not to rest or relax in this world, but to do so in the next world! Wesley emphatically taught and was famously known for this proverbial truth: earn all you can (by diligence and industry); save all you can (by thrift and frugality); and give all you can (with liberality and generosity)! All this was to be done with religious enthusiasm for the Lord and with intensity and urgency for the advancement of the Kingdom of God on earth while there was still a little time left!

According to R. H. Tawney (P. 164), the Puritans held certain strong religious theories and ideals that defined their reality, especially their economic reality for the rise of capitalism. They heavily opposed any forms of the sin of avarice or covetousness (PP. 39-54). They were to glorify God through their works in a world given over to the powers of darkness. Constant prayers, toils and Godly disciplines of both the self and others were an absolute necessity. Spiritual discipline was indeed the very ark of the Puritan covenant. Puritans attuned their hearts to the will of God by an immense effort of concentration and abnegation: to win all, he renounces all! The Puritan life was likened unto a soldier in a hostile territory. The individual was to be personally responsible, active, proactive, and productive in his calling! (P. 189). Although this form of puritan radicalism upset the order of the established churches then , and thus they suffered persecution, yet there was no denial that these very puritan virtues and ethics brought them also spiritual victory and economic prosperity (P. 233). They constantly studies, emphasized and modeled themselves after the excellent biblical steward of Joseph (Gen 39:2) who greatly prospered!

John Wesley on Money and Giving

For the Reverent John Wesley, stewardship was always at the heart of the Wesleyan revival. Financial stewardship was considered an integral part of Christian discipleship and leadership, and it was always a consistent theme in both his life practice and his preaching and teaching ministries. Giving of financial resources was emphasized as an important part of the Christian spiritual discipline. For Wesley, no one was to be exempt from the Lord's commandment to both love and to give. Loving God and one's neighbors is a must, and giving is a visible and tangible expression of that love. Giving is a natural extension of loving.

My personal interactions over the years with many Wesleyan and United Methodist ministers and leaders around the world raised several serious causes of concern in terms of leadership, liberalism, wealth and doctrinal shifts. An article by Bishop Kenneth L. Carter about "John Wesley I read on line on giving" is very revealing (www.interpretermagazine.org). Wesley himself once said, "I am afraid, lest they (the Methodists) only exist as a dead sect, having the form of religion without power. And this undoubtedly will be the case, unless they hold fast both the doctrine, spirit, and discipline with which they first set out." The most evident threat to his movement both in the USA and his nation came not from without, but from within the church, namely, the growing wealth of the Methodists. Wesley believed that "Christianity has within it, the seeds of its own demise," in that while discipleship makes us diligent and frugal, it also makes us increasingly wealthy with our diligence and frugality. With their increase in goods, they also proportionately increase in pride, in the desire of the flesh and the desire of the eyes. Wealth changes our priorities and our relationships. We begin to assume an unrealistic independence and self-reliance, and we forget how to give. While the people observed the first two rules concerning the use of money (Gain all you can, and save all you can), most of them did not observe the third rule, "Give all you can." "And yet nothing can be more plain than that all who observe the first rules without the third will be two fold more the children of hell than ever they were before", declared John Wesley in no uncertain terms.

The life and ministry of John Wesley exemplified the spirit of generous giving and sacrificial living. He preached what he practiced and always practiced what he fervently preached. Only by observing the third rule of stewardship (give all you can), can one find the true meaning and significance of the first two rules. We are to gain all we can and save all we can so that we can give all we can. The first rule emphasizes diligence and industry; and the second rule emphasizes thrift and frugality by living a simplified lifestyle with no extravagance, opulence and self-gratification, not to waste any resources as wise and responsible Christian stewards. It is the third rule of the Wesleyan Christian stewardship that really gives meaning and purpose to the first two because:

1. Giving is rooted in God's very being. For God so loved the world that He gave...
2. Giving is indispensable to Christian discipleship;
3. Giving includes more than the products of our labor;
4. Giving involves friendship with the poor;
5. Giving moves beyond individual charity to building communities of shalom --- communities of interconnectedness and compassion. Giving our voices on behalf of the voiceless, giving insights and influence to build communities that reflects God's reign of justice, generosity and joy.
6. Giving expresses tangibly and visibly our gratitude for God's generosity and God's mission.

Be Money Wise, for Money Matters:
Powerful Proverbial Wisdom on Work and Wealth

I love proverbs of all countries and cultures of the many centuries, and have been an active collector and applier of all the profound insights contained in them. I've benefited so much from its wisdom applied to real life, and I still have much more to learn and a long way to go. Proverbs are short sentences from long experiences, and they encapsulate big ideas in few words. In other words, they always speak so much with so little. These great quotes I have intentionally selected here below for you in the area of faith and finances have bountifully blessed me over the years and I pray and hope that as you learn and apply them in your own money and ministry lives, they will inspire, motivate, encourage, challenge, empower and bless you as well to grow in His grace and glow in His glory.

1. Watch the pennies, and the dollars will take care of themselves! --- Benjamin Franklin
2. A penny saved is a penny earned! --- Benjamin Franklin A penny saved is actually better than a penny earned, because frugality is the cornerstone of wealth creation. Frugality causes prosperity. He who can hold on to his money is worth more than the one who earns it.

3. If you want to sell, you must learn to tell, for it has to be told before it can be sold! Meaning: communication is crucial in faith and finances.
4. Always increase your income and decrease your outgo; if your outgo is greater than you income, then, your upkeep will be your downfall!
5. There are three conversions necessary for the Christian: of the heart, of the mind and of the purse. Of these three conversions, of the purse is the most difficult --- Martin Luther.
6. Work keeps us from three evils: boredom, vice, and poverty. --- Voltaire.
7. The only place where success comes before work is in the dictionary. – Vidal Sassoon.
8. Work like it all depends on you, and pray like it all depends on God --- St. Ambrose
9. Nature gave us two ends --- one to sit on and one to think with. Ever since then, man's success or failure has been dependent on which one he used most --- George Kilpatrick.
10. There are generally four things you can do with your hands: put them in your pockets for safekeeping; fold them in apathy; wringing them in despair; or lay them on a job that needs doing!
11. The recipe for anyone who has gotten to the top is hard work – Margaret Thatcher. (Meaning: diligent industry causes financial prosperity. The one sure place to go and get money is called work).
12. The Samaritan's Purse: The truth of the matter is that no one would have remembered the Samaritan, were it not for his purse – Margaret Thatcher.
13. A workman on his feet stands taller than a gentleman on his knees – Ben Franklin
14. An investment in knowledge always pays the best interest --- Ben Franklin.
15. You must first learn before you can earn! Self-investment is the best investment.

16. Money is an excellent servant, but a terrible master!
17. Master your money before your money masters you! Gain control over your money or your money will forever control you!
18. As vision brings provision, so does money follow ministry!
19. Faith and Finances: Faith increases finances, and finances increase faith!
20. A wise person should have money in the head, but not in the heart. --- Jonathan Swift.
21. Wealth consists not in having great possessions, but in having few wants. --- Epictetus.
22. When you have more to live for, you will need less to live on!
23. Be content with what you have and you will be happy. No greater blessing than contentment; No worse curse than greed --- Chinese proverb.
24. A heart of discontentment is like a snake trying to swallow up an elephant --- Chinese Proverb.
25. Whoever loves money never has enough; whoever loves wealth is never satisfied with his income (Eccl 5:10). He that is of the opinion money will do everything may well be suspected of doing everything for money (Benjamin Franklin)
26. The Jewish shrewdness with money is the stuff of legend. This does not happen by mere chance, but by wise choice, not by default, but by design!
27. Many complain about the lack of money, but none complain about the lack of brains!
28. If charity costs nothing, everyone would be a philanthropist!
29. Do your will while you are living, and then you will be knowing where it's going.
30. Right makes might, but haste makes waste.
31. Team spirit: Your current network will determine your future net-worth. If you are not net working, you are simply not working.
32. Procrastination is the grave in which opportunity is buried.

33. Harmonious human interaction and cooperation are one of the foundations of wealth creation. Interdependence is a higher virtue than independence. If one wants to get ahead financially, he must learn to get along relationally.
34. It is not so terrible when you lose money; but all is lost when courage is lost.
35. Lend money and acquire an enemy.
36. The quickest way to double your money is to fold it over and put it back in your pocket.
37. A habit becomes a hobby when it starts costing you money.
38. Having been poor is no shame, being ashamed of it is (Benjamin Franklin). The lesson: Remembering the crushing weight of debt or poverty is a necessary motivation required of you to sustain frugality and ensure prosperity.
39. Rather go to bed without dinner than to rise in debt (Benjamin Franklin). The lesson: Don't ever live beyond your means, and get out of debt as quickly as possible.
40. Money has never made man happy, nor will it. There is nothing in its nature to produce happiness. The more of it one has, the more one wants. – Benjamin Franklin.
41. Secure the personal virtues of industry and frugality, for they are the way to wealth – Benjamin Franklin.
42. Creditors have better memories than debtors --- Benjamin Franklin.
43. A penny is a lot of money --- if you haven't got a penny. --- Jewish Proverb.
44. Do not be wise in words. Be wise in deeds. We are what we do.
45. Charity is the spice of riches. ---Jewish proverb.
46. If the rich could hire the poor to die for them, the poor would make a very good living. --- Jewish proverb.
47. While having money may not bring you happiness, the lack of it will surely bring you unhappiness. --- Jewish proverb.
48. A heavy purse makes a light heart; and a light purse makes a heavy heart.

49. A righteous man falls down seven times and get up (Prov 24:16) – King Solomon. The lesson: If you get up one more time than you fall, you will make it through. Fall seven times, but stand up the eighth time. According to the Torah, the righteous person is defined, not as someone who has succeeded, but someone who has persevered. Always do what's right, get up from failure, keep on moving forward, and never ever give up!
50. Life must have meaning and purpose! "If you don't know what you are living for, you have not lived." --- Rabbi Noah Weinberg
51. An inch of time is worth an inch of gold, but it is hard to buy one inch of time with one inch of gold! Time is more precious than money --- Chinese proverb.
52. Money could make demons turn grindstones --- Chinese proverb.
53. Give a man a fish and you feed him for a day; teach a man to fish, you feed him for a lifetime! Don't stand by the water and long for the fish, go home and weave a net. --- Chinese proverbs.
54. If you save the green mountain, you will not worry about having no firewood to burn. --- Chinese proverb (CP).
55. In every crisis, there is opportunity (CP).
56. Sow a thought, reap an action; sow an action, reap a habit; sow a habit, reap a character; sow a character, reap a destiny (CP).
57. If you want one year of prosperity, grow grain. If you want ten years of prosperity, grow trees. If you want one hundred years of prosperity, grow people. (CP). The best time to plant a tree was 20 years ago. The second best time is now!
58. A bad workman blames his tools (CP).
59. A closed mind is like a closed book; just a block of wood (CP).
60. To fall into a pit is to gain a bit of wit. Don't be afraid of making mistakes as long as one learns from the mistakes (CP). It is good to learn from your own mistakes but it is better to learn from others' mistakes.

61. A jade stone is useless before it is processed; a man is good for nothing until he is educated (CP).
62. A journey of a thousand miles begins with a single step. --- Lao Tzu of China
63. A single conversation with a wise man is better than ten years of reading books (CP).
64. All cats love fish but fear to wet their paws --- meaning that all people love to make money but few pursue it due to the many challenges, efforts and risks.
65. To pen a shop is easy but to keep it open is an art (CP). He who cannot smile should not bother to open a shop.
66. He who is not satisfied with himself will grow, and he who is not sure of his own correctness will learn (CP).
67. Find a job you love and you will never have to work a day in your life --- Confucius of China. Do what you love and you will love what you do. Your passion will turn your vocation into a vacation!
68. The emperor is rich, but he cannot buy one extra year. Meaning: money and riches are not the most important things in life, and the most important things in life are not things (CP).
69. It's how you deal with failure that determines how you achieve success. – David Feherty
70. Opportunity is missed by most people because it is dressed in overalls and looks like work. – Thomas Edison.
71. Formal education will make you a living; self-education will make you a fortune. – Jim Rohn
72. Money is only a tool. It will take you wherever you wish, but it will not replace you as the driver. – Ayn Rand
73. He who loses money loses much; He who loses a friend loses much more; He who loses faith loses all. – Eleanor Roosevelt
74. I'm a great believer in luck, and I find the harder I work, the more I have of it… Never spend your money before you have it. -- Thomas Jefferson
75. Every time you borrow money, you are robbing your future self. – Nathan Morris.

Faith and Finances

76. Rich people have small TVs and big libraries, and poor people have small libraries and big TVs... It's not the situation, but whether we react (negative) or respond (positive) to the situation that's important... People often say that motivation doesn't last. Well, neither does bathing – that's why we recommend it daily. -- Zig Ziglar
77. Wealth is not his that has it, but his that enjoys it. – Ben Franklin
78. Many people take no care of their money till they come nearly to the end of it, and others do just the same with their time. – Johann Wolfgang von Goethe
79. The habit of saving is itself an education; it fosters every virtue, teaches self-denial, cultivates the sense of order, trains to forethought, and so broadens the mind. – T.T. Munger (Frugality includes all the other virtues – Cicero)
80. We make a living by we get, but we make a life by what we give. – Winston Churchill
81. Wealth is a relative thing since he who has little and wants less is richer than he that has much and wants more. --- Charles Caleb Colton.
82. Not everything that can be counted counts, and not everything that counts can be counted. – Albert Einstein
83. As long as you are going to be thinking anyway, think big. – Donald Trump
84. Early to bed and early to rise, makes a man healthy, wealthy and wise. – Ben Franklin
85. Women and wine, game and deceit, make the wealth small and the wants great --- Ben Franklin.
86. Don't worship your work, work at your play and play at your worship.
87. Proper physical exercise increases your chances for health, and proper mental exercise increases your chances for wealth. Laziness decreases both health and wealth --- Robert Kiyosaki
88. The Japanese are always aware of three powers: the power of the sword (military/weaponry), the power of the jewel

(money), and the power of the mirror (self knowledge and reflection) --- Robert Kiyosaki.
89. Think and Grow Rich: Remember it is what is in your head that determines what is in your hand --- Robert Kiyosaki
90. Get to know two things about a man, how he earns his money and how he spends it. You will then have a clue to his character. You will have a searchlight that shows up the inner recesses of his soul. You know all you need to know about his standards, his motives, his driving desires and his real religion --- Robert J. McCracken.
91. First I was dying to finish my high school and start college. And than I was dying to finish college and stRt working. Then I was dying to marry and have children. Then I was dying for my children to grow old enough so I could go back to work. But the. I was dying to retire. And now I am dying... and suddenly I realized that I forgot to live. To make Maloney, we lose our health. And the to restore our health, we lose money... We live as if we are never going to die, and we die as if we never lived... Please do not let 5is happen to you. Appreciate your current situation enjoy each day. Enjoy our life now for it is not a rehearsal. — Anonymous Jewish Proverb
92. The blessing of the Lord brings wealth, without painful toil for it (Prov 10:22).

Biblical Proverbs on Wisdom and Wealth

Prov 3:9-10, 13-14 --- Honor the Lord with your wealth, with the first fruits of all your crops, then your barn will be filled with overflowing and your vats will brim over with new wine... Blessed is the man who finds wisdom, the man who gains understanding, for she is more profitable than silver, and yields better returns than gold.

Prov 8:10-11, 18-21 --- Choose my instructions instead of silver, knowledge rather than choice gold, for wisdom is more precious than rubies, and nothing you desire can compare with her... With me are riches and honor, enduring wealth and prosperity. My fruit is better than fine gold; what I yield surpasses choice silver. I walk in the way of righteousness along the path of justice, bestowing wealth on those who love me and making their treasures full.

Prov 10:22 --- The tongue of the righteous is choice silver, but the heart of the wicked is of little value.

Prov 14:24 --- The crown of the wise is their riches, but the foolishness of fools is folly.

Prov 16:8, 16 --- Better a little with righteousness than much gain with injustice... How much better to get wisdom than gold, to choose understanding rather than silver.

Prov 19:4 --- Wealth brings many friends, but a poor man's friend deserts him.

Prov 20:15 --- Gold there is and rubies are in abundance, but lips that speak knowledge are a rare jewel.

Prov 22:4 --- Humility and the fear of the Lord bring wealth and honor and life.

Prov 23:4-5 --- Do not wear yourself out to get rich; have the wisdom to show restraint. Cast but a glance at riches, and they are gone, for they will surely sprout wings, and fly off to the sky like an eagle.

Biblical Proverbs on Work and Wealth

Prov 6: 6-8 --- Go to the ant, you sluggard; consider its way and be wise! It has no commander or overseer or ruler, yet it stores its provision in summer and gathers its food at harvest.

Prov 6: 10-11 --- A little sleep, a little slumber, a little folding of the hands to rest --- and poverty will come on you like a bandit and scarcity like an armed man.

Prov 10:4-5 --- Lazy hands make a man poor, but diligent hands bring wealth. He who gathers crops in summer is a wise son, but he who sleeps during harvest is a disgraceful son.

Prov 12:11 --- He who works his land will have abundant food, but he who chases fantasy lacks judgment.

Prov 13:4,11 --- The sluggard craves and gets nothing, but the desires of the diligent are fully satisfied... Dishonest money dwindles away, but he who gathers money little by little makes it grow.

Prov 14:23 --- All hard work brings a profit, but mere talk leads only to poverty.

Prov 20:13 --- Do not love sleep or you will grow poor; stay awake and you will have food to spare.

Prov 21:5 --- The plans of the diligent lead surely to plenty, but those of everyone who is hasty surely to poverty.

Prov 22:29 --- Do you see a man who excels in his work? He will stand before kings; He will not stand before unknown (obscure) men.

Prov 24:33-34 --- The same as Prov 6:10-11, repetition here is for emphasis and not as redundancy

Prov 28:19 --- He who works his land will have abundant food, but the one who chases fantasies will have his fill of poverty.

Wisdom on the Rich and the Poor

Prov 10:15 --- The wealth of the rich is their fortified city, but poverty is the ruin of the poor.

13:7-8 --- One man pretends to be rich and yet has nothing; another pretends to be poor and yet has great wealth. A man's riches may ransom his life, but a poor man hears no threat.

14:20 --- The poor are shunned even by their neighbors, but the rich have many friends.

17:5 --- He who mocks the poor shows contempt for their Maker; whoever gloats over disaster will not go unpunished.

18:11, 23 --- The wealth of the rich is their fortified city; they imagine it as an unscalable wall.

19:7 --- A poor man is shunned by all his relatives - much more do his friends avoid him! Though he pursues them with pleading, they are nowhere to be found.

21:17 --- He who loves pleasure will become poor; whoever loves wine and oil will never be rich.

22:2 --- Rich and poor have this in common: the Lord is the Maker of them all.

28:6, 11 --- Better a poor man whose walk is blameless than a rich man whose ways are perverse... A rich man may be wise in his own eyes, but a poor man who has discernment sees through him.

Warnings Against Dishonesty and Greed

Prov 1:19 --- Such is the end of all who go after ill-gotten gain: it takes away the lives of those who get it.

11:28 --- Whoever trusts in his riches will fall, but the righteous will thrive like a green leaf.

15:27 --- A greedy man brings trouble to his family, but he who hates bribes will live.

22:16, 22-23 --- He who oppresses the poor to increase his wealth and he who gives gifts to the rich --- both come to poverty.

23:4 --- Do not wear yourself out to get rich; have the wisdom to show restraint.

28:8, 20, 22, 25 --- He who increases his wealth by exorbitant interest amasses it for another …. A faithful man will be richly blessed, but one eager to get rich will not go unpunished… A stingy man is eager to get rich, and is unaware that poverty awaits him… A greedy man stirs up dissension, but he who trusts in the Lord will prosper.

Warning against Idleness and Laziness

Prov 6:10-11 --- A little sleep, a little slumber, a little folding of the hands to rest --- and poverty will come on you like a bandit and scarcity like an armed man.

Prov 12:24 --- The hand of the diligent will rule, but the lazy man will be put to forced labor.

Prov 13:4 --- The soul of a lazy man desires, and has nothing; but the soul of the diligent shall be made rich.

Prov 14:23 ---In all labor there is profit, but idle chatter leads only to poverty.

Prov 19:15 --- Laziness casts one into a deep sleep, and an idle person will suffer hunger.

Prov 22:13 --- The lazy man says, "There is a lion outside! I shall be slain in the street!"

Prov 26:14-16 --- As a door turn on its hinges, so does the lazy man on his bed. The lazy man buries his hand in the bowl; It wearies him to bring it back to his mouth. The lazy man is wiser in his own eyes than seven men who can answer sensibly.

Warnings Against Debt and financial Lending

Prov 6:1-5 – My son, if you have put up security for your neighbor, if you have struck hands in pledge for another, if you have been trapped by what you said, ensnared by the words of your mouth, then, do this, my son, to free yourself, since you have fallen into your neighbor's hands: Go and humble yourself, and press your plea with your neighbor! Allow no sleep to your eyes, no slumber to your eyelids. Free yourself like a gazelle from the hand of the hunter, like a bird from the snare of the fowler.

Prov 17:18 --- A man lacking in judgment strikes hands in pledge and puts up security for his neighbor.

Prov 22:7 --- The rich rules over the poor and the borrower is a servant (slave) to the lender.

Prov 22:26-27 --- Do not be one of those who shakes hands in a pledge, one of those who is surety for debts. If you have nothing with which to pay, your very bed will be snatched away from under you.

Prov 27:13 --- Take the garment from him who is surety for a stranger, and hold it in pledge when he is surety for a seductress.

Psalm 37:21 The wicked borrow and do not repay, but the righteous give generously;

Wisdom on Living a Righteous Life of Balance

Prov 10:2 --- Ill-gotten treasures are of no value, but righteousness delivers from death.

Prov. 11:4,8 --- Wealth is worthless in the day of wrath, but righteousness delivers from death.

Prov. 15:6 --- The house of the righteous contains great treasure, but the income of the wicked brings them trouble.

Prov. 17:3 --- The crucible for silver and the furnace for gold, but the Lord tests the heart.

Prov. 19:1 --- Better a poor man whose walk is blameless than a fool whose lips are perverse.

Prov 20:7 --- The righteous man walks in his integrity; His children are blessed after him.

Prov. 22:1 --- The king's heart is in the hand of the Lord; He directs it like a watercourse wherever He pleases.

Prov 30:7-9 --- Two things I request of you (Deprive me not before I die): Remove falsehood and lies far from me; give me neither poverty nor riches --- feed me with the food allotted to me; lest I be full and deny You, and say, "Who is this Lord?" Or lest I be poor and steal and profane the name of my God.

The Gift of Generosity Strongly Encouraged

Prov 3:27 ---Do not withhold good from those who deserve it, when it is in your power to act.

Prov 11:24-25 --- There is one who scatters (gives), yet increases more; And there is one who withholds more than is right, but it leads to poverty. The generous soul will be made rich, and he who waters will also be watered himself.

Prov 14:21, 31 --- He who despises his neighbor sins, but blessed is he who is kind to the needy... He who oppresses the poor shows contempt for the Maker, but whoever is kind to the needy honors God.

Prov. 19:17 --- He who is kind to the poor lends to the Lord, and He will reward him for what he has done.

Prov 22:29 --- A generous man will himself be blessed, for he shares his food with the poor.

Pro. 28:27 --- He who gives to the poor will lack nothing, but he who closes his eyes to them receives many curses.

Wisdom on Stewardship and Investments

Prov 6: 6-8 --- Go to the ant, you sluggard; consider its ways and be wise! It has no commander, no overseer or ruler, yet it stores up provision in summer and gathers its food at harvest.

Prov 10:16 --- The wages of the righteous bring them life, but the income of the wicked brings them punishment.

Prov 13:22 --- A good man leaves an inheritance to his children's children, but the wealth of the sinner is stored up for the righteous.

Prov 19:14 --- Houses and wealth are inherited from parents, but a prudent wife is from the Lord.

Prov 20:21 --- An inheritance gained hastily at the beginning will not be blessed at the end.

Prov 27:23-24, 26-27 --- Be diligent to know the state of your flocks, and attend to your herds; for riches are not forever, nor does a crown endures to all generations… The lambs will provide your clothing, and the goats the price of a field; You shall have enough goat's milk for your food, for the food of your household, and the nourishment of your maidservants.

Prov 31:10, 14-16, 20 --- Who can find a virtuous wife? For her worth is far above rubies… She is like the merchant ships, she brings her food from afar. She also rises while it is yet night. And provides food for her household, and a portion for her maidservants. She considers a field and buys it; From her profits she plants a vineyard… She extends her hands to the poor, yes, she reaches out her hands to the needy.

Reflections and Applications

Over the years I have observed and experienced the amazing phenomenon known as "the immigrant mentality", with us being among them. This mentality is the polar opposite from the entitlement mindset and ingratiate mentality of too many people, especially among our youth. The new immigrants seize all available opportunities vey seriously and work hard with diligence to make it a success. They are smart, thrifty and frugal, take nothing for granted, and they do not complain about their circumstances, but they endure hardship so as to create and enjoy a bette and brighter future for themselves and their families.

We as a couple and later a family lived with such a mentality and personal discipline with consistency over 33 years now, and to a large degree, still live with this healthy and positive mindset. Your mentality determines both your economy and even your destiny! We started out in this great blessed nation the USA as poor foreign students with nothing except $20 in our pockets. But we came by faith in the Lord and His goodness, knowing that He blesses and favors those who trust and obey Him with perseverance and actions. While studying at the seminary, we actively worked on various menial jobs with minimum pay at only $3.25 an hour, living gratefully with a wonderful host couple Drs Caroline and Murl Dirksen. At the end of the month, I excitedly received my first pay check at about $160. I was so overjoyed as a little janitor to make more money than my professors in China at that time. As I tried to give the check with thanksgiving to the Dirksens, they refused to take it but advised to save it, and helped me open my first American saving account at the local First Citizens Bank!

As the years passed by, we always keep the same saving mentality even at only $1000 monthly missions allotment for a family of four. We sought after and served every possible opportunity to work, preaching and teaching the Word all over the places, never ever asking for a fee to minister but fully trusting god to take care of us. The Lord Jesus Himself saw our faith as dedication in action, entrusted and rewarded us with a lot more growth and increases. By the time we bought our first house, we almost paid it fully in cash! Praise the Lord! Even since then, we have been blessed with much more abundance of peace and prosperity in all things, and being purpose driven and passion packed, we have been mightily blessed used of Him to serve and lead with passion and integrity and influence all over the world I. Over a hundred nations. We are so grateful that we have been truly blessed to be a blessing to many others just as Proverbs 10:22 affirms correctly and precisely that the blessings of the Lord have brought us wealth and He adds no sorrow to it! Praise the Lord forevermore.

Here are a few key questions for you to ask yourself for application:

1. What opportunities do you see around you to grasp and utilize to improve your life and increase financial income?
2. What is your gut feeling about the situation you are I right now?

3. What's the number one faith and finance lesson you take for this chapter for your immediate application and improvements?

Chapter 7

Money Matters
Erroneous Religious Folklore vs
Solid Spiritual Principles

Proverbs 23:7 --- As a man thinks in his heart, so is he.

What is in the head will determine what is in the hand!

Your THOUGHTS impact your DESTINY. Watch your thoughts for they become your words. Watch your words for they become your actions. Watch your actions for they become your habits. Watch your habits for they become your character. Watch your character for it impacts your Destiny!

As the mind goes, the man follows! As the mind goes, the money follows!

We become what we think about --- Earl Nightingale

Whatever the mind of man can conceive and believe, it can achieve --- Napoleon Hill

In order for Christians to get out and stay out of debt, which shall be dealt with in details in the next chapter, and in order for the children of God to not just barely survive but successfully thrive, and with the right biblical spiritual priority and the higher purpose for His greater glory, we must seriously examine and correct any wrong mindset as we are a sum total of our mentality. And our mentality determines our economy and mobility which in turn will decide the scope and the influence of our ministries. We must first expose and dispel some of the deeply-seeded "religious" misconceptions, wrong attitudes, and erroneous (not to mention illogical and irrational) folklores that are common place among so many in the churches and other faith communities. The following represent a list of eight major ones that do not help but hurt and hinder true followers of Christ from reaching their God-given potential in faith and finances in their services for the cause of Christ.

Some Misconceptions

1. Money is the root of all evils, the Bible says it somewhere!

This is quite common, erroneous and even ridiculous, and yet quite a few Christians, being ignorant of the Word of God and thus not knowing what the Bible really teaches, have bought into this belief and formed this wrong attitude towards money. Money in and of itself is not at all evil. In fact, money is not just neutral. Not only is it essential for a victorious life and multiplied missions and ministries, money is even deeply spiritual in its final analysis. The Scripture clearly teaches us not to love money as it would be idolatry, for the "love of money" is a root of all kinds of evil, and one's eagerness for money will cause him or her to wander from the faith and to be pierced with many sorrows (I Tim 6:10). And we are to keep our lives from the "love of money" and be content with what we have (Heb 13:5). The Lord Jesus emphatically instructs us to "Watch out! Be on your guard against all kinds of greed!" (Lk 12:15). However, nowhere in the whole Bible does it teach that money is evil or is the root of all evils.

2. Poverty is next to true spirituality!

More poor, more pure! Living with poverty is a clear sign of true spiritual purity. This is far from the truth of the Scripture that never teaches that God intentionally impoverishes anyone in order to enhance his or her spirituality and thus the level of religious purity. In fact, there is no inherent virtue in being poor, except that the only possible purpose for the existence of poverty is so that the rich can get a chance to exercise a bit of their charity (Jewish proverb paraphrased). Nothing is more painful than poverty as those who are under its miserable bondage of it cannot even help themselves, let alone assisting or blessing anyone else. Since Romans 12:5-8 describes the gift of giving, it must be true then that there is also the gift of gathering, for no one can give what he or she has not gathered.

Every good gift we have gratefully gathered is given to us from our compassionate and merciful Father above who is the epitome of gracious generosity. While God condemns the human preoccupation and obsession with, the misuse and the abuse of money, He never condemns money itself. As a matter of fact, it was God who personally declared that gold was good in Genesis 2:12. "God never once relates spirituality to poverty. Therefore, there is no way Christians can attain spirituality by impoverishing themselves or their families." (Burkett, P. 32). Even in the case of the suffering Job as a test of his unwavering faith when the devil by God's permissive will, destroyed all his family and finances, the good great gracious glorious and generous God we serve personally returned to Job, forcefully removed the devil, and marvelously restored Job and his fortune for twice as much as he ever had, as a beautiful testimony to God's glory and a wonderful witness to God's faithfulness. Instead of holding any grudges or vengeance against his three miserable comforters and judgmental friends due to erroneous theology, Job kindly prayed for them, and his prayers were accepted of the Lord. In return, the Lord made Job prosperous again, and gave him "Double for all his trouble" (Job 42:10)

3. Christians should not strive for prosperity and financial successes for they are all just secular and too worldly!

Doubly wrong again both in thoughts and in attitude. While I stand firmly and categorically against the so-called Prosperity Gospel which has deceived and disillusioned many believers especially in the USA, I also vehemently and adamantly believed that our God delights in the prosperity of His servants! Jesus assures His servants in Mark 10:28 Peter said to him, "We have left everything to follow you!"10:29 "I tell you the truth," Jesus replied, "no one who has left home or brothers or sisters or mother or father or children or fields for me and the gospel10:30 will fail to receive a hundred times as much in this present age (homes, brothers, sisters, mothers, children and fields--and with them, persecutions) and in the age to come, eternal life. The truth of the matter is that as we keep our spiritual priority and focus on seeking first the Kingdom of God and His righteousness as the center of our faithful service (Matt 6:33), it is the delight and the pleasure of the Lord to prosper His servants who please Him through their bold exercise of the faith and their demonstrated faithfulness (Ps 35:27, Heb 11:6). God always promises what He performs, and He always performs His promises as long as we do our part in fulfilling the conditional premises.

Josh 1:8-9 infallibly declares to us all that if we will sincerely trust the commands of the Word of God, daily prayerfully meditate on it, and IF we are careful to observe, obey and do everything written in it, "THEN you will be prosperous and successful." Instead of becoming discouraged or terrified by our circumstances or the enemies, on the contrary, we will also become strong, very courageous, victorious and prosperous, knowing with full faith and complete confidence that the Lord will never leave us or forsake us. Neither will He ever forget us or fail us. And as He was with Moses and Joshua, He will always be with us wherever we go! We will, in Him, through Him, and for Him, have More than enough so that we can, in all these things, become More than conquerors through Him who loves us (Rom 8:37). You and I can do all things through Christ who strengthens us because we know beyond the shadow of a doubt that our God who reigns omnipotently over all things, shall supply all our needs according to the riches of His glory in our Lord Christ Jesus (Phil 4:13, 19). As we faithfully apply His principles, He will always fruitfully supply all the provision and protection, correction and direction that we need. I am more convinced these days than ever before that if we faithfully apply our very best, Christ will abundantly supply all the rest! And God's work done God's way will never lack God's supply! These are the unfailing universal laws of the Kingdom of God! God our loving Father delights in His children's victories, successes and prosperity for His glory even as our life prospers in all things and our soul prospers in the Lord with fullness of love joy and peace (III John 2)! All of this will make our life witnesses more convicting and more compelling to this u believing and even hostile world of scarcity, poverty, hate and revenge!

4. Giving money is always spiritual, but for Christian even just talking about money especially about making money is very secular, worldly and sinful, especially in the church.

Wrong once again. Be careful with the use of "labels" for the labeling effect can be very harmful as it often creates and propagates a wrong narrative. . God does not clearly distinguish the "secular" from the "spiritual" as we humans often do. As long as our labor or work is done with excellence of quality as a means of making a living to provide for legitimate needs and as a calling to serve God and serve God's other children, it is just as honorable and dignified as the ministerial assignments if not more so. While we must emphasize the biblical virtue of generosity of caring and sharing (II Cor 8 & 9) through the grace of loving and giving, it is really high time that Christian leaders preached and practiced the art and science of earning all we can by diligence and industry, saving all we can by thrift and frugality, and giving all we can with love and generosity, by both our authoritative scriptural precepts and by our authentic personal example. Without ever missing, losing, straying or drifting away from the centrality and priority of Jesus and His Mission, the Great Commission, the furtherance of the glorious great Gospel of God's grace, until all have heard, we must be ourselves seriously and strongly, profoundly and prolifically trained in matters of faith and finances: how to make, save, invest, enjoy, diversify and distribute monies and material resources! Only in this way, can we ever hope to be equipped and empowered sufficiently to train the church to achieve economic peace and prosperity, financial fitness, freedom and force, to glorify God and to benefit God's other children around the world. While giving money with the right attitude of joyful gratitude and generosity is indeed spiritual, diligently and intelligently making money, and frugally saving money in order to give more substantially is not worldly or sinful, but equally spiritual, for you can't do one without the other.

5. Financial planning is not necessary for the Bible says that God will supply all our needs when we need it. Just trust and pray!

Yes it is essential to trust and pray, but it is more crucial and critical to simply obey! Obey the Word of God in learning from the principles of the bees and ants in the Proverbs, and in the parables of Jesus especially in Luke 14 before one builds a house or prepares to go to war! Pray, trust and obey. Sit down and count and calculate all the possible and potential costs involved, with a seriously thought-through, written budget, and even seek out wise guides before one decides. If we have failed to plan, then we have planned to fail. If we do not organize, we will agonize. Noah taught us many life lessons through the building of the ark, and one of them is that we must build our ark and fix our roof before the rain! The book of Acts is not a book of talks. It is a divine authorization and commission for bold action, with no reservation or hesitation or distraction or procrastination. Always pray, plan, prepare and by faith courageously proceed and you will by His grace and for His glory, surely succeed!

6. To be wealthy, you have to be sinful! In other words, since God does not want us to get rich, it is simply sinful then to be rich.

This is just another erroneous concept with God's name mixed in it to try to justify the other misconception that for the true followers of Jesus, only living in material scarcity and financial poverty counts for some type of real spiritual purity. The Holy Bible does not condemn the rich for their richness sake. As a matter of fact, there were quite a few leaders in the Bible who have become extremely wealthy due to the favors of God on His part and their intelligent diligence on their parts such as Father Abraham, the faithful Job, Zacchaeus (Lk 19:1-10), and King Solomon, to name just a few. The blessing of the Lord brings wealth and He adds no trouble, painful toil or sorrow to it (Pro 10:22). This scriptural promise and truth is doubtlessly the spiritual peace with material prosperity with a divine priority! The Apostle Paul did not condemn the rich Christians either, but rather he commands them not to put their hope in their wealth, or to become arrogant because of the uncertain riches. The rich believers are to trust in the Lord and enjoy their God-given abundant provision. They are to be rich not only in material wealth, but also rich in good deeds, in their generosity and in their willingness to care for and share with the needy. In this way, they will be laying up treasure for themselves for the coming age and will be taking hold of the life that is truly life (I Tim 6:17-19).

7. Money brings happiness as the Bible says that money is the answer to everything (Eccl 10:19).

This obviously indicates the other extreme on the money spectrum, and it is borderline to the enticingly deceptive theology of the so-called "prosperity gospel" which is way out of balance, stresses materialism at the neglect of the spiritual priority of money, wealth and possession as an indispensable and effective tool to glorify God and advance the cause of Christ. Even the often-quoted verse from Ecclesiastes 10:19 has been taken out of context to justify a lavish lifestyle, while King Solomon was merely experimenting with power, pleasure, fame and fortune in search for the real answer to the true meaning and purpose of human existence in the midst of the complexity and perplexity of life itself. Hear please his definitive and final thought. Now all has been heard; here is the conclusion of the matter: Fear God and keep His commandments, for this is the whole duty of man. For God will bring every deed into judgment, including every hidden thing, whether it is good or evil (Eccl 12:13-14). As the wise man Benjamin Franklin famously said, "Money has never made man happy, nor will it. There is nothing in its nature to produce happiness. The more of it one has, the more one wants."

8. It is not good, and actually terrible, if you allow your bank accounts, either personal or ministerial, or both, to grow, accumulate and maintain a "big" surplus, for that would be hoarding. When supporters knew about this, they would stop supporting you!

Now while this belief and attitude may be typically American and highly cultural, but it's not biblical at all. The truth regarding this money matter is that the Bible strongly teaches against the "barely enough" mentality of scarcity, but emphatically encourages savings and surplus and living in abundance with "more than enough", as in "my cup overflows" (Ps 23). In the house of the wise, are there all kinds of wealth and treasures, but he or she is definitely a fool who spends and squanders it all (Prov 21:20), only to live anxiously from hand to mouth, and to struggle for survival from pay check to paycheck, with all kinds of side effects of anxieties, quarrels, worries and fears, dreadful days and sleepless nights, to mention just a few!

On the other hand, when donors hear your success stories, and know the faithfulness and fruitfulness of your life and ministry, and trust your Godly stewardship of plentiful prosperity, passion with purity, purpose and priority, success and abundance, they feel so happy and blessed to be a part of your victorious life and abundant ministries through their generous giving. They also recruit and enlist others with confident credibility for you through words of mouth. This is known psychologically as the Law of Attraction and economically famous as the Matthew Effect, the power of the snowball! And that is why "sorry stories" of negativity and pessimism never inspire anyone to become passionate partners in life and ministries, for no one wants to put his hard-earned money in to a bank that's not stable or strong or prosperous, or on the brink of bankruptcy. Passionate positivity propels powerful pro activity and persuasive productivity while negativity and pessimism only produces sad scarcity and powerless poverty! This scriptural and spiritual truth, which is life-giving, both psychological and financial, has been proven right time and again in our lives and ministries of more than 30 years for the glory and praise of the Lord Jesus! Hallelujah! Amen, Amen and Amen! Glory to God!

Sound and Solid Scriptural Principles for Making and Managing Money

Here are ten of the most powerful and thus productive principles we have learned and multiplied to others for the past three decades of humbly and faithfully serving the Lord Jesus all over the world. Please study and use them yourselves to become more effective and more fruitful (John 15:2) in your own lives as God sees your faith in practice (Mk 2:5) and will reward you accordingly.

1. Character counts the most in money matters!

Consistency, constancy, and undeviating diligence to maintain the Christian character of integrity are a must if the older generation is to command respect, or even a hearing, from the young. --- Billy Graham.

Psalm 37:21 declares that the wicked borrows money from others and yet does not pay back. It is the righteous that always shows mercy and gives generously. A good name is more desirable than great riches, and to be esteemed is better than silver or gold (Prov 22:1). In business and finances, as in various aspects ministries, our character and reputation count and matter the most. It is foundational for success, abundance, peace and prosperity in all the other areas of human endeavors and life too! Our character of brutal honesty and trustworthy integrity must go before all the charismas, for charisma without character to guide and guard it, as has been observed by the authors of this book, way too many times, will sooner or later, cause much regrettable calamities and even countless catastrophes! The Bible says that wealth gained by dishonesty will be diminished or dwindled away, but he who gathers by little by little makes it grow (Prov 13:11). We are created to be Christ-like, and we must become more and more Christ-like in our truthfulness, transparency, being ethical in our dealings with everyone, and have absolutely nothing to do with dubious duplicity and devilish deception with stealing, cheating and lying to others for greedy and selfish gains that will lead only to our utter ruins.

The first and the most important and essential characteristic of Scriptural stewardship is none other than character, Godly and Christ-like character, known as the character stewardship with a solid, trustworthy and reliable name and reputation (your indispensable social and relational capitals). In the NIV Stewardship Study Bible, John Luther (P. 625) writes that one's good character is to be more praised than outstanding talent. Talents are gifts endowed by the Creator, but character, in contrast, is not given to us. We have to build our character piece by piece --- by thought, choice, courage and determination. And this takes a long time, even a lifetime. Just as money cannot buy happiness, neither can money buy us character! Character must be developed little by little, day after day, over a long period of time with intentional accountability and strategic investments. As the good ole Christian saying goes: be all means, be holy! But you can't be holy in a hurry! In other words, it takes time to construct such building blocks of character like a good work ethic with discipline, diligence, endurance, humility, teachability, responsibility, accountability, loyalty, morality, and integrity. These so-called "social capitals" that lead to serious success and plentiful prosperity are not only developed over time, these also flow from one's "spiritual capital" such as one's faith system, core values, spiritual laws, sound principles and solid daily practices! Chuck Colson (P. 625) observes that values are foundational to any society and one's value system is closely related to his or her economic situation. "The values erosion is largely responsible for the economic problems now facing the nation." The breakdown of values in the USA has caused not only billions of dollars, but also the breakdowns of marriages and families. The deterioration and even abandonment of the traditional work ethic have resulted in the loss of billions of dollars in productivity.

2. Diligence and industry matter seriously!

Someone once said it so succinctly that "diligence is the mother of good fortune." Thomas Edison the great American inventor was quoted as saying that, "opportunity is missed by most people because it is dressed in overalls and looks like work!" No matter how smart or intelligent one really is, nothing can take the place of hard work in money matters and in any worthwhile human endeavors. There is one sure place to go and get some money, and that place is called WORK! No perspiration, no inspiration, for much of our human inspiration comes from human perspiration! No one can acquire if she or he refuses to perspire! Laziness casts one into deep sleep, and an idle or shiftless person will suffer hunger (Prov 19:15). The lazy sluggard will not plow because of winter; he will beg during the harvest and have nothing! As one of the traditional seven (7) deadly sins (the other six being pride, greed, envy, anger, lust and gluttony), sloth in the Bible has been completely condemned as a vice to be avoided. We are to go to the small and simple insects like bees and ants and observe their ways so as to learn and apply industry and diligence to our own lives. The Bible warns us not to love sleep, or we will grow poor; rather we are to always stay awake and alert so that we will have food to eat and even to spare (Prov 20:4, 13). The apostle Paul, having preached what he practiced and practiced what he preached, by example, sternly commanded the Thessalonians that "if anyone will not work, neither shall he eat!" (II Thes 3:10).

3. Debt-free living matters!

Avoid any debt at any cost! The rich rules over the poor, just as the borrower is a servant, a slave to the lender (Prov 22:7)! Romans 13:8 admonishes us as Christ followers and His true disciples to "owe no one anything except to love one another." The book of Proverbs warns us over and over again against the danger of borrowing and lending as surety that results in debt and bondage. We are to be wise and stay away from any of such traps that hinder us from ever reaching financial freedom. Debt and poverty are like a python that chokes the life out of the devastated debtor even to death. Therefore, avoid debts as if it were a killer python. On the contrary, The promise of God for His children both in the Old and New Testaments is that we shall prosper in all things, in good health even as our soul prospers in the Lord (III John 2)! Why? Because the Lord loves us and promises to provide for all our needs with sufficiency and with more than enough as He is pleased, delighted and even magnified "in the prosperity of His servant" (Psalm 35:27). In Deut 8:18 and chapter 28, the generous and gracious Lord made and kept His promises as His children adhered to the premises of trust and obedience. It is the Jehovah Jireh our God who provides us His people the power to get wealth, to be the head and not the tail, to be above all the circumstances and not beneath them, to lend to many nations and borrow from none (28:12-13). Our God is faithful in that He always delivers what He declares, and performs all that which He has promised as long as we heed commands and obey His clear instructions --- the BIBLE (Basic Instructions Before Leaving Earth!). I am more convinced now than ever before that our obedience brings down His abundance! Next only to holy living and Godly living for us His real and true disciples of disciplines, is the debt-free living! Christians must get out and stay out of debt once and for all, before they can have the liberty to give, save, enjoy and invest.

4. A slow but steady strategy matters!

One is not only to be industrious to make money and be frugal to save money before he can accumulate money and give money and invest money to grow the money, this person must be completely committed to daily living according with disciplined consistency and constancy! A wise ole Chinese proverb says it well: "Be not afraid of growing slowly; be afraid of standing still!" The Lord in the Old Testament showed the Israelites the precious Promised Land for their inheritance, but He also told them that He was to give it to them little by little. Hw would not give all of it to them all at once and all of a sudden as it would overwhelm them and they had no wisdom or ability to handle it. Likewise, a large amount of inheritance given all at once at the beginning will not be blessed in the end for the heir has not developed the capacity needed to mange it. It would spoil them and ruin them in the end, not an a blessing but as a curse. Proverbs 21:5 teaches that the plans of the diligent who steadily plod will surely lead to plenty of profits, just as surely as everyone who is hasty leads to poverty! Haste makes waste! That is why so many of those Get Rich Quick schemes get numerous greedy people into deep financial losses and debts too. We are to get into our fields and stay and work in it patiently with endurance until it pays off with dividends. Stay away from any triviality, frivolity, and vanity as they together will not bring you prosperity, but certainly will cause you enough poverty! The Lord punishes those who always hastens after riches, but prospers them that are steadfast and perseverant! (Prov 28:19-22). Haste also makes waste. Dishonest money dwindles away, but he who gathers money little by little makes it grow (Prov 13:11). Patience and perseverance always pay off profitably.

5. Saving and surplus matter!

In order to be abundant and even affluent (as more affluence definitely produces more influence!) for the cause of Christ, we as the disciples of Jesus must be daily disciplined (Lk 9:23) like soldiers of Christ to do all that we can to earn money, save money so that we can cheerfully and generously give money! In the house of the wise, are there all kinds of desirable treasures, but the fool squanders all that he has (Prov 21:20). By wisdom a house is built and through understanding it is established. And through knowledge its rooms are filled with rare and beautiful treasures (Prov 24:3-4). We must be diligent and disciplined disciples of deep discernments to acquire the knowledge and to apply the wisdom with spiritual understanding which are readily available to us all in the Word of God! In matters of saving and surplus, faith and finances, for ignorance is no bliss as the people of God are destroyed for their laziness and thus their lack of knowledge (Hosea 4:6). We must learn and grow in this vital area of money matters so that we can go and glow and glorify the Jehovah Jireh our Provider!

6. Wise counsel matters!

He who walks with the wise will be wise, but the company of fools will suffer harm and even be destroyed (Prov 13:20). Plans fail for lack of counsel, but with many advisers they succeed (Prov 15:22). For by wise counsel you will wage your own war, and in the multitude of counselors there is safety (Prov 24:6). Jesus commands us in Luke 14 to sit down, carefully and prayerfully consider, count and calculate all the possible costs and alternatives before we should start anything, lest we could not finish what we begin and thus become a laughing stock for all to see and mock! Let us get the full counsel of God from the Word of God, and all the wise counsel from Jesus who is not only the Power of God but also the Wisdom of God from above for us. He is the Wonderful Counselor who will guard us every step of the way and will guide us every moment of the day to choose and decide wisely and to act faithfully and fearlessly with much fruit to show for it! He will never leave us or forsake any of us (Heb 13:5) and He will never forget you and never fail you as you wholeheartedly follow His infallible instructions through both the Word of God and the wise and Godly spiritual counselors, advisors, mentors and models.

7. Diversified investments matters!

Not only are we to quickly get out and forever stay out of debt in our living, and not only are we to start a saving and giving plan (as one can not give what he does not have!), to be a blessing to the needy and to have strong and lasting impact and influence for the advancement of His Kingdom, we are further commanded to go deeper, and aim higher and do better to invest and grow with diligence, intelligence, responsibility and a sense of urgency. There is no better model or example in the whole Bible than the smart and spiritual stewardship of Joseph and the well-known Parable of the Talents in Matthew 25, with the Matthew Effect (25:29), which we are to delve deep into in two separate chapters of this book!

In order to thrive and prosper, we are to prepare ourselves and get ourselves ready early on and way ahead of time, for the work both outside and inside (Prov 24:27). As the good ole saying goes that if we have failed to prepare, then we are prepared to fail! Ecclesiastes 11 verse 1 stresses the importance of investments with a long-term perspective and strategic patience, which is crucial and indispensable for our financial freedom; verse 2 emphasizes the need for diversification in our financial investment (as it is true also of our spiritual investment in Christian discipleship), and verse 4 commands us to do the sowing and the reaping now with bold, decisive and urgent actions with no hesitation, reservation, distraction, procrastination or any vain speculation. This is so because whoever watches the wind will not sow, and whoever looks at the cloud will not reap. Those who will wait for the "perfect" time or condition to come before they will try to do thing, will end up always speculating, anticipating and eventually dissipating for this is no perfect timing or conditioning in this imperfect world with imperfect people!

Cast your bread decisively and determinedly upon the waters, for after many days you will find it. "Give portions to seven, yes to eight, for you do not know what evil will be on earth or what disaster may come upon the land." (Eccl 11:2). Just as the old sages of real estates investing emphasize their three important keys before purchasing, Location, Location and Location, so to protect and preserve your investment and reduce its potential risk depends also on three key factors: Diversification, Diversification and Diversification. This wisdom, revealed to us through the wise and wealthy King Solomon thousands of years ago in the previous verse, still holds true for our roller-coaster economy. Diversification is spreading your hard-earned money among different types of investment alternatives so that if any of them suffers, the entire investment portfolio does not shrink. Although it does not guarantee you a better return, diversification does substantially reduce and diminish your over all investment risks. Diversification of funds therefore, is your seat belt and your safety bar against potential losses and for the protection and preservation of your capital (Blue & White, PP. 95-96). Again as the ole saying of the ole sage goes, "Don't put all your eggs in one basket." So embrace this wisdom, and you will enlarge your wealth to be financially fit for His kingdom services.

8. Good and accurate financial record-keeping matters!

Proverbs 27:23 clearly commands us to be both diligent and sure to "know the condition of your flocks, and give careful attention to your herds". As good shepherds, we must be like Jesus to know the will of the Father and to know our sheep (John 10:14-15). What you don't know will not help you; rather it will hinder you and even hurt and harm you! As beloved and trusted stewards of the Lord's resources, we are to be held responsible for their proper uses, wasteful misuses and even unfortunate abuses! Budgeting is essential to effective stewardship and responsible leadership, and with a carefully planned SMART (an acronym for Specific, Measurable, Attainable, Realistic and Testable!) budget in smooth operation, you will tell the money where to go to accomplish a specific purpose instead of you later wondering aimlessly where all your money went! This is a serious and important responsibility that will ensure and result in accountability. In turn, accountability will produces spiritual integrity and a good Godly legacy of impact and influence (Lk 16:10), starting with me, now, from here and start small! This is the law of the process necessary and indispensable for proportionate peace and prosperity, and it ensures the successes in all matters of life including of course, the money matter.

9. Quality goods with consistent and excellent services matter!

Casual and nominal Christianity does not work in the real world, especially in the competitive business and financial world. In order to create wealth, one must be willing to go and follow the Extra Mile principle: doing more than he is asked for, expected, or paid for, and going above and beyond the basic requirements for the job with quality product and excellent service. And going and doing so with a grateful and joyful and enthusiastic attitude, predictable good quality, constant consistency and extraordinary excellence! Proverbs 22:29 provides an amazing observation that successful Jews have always followed in numerous examples: Do you see a man who excels in his work? He will stand and serve before kings; He will not stand or serve before unknown or obscure men! Wow, what truth about excellence! This will naturally lead us to the last money matter.

10. A higher calling matter!

This refers to the importance of a kingdom perspective that produces passion, power and profitable productivity. There is much more to this world than what is tangible and visible in the world. We would be of all men most miserable if we did not have a hope beyond the here and now. But praise the Lord who gives us the victory here and now (I Cor 15:57) but also the hope of His glory there and then with Him (Col 1:27). As Christians who have been raised with Christ, we are strongly urged by the Apostle Paul in Col 3:1-2 to set our hearts, minds and affections and devotions on the things above where Christ is seated, and not the earthly things below. In other words, we are to be purposed as our divine calling in whatever we do to do it with joyful excellence as unto the Lord who demands and deserves our very best. This is because Christ Himself so loved us that He gave Himself totally to us (Gal 2:20). Therefore in all aspects of our lives and work, we are to do our uttermost and give our best to please and glorify God as our divine duty and our higher calling! As Paul the apostle to the Gentiles eloquently proclaims that whatever we do, whether in words or deeds, we are to do it all with the attitude of gratitude in the hearts, and do it all not for men, but working for the Lord, "since you know that you will receive an inheritance from the Lord as your reward.

It is the Lord Christ you are serving." (Col 3:16-17, 23-24). It was exactly this typical and central puritan and protestant belief, spirit and work ethics that caused the rise of prosperity and success in Europe and America as we will discuss this issue in much more details in a separate chapter of this book.

Reflections and Applications

Developing a proper perspective and maintaining the right attitude is very crucial and critical in all spheres of the Christian life. There is a very good sayings that goes like this, "money is a very good servant but a very bad master". How we treat money can either make us or break us. It's all about our perspective and our attitude towards it. As the Lord says, one can not serve two masters: God or Mammon. One has to make the right choice before he or she can live a life of fulfillment and success. When money becomes your master, it will rule your life with greed and destruction.

But when we have the proper perspective, money becomes an effective useful and powerful tool to improve our lives and bring blessings unto many others to glorify God. Therefor our heart attitude toward is extremely important. As Proverbs 4:23 clearly warns us that above all things guard your heart, for it will affect everything you do. Indeed we must guard our hearts against all forms of covetousness and greed so we can live an overcoming life.

Here are a few key questions to ask of yourself:

1. Have I ever been tempted by money and greed? If yes, how did you overcome it?
2. What is your personal attitude towards money? Are you a master over it or a slave under it?
3. Of the ten above discussed money matters, which one speaks more relevantly to you and why?

Chapter 8

Digging Your Way Out of Debt: Causes, Consequences and Cures for Financial Indebtedness

II Kings 4:1: The wife of a man from the company of the prophets cried out to Elisha, "Your servant my husband is dead, and you know that he revered the Lord. But now his creditor is coming to take my two boys as his slaves."

Proverbs 22:7: Just as the rich rule over the poor, so the borrower is a slave to the lender.

Deut 28:1-2, 12: If you fully obey the Lord your God and carefully follow all His commands I give you today, the Lord your God will set you high above all the nations on earth. All these blessings will come upon you and accompany you if you obey the Lord your God ... The Lord will open the heavens, the storehouse of His bounty, to send rain on your land in season and to bless all the work of your hands. You will lend to many nations but will borrow from none.

Rom 13:8: Let no debt remain outstanding, except the continuing debt to love one another, for he who loves his fellow man has fulfilled the law.

Psalm 37:21: The wicked borrow and do not repay, but the righteous show mercy and give generously.

Debt is never the real problem. It is symptomatic of the real problem: greed, self-indulgence, impatience, fear, poor self-image, lack of self worth, lack of self-discipline, or something else —Ron Blue.

More debt, more sweat; No debt, no sweat! No debt, no regret: live your life with no debt and your life will have no regret!

I'd rather go to bed without dinner than to rise with debt. --- (Benjamin Franklin). The lesson: Avoid debt at any cost by living within your means and even intentionally below your means. Get out of debt as quickly as possibly.

Nothing is more painful than poverty! The only reason for the existence of poverty is to remind the rich to practice their charity. --- Jewish proverbs.

Too many people spend the money they don't have, to buy the things they don't need, to try to impress the people they don't even like. --- Will Rogers.

Debt is a merciless master, a fatal enemy of the savings habit. Poverty alone is sufficient to kill off ambitions, destroy self-confidence, and destroy hope. All victims of these two cruel taskmasters (debt and poverty) are practically doomed to failure --- Napoleon Hill.

Annual income twenty pounds, annual expenditure nineteen six, result happiness. Annual income twenty pounds, annual expenditure twenty pounds ought and six, result misery. --- Charles Dickens

Financial peace isn't the acquisition of stuff. It is learning to live on less than you make, so you can give money back and have money to invest. You can't win until you do this. --- Dave Ramsey

He who loses money, loses much; He who loses a friend, loses much more; He who loses faith, loses all. – Eleanor Roosevelt.

He that goes a borrowing goes a sorrowing --- Benjamin Franklin

Definition of Debt

The scriptural definition of debt is a person's inability to meet the "agreed-upon" obligations. When a person buys something on credit, it is just a contract, and not necessarily a debt. But when the terms of that contract are violated, then that contract becomes a debt. Debt has occurred (Burkett, 1975 P. 56). The dictionary definition of debt refers to money or property which one person is obligated to pay to another. This may include money owed to credit card companies, bank loans, money that one borrowed from other people, any bills past due and the home mortgage. Monthly bills such as gas, water, electricity are not considered debt if they are paid on time (Dayton, 2011, P. 29). Lenders and advertisers use all kinds of attractive definitions of debt to try to mask the harsh and brutal reality. But the truth of the matter is that indebtedness is a terrible bondage tantamount to a modern-day version of ancient slavery.

While the Word of God does not speak against borrowing as a sin, it does not encourage it either. It is not wise to borrow from others as it creates the possibility of falling into the debt trap. There is zero promise from God to bail out the debtor. Causing a debt to exist is not a spiritual test or an exercise of faith; rather it is an act of stupidity and a habit of fatality as the debt bondage tightens its noose around the debtor's neck. It warns against those who borrow and do not repay back on time as people who are wicked (Ps 37:21). It is better not to loan money to people either, as it does change the nature of your relationship with the people who owe you money, especially when they fail to pay back behind various scenarios.

It is also dangerous and foolish to strike hands in pledge with someone by cosigning to guarantee another person's loan (Prov 11:15). If you put up financial security for another, you will surely suffer. Just as you deal with debt, you must humble yourself to go and get out of the surety situation as quickly as possible, with serious intensity, running for your life like a gazelle from the hand of the hunter, and like a bird from the snare of the fowler (Prov 6:1-5). While the Lord desires for us to know and obey His truth and thus live in His freedoms, including financial freedom (John 8:31-32), the evil devil always wants to trap us into the bondage of excessive debts, where we are too immobilized to do anything for The cause of Christ or others we love and care about. Indebtedness violates the principles of God's word in that it presumes upon the future with boastful arrogance and presumption that are dangerous and even reckless (James 4:13-17). Additionally, borrowing money without the ability to repay denies the Lord the opportunity from doing a miraculous provision for us (Dayton, 2011, PP. 31-32), and it becomes a disgrace and shame to His name because our testimonies as the children of God are tarnished and discredited even by the sinful and greedy world.

When Is "Possible Debt" Permissible?

The Holy Scripture is always loud and clear on its commandments for us to be diligent in making money, to be thrifty in saving money, to be faithful and wise in managing money, and never ever to waste any money or resources as His wise and responsible stewards, to be diversified in our approach to investing money, and particularly to be generous and sacrificial for us to give money to the needy and the cause of Christ. The Bible also warns us against lending or loaning money to others as the practice changes the nature of human interactions and relationships in a negative and unhealthy way. Yet on the subject of us borrowing from others or owing money to others, the Word of God is kind of silent. According to the highly respected Christian financial advisor and counselor Howard Dayton (2011, P. 32), it is possible and implicitly permissible for Christians to owe money when it comes to a home mortgage, or for your business, or your vocational preparation such as education. Remember that a "debt" is not really a debt when it's intentionally created for some advantageous benefits and when you have the money reserved to pay it off at any time you want. However, this "possible debt", although by no means encouraged and of necessity to be repaid as soon as possible, is allowed only if the following three criteria are satisfied:

1. The item that you purchase is an asset with the potential to appreciate in value and/or produce an income;
2. The value of the item purchased equals or exceeds the amount owed against it, such as one's loan as an investment in education and in preparation for a profession;
3. The debt is not so large that repayment puts undue strain on your budget.

The Myths of Debt

A major barrier to our winning in life is our view of debt! According to the Christian financial guru Mr. Dave Ramsey of Financial Peace University (2007, PP. 17-51), several major myths about debt have to be carefully examined and fully exposed and brutally dealt with in light of the truths, so that we can be financially fit and free to serve the Lord and bless others out of our prosperity and abundance.

Let's take a close look at each of these twelve myths he pinpointed below:

1. Debt is just a tool to be used to create prosperity. The truth of this money matter is that using debt or borrowed money to create wealth is presuming upon the future that is highly changeable and extremely uncertain. This myth creates considerable risk and most often does not bring prosperity.
2. If I loan money to friends or relatives in debt, I'm helping them out. The truth of the matter is that once money is loaned, the relationship will be strained and can even be ruined as one becomes the master and the other party the servant or slave.

3. By cosigning a loan, I'm helping a friend or relative. The truth is that once you cosign, you better be ready to repay the loan as the banker and the law will be asking you the cosigner to pay in case of debt. You will be personally held accountable for this matter until the last penny is paid.
4. Cash advance, payday loans, rent to own, title pawning are needed to help the poor people to get ahead. Wrong! These are rip-off examples of predatory lending to take advantage of the lower-income folks to benefit only the owners of the businesses.
5. Car payments are a way of life; you'll always have one. The truth of the matter is to never secure a loan for a new car. Driving a reliable used car is what the average millionaire does. In fact, this is exactly how she or he became a millionaire in the first place.
6. Leasing a car is what sophisticated people do. Wrong! Consumer experts all confirm that car lease is the most expensive way to operate a vehicle.
7. You can get a brand new car at 0 percent interest. The truth is that a new car loses 60% of its value in the first four years; that isn't exactly 0 percent.
8. You should get a credit card to rent a car, check in a hotel, or buy on line. Nope, a debit card will do all that, and it is no more risky than a credit card. In fact, 60% of the people do not pay off their credit cards every month!
9. Make sure your teenager gets a credit card as he or she will learn to be responsible with money. The truth of the matter is that your doing so is an excellent way to teach the teenager to be financially irresponsible. That's why teens are now the number-one target of credit card companies.
10. Debt consolidation saves interests and you have one smaller payment. The truth is that debt consolidation does not solve the debt problem as it just superficially and deceptively treats only the symptom and not dealing with the real issue: the root cause.

11. If no one uses debt, then our economy will collapse. Nope, it would prosper!
12. Debt is a tool for life. Nope. Debt is an effective method to make the bank wealthy and to make you poor. Debt is bondage that keeps you from prosperity and drags you down into the scarcity snares and the poverty pits.

The Root Causes of Debt

It has been widely reported by financial researchers and respected experts that in the U.S.A, the average household personal debt (not including mortgage) is anywhere from $8000 to $22,000. Average Americans spend much more than they earn --- 132% of what they really make. One in seven credit card holders report that they are over stressed with making minimum monthly payments. When your debt is way over your head, it is the main and major obstacle to balancing your budget even if you established one. There are many causes of indebtedness that result in material scarcity and financial poverty. Some of them are: sudden loss of one's gainful employment due to various reasons, unexpected physical development of sicknesses and medical bills, major accidents and unforeseeable natural disasters that cause huge losses or horrible damage to houses and cars with no previous insurance coverage. However, the following list of 6 major factors deal with some major preventable and personal causes. They all start with the letter "I" to pinpoint and discuss the issues. Let us take a serious look at them:

1. Ignorance --- "My people are destroyed for lack of knowledge." (Hosea 4:6). People become ignorant because they have willfully ignored and rejected the Word of God to their own demise and destruction.   Proverbs 22:3 says that the prudent sees evil and hides himself by taking the necessary and proper refuge, but the naïve or the simpleton go on and are punished for it with much suffering. Ignorance is by no means bliss but thankfully, ignorance is not stupidity; it is just the lack of required knowledge or specialized training. While ignorance is not bliss; it is a burden and bondage seriously preventing one from reaching his or her potential. If one does not want to learn, no one can help him; but if he is willing to learn, nothing can stop him. That I'm very convinced of! And in order to really earn, one must first be ready to learn, for what you learn will determine how much you will earn. By one's willingness to be educated and trained, unrealistic and unbiblical desires for self-fulfillment or instant gratification can be removed or easily overcome. The best investment you can ever make is to invest in yourself through the powerful fortification of education. As the wise ole Benjamin Franklin said, "Am investment in knowledge always pays the best interest." And what you do not know will hurt you. There is always hope to those who are willing, ready and eager to embrace the unfathomable knowledge of the Word of God as we serve the God of wisdom and hope (Rom 15:4, 13).

2. Indulgence --- As a rule of life for us, the wise man Benjamin Franklin writes, "Nothing brings more pain than too much pleasure; nothing more bondage than too much liberty." "Whoever loves pleasure will be a poor man; he who loves wine and oil will not be rich." (Prov 21:17). Everything in life must have moderation and a proper balance. With the proper balance, even what seems to be a curse can turn out to be a blessing; and without the proper balance, too much blessings can become a terrible curse, as many experiences of ours have demonstrated. When people go to the extremes and excesses for their so-called successes, their lives are quickly thrown out of balance with painful instabilities and harmful even irreversible consequences. The drunkard and the glutton will come to poverty, and the slumber will clothe them with rags (Prov 23:21). God does not bless the lazy and the idle.

Jesus the Lord, in one of his 8 hard woes and curses in Matt 23, rebukes the Pharisees and the scribes as "hypocrites", for they only clean the outside of the cup and the plate, "but inside they are full of greed and self-indulgence (V. 25). Due to our fallen nature, humans are infected with hedonism, meaning that we all naturally seek pleasure and avoid pain for ourselves. In a sense and to some degree, honestly, we are all self-indulgent in feeding the passions and desires of the flesh. And to successfully fight indulgence, we must understand what really fuels it. As the Lord Jesus precisely pinpoints to us in the previous verse, the root cause of this indulgence is greed based on unscriptural and unspiritual folklores around us, many of which are lies from the world and its prince the devil himself, the father of all lies. Greed causes people to go shopping on impulse, and pushes the naïve and ignorant and the selfish to fall into the traps of all kinds of get-rich-quick schemes and scams (I Tim 6:9). Greed corrupts Godly contentment, as godliness with contentment is great gain (I Tim 6:6), and this idolatrous greed for more fame and fortune, and for more power and pleasure has ruined far too many individuals, marriages and families spiritually, relationally, and financially.

3. Impulsive Purchases --- It is human nature to want "stuff", and to want more of it, and want it all right now. The deep desires for more pleasure and for the instant gratification of the flesh (I John 2:16) are within us all. Being willing and being disciplined to delay pleasure for a greater purpose is a sure sign of personal maturity and Christian spirituality. The lack of a realistic budget and/or a lack of disciplines to live within one's means by always spending less than you earn often results in a shopping spree on impulse. A mutually agreed-upon and realistic and thorough budget between the couple and in the family is quite necessary, essential and even indispensable these days in channeling and directing us to keep accurate records of our incomes and outgoes. It is critical to live within the budget with strict personal disciplines and mutual accountability so that one will not overspend through seductive advertising and impulse shopping, with the money we don't really have, to buy the stuff we don't really need, only to try to impress the people that we don't even like. The Lord Jesus promises to supply us all our need and not any of our greed according to His glorious riches in Jesus (Phil 4:19). There is indeed a huge difference between a need and a greed.

4. Indolence, inaction and Idleness --- Proverbs 6: 6-8 commands us to go to the ant and consider its ways and learn from its wisdom of diligence, intelligence and organizing and saving in preparation for the harsh and bitter times when there would be no food to eat outside. Poverty and scarcity will come to those who are sleepy, idle and lazy, like a bandit robbing them all they might have. Laziness brings on deep sleep, and the shiftless and idle man goes hungry (Prov. 19:15) and suffers much devastating poverty. The Apostle Paul, who was always busy working to make tents as a product to fund and finance the ministries as an example and a model for others to follow, sternly warns the leaders in Thessalonica to teach all the others that, "If a man will not work, he shall not eat." (II Thess 3:7-10). God will never favor idleness or bless laziness. As a matter of fact, idleness is the devil's workshop. Indolence is the mother of poverty just as industry is the mother of prosperity, and diligence is the mother of success!

5. Indifference --- The longer I live and learn, the more I am convinced that the opposite of love is actually not hate. It is the attitude and the spirit of indifference. Indifference basically says that "I don't know, and I don't care to know!" "Who cares?" "Why should I care?" This calloused and selfish heart is devoid of passion for anything as it does not care about anyone but the self. A passionless life is a purposeless life and a pathetic life of powerlessness. This kind of spirit will not be proactive or productive in any area of life. It will cause one to have scarcity, poverty and go deeper in debts. The opposite of this type is spirit of loving and giving, sharing and caring and daring. The more we care, the more we share. And as we lovingly and generously share, we show that we deeply care. What goes around does come around, as the law of the harvest teaches. And as one sows, so will he reap. Let us dare to share and care, and I know more will come back to you with increased measure (Eccl 11:1, Lk 6:38).

6. Incooperation with others --- In order to get ahead financially, you need to get along with others relationally. Interdependence is a higher virtue than independence when it comes to wealth creation and financial accumulation. Harmonious cooperation and collaboration with proven, trusted and effective key relationships is the foundation for money making and wealth creation, for it is in the context of people you like, know, and trust, along with your good services and/or quality products, that money is made and riches are created and accumulated little by little and day by day. But if you are not able or willing to serve and work with others, you will be isolated relationally and emotionally and financially from all the others who do not want to associate with you or do any business with you. Financial prosperity or poverty is not a lack of individual IQ, but a lack of healthy interpersonal and relational skills. The famous universal Golden Rule of human relationships given by the Lord Jesus in Matthew 7:12 must always be remembered and applied to have healthy interaction for wealth creation, "So in everything, do to others what you would have them do to you, for this sums up the Law and the prophets." Treat others sincerely, fairly and kindly with respect, empathy, compassion and generosity, and all of these will come back to you in increasing measures with greater abundance and a funnel of fabulous favors (Lk 6:38).

7. Insolence --- People including Jesus followers get into drowning debts not only because they want to catch up with the Jones, but also because they want to have more than the Jones, much more than the current level of God's divine provision for the lives. This is due to spiritual pride, economic pride, emotional pride and family pride in an attempt to project a false image and a fake appearance of wealth. Indeed price demands a high price for its maintenance. God hates pride and pride goes before the fall and the destruction. Learn the Number One Spiritual and Practical Lesson from the fall of Lucifer in Isaiah 14. While we know that humility is truly our best friend in life and ministries, pride is our worst enemy and can be our worst nightmare. God does not want to hurt our pride; God wants to kill our pride, before it kills us!

The Devastating Consequences of Debt:
I owe, I owe. Off to work I go!

In the ancient times, indebtedness carried much worse consequences from culture to culture. If you owed money to someone that you could not pay back on time, by law, the creditor could put you in debtors' prison. You could be forcibly taken away and be made a slave for hard labor as in the case of II Kings chapter 4 with the sons of the widow lady. The lender had the right to not only imprison the debtor but also to take possession and own everything that once belonged to the debtor, including all his family and properties. You could also lose your citizenship due to your excessive debt. In old India and Nepal, creditors would hold a fast on the debtors to force them to pay back what they owed. Creditors would essentially go on a hunger strike at the doorway of the debtors for all to see until they had paid their debt in full. This extremely humiliating ancient practice of debt collection would cause the debtors and their families to lose face and suffer shame and public dishonor tantamount to psychological death. In case the creditor on hunger strike died while fasting for his money to be paid back, the rest of the community would take out the debtor and beat him literally to death (Blue & White, P. 75). If you are in debt today, you'd better be grateful that you live in this modern time. Yet in our modern days with so much social polarization, divisiveness, and unrests, terrorist threats, wars and rumors of wars, major natural disasters, and high economic uncertainties, there are still many devastating consequences for those who are in debt, as the economy can suddenly decline, employment can be terminated due to reductions and cuts, and even one's investments can sour very suddenly. There are indeed very few guarantees or certainties in this life except death and taxes.

We've always believed and practiced this value that next to holy living is a debt-free living. Avoid debts of any kind at any cost. Excessive debts, as a financial bondage, will result in many terrible consequences for the debtor and his family. Let us look at this terribly enslaving issue from the Christian perspective, and let us carefully and prayerfully examine all the devastating consequences spiritually, psychologically, physically, emotionally and relationally with marriages, families and friends both with God and with people.

Spiritual Bondage

Spiritually speaking, the debtor is denounced of the Lord as being not only irresponsible, but also "wicked" as he or she borrows but cannot and will not pay back. While borrowing money may not be sinful, and at times may be temporarily permissible with the promise to pay back as soon as possible, debt is doubtlessly a spiritual burden and curse. The Lord our God nowhere in the Scriptures speaks positively or favorably about borrowing or co-signing that often results in debt. He is not pleased at all with his children who live irresponsibly and unproductively. And if the Lord is not pleased with the rampant indebtedness among his children and in many of His churches, how then can He go ahead and prosper them and favor them with more successes?

The root problem of most of the Christian debtors, in our observation and estimation, is that people have consistently disobeyed and thus willfully violated the principles of the Scriptures regarding faith and finances. They are spiritually responsible to their excessive and paralyzing debts. People in excessive indebtedness have drifted further and further away from both the presence and the Word of God. Their lives are a poor testimony to the promises of God as they gradually lose their power to be credible witnesses for Jesus who promises the "abundant life" of prosperity in all senses of the words (John 10:10, III John 2). God Himself will hold them strictly accountable and will not consider them guiltless both in this life and in the life to come.

Chuck Bentley (2013, P. 45) further warns Christians of the spiritual costs of indebtedness, saying that debt often inhabits our liberty to follow God's will in that when we are so heavily encumbered by debt, we are in bondage with no freedom to respond to God's leading and calling. We will miss opportunities to serve God and His purpose for our lives when we have two masters. No servant can serve two masters, as Jesus warns us in Luke 16:13. He will either hate the one or love the other, or else he will be loyal to the one and despise the other. I am convinced that the credibility of our testimony diminishes outside the church in the unbelieving world , and our reputation even in the spiritual community of faith also suffers greatly if we are unable to repay the debt we owe and when we are eventually forced to file for bankruptcy. Our character is in question as our money problem is often a clear indication, as one's personal economy is closely correlated with her or his life philosophy.

Literal and Physical Bondage

Physically speaking, the Lord Jesus advises the debtors in Matthew 5:25-26: "Make friends quickly with your opponent at law while you are with him on the way; in order that your opponent may not deliver you to the judge, and the judge to the officer, and you will be thrown in prison. Truly I say to you, you shall not come out of there, until you have paid up the last cent." Financial bondage literally becomes physical bondage because failure to repay a debt in a timely manner was equated with personal dishonesty. Why? A man's word is his mark of honor. When a man gives his word, he is expected to keep it; and anyone who fails to do so can no longer be trusted. Unfortunately our modern society only winks at debts and debtors today. We have become too sophisticated to incarcerate someone simply because of debts (Burkett, 1975, P. 54). What a shame and disgrace this really is!

Psychological and Mental bondage

Every year, millions of Christians, like the rest of the world, encumber themselves with credit card debts with no abilities to repay, due to lack of mental and financial disciplines and therefore impulsive shopping and emotional purchases. They put themselves and their families under bondage with heavy financial burdens that cause them to have many sleepless nights and stressful days! Physical bondage and psychological burdens often work together on the debtor with harmful psychosomatic disorders beyond the individual's ability to bear. He thinks that he has become a laughing stock to be looked down upon by all those people around him, a worthless failure, defeated and hopelessly suffering mental agony, aguish and anxieties.

Digging Your Way Out of Debt:

Emotional Bondage

Emotionally speaking, the debtor becomes very unstable, manic-depressive with the ups and downs of his emotions, affections and feeling of heaviness. When a person is stressed out with monetary problems, in light of the many unpaid bills and endless phone calls from the collectors and creditors who have much stronger memories and stamina to get their monies back, it has a huge negative consequence on his identity as his self-worth is being challenged, attacked and soon to be down trodden. This is especially true of men whose identities and self worth are so closely connected with their jobs and employments and income as the sole breadwinners and primary providers for the families. Their lives are devoid of the sense of peace and purpose that are so needed for a healthy and productive person. This excessive financial depression and even economic devastation have taken its toll on many individuals with desperation and destruction of the worst kinds: homicides and suicides. Desperate people with a feeling of helplessness and hopelessness tend to often think desperate thoughts and do desperate things that have disastrous personal, marital, familial and social consequences that are often irreversible and irreplaceable. All this has unfortunately and repeatedly happened all too often and too close around us as one watches the daily news and even personally knows the tragedies.

Relational Bondage

Numerous research studies have consistently demonstrated these following ugly truths in the United States that expenses, borrowing and debts have spun out of control both personally and nationally. The number one cause of debt is the use of credit cards for unbudgeted and undisciplined purchases on impulse with no thought on the financial abilities or monetary availabilities to pay for it on time. Over 50% of marriages end up in ugly divorce, and the number reason for marital fights that lead to separation and divorce is the money fight due to financial tensions and debts, and thus the number problem in all the divorces (70%) is the money problem --- indebtedness. It has not only affected the debtor in various ways personally, it has also seriously damaged their marital harmony and split family unity. Single moms with kids have become a new category of economic poverty and social welfare, as they struggle to make ends meet with zero savings for any type of emergency needs. Of the approximately 300 million people in the USA, one third live on some types of governmental welfare. Surveys show that these people do not even have $500 in cash to their name and existence. Debt has become a serious social problem for the nation with millions of damaged, paralyzed and broken family relationships. This resulting hopelessness has greatly contributed to all kinds of abuses, violence, and other vices all over the places. Excessive indebtedness destroys reputations, partnerships, profitable opportunities, marriages, families, and friend relationships. What a horrific consequence it is all because of the debt bondage, an ancient and a modern slavery!

Cures of Debt:
How to avoid debt, and get out of debt, and forever stay out of debt

Now that we have learned of the many curses of the bad and devilish debt, we must do our uttermost, by prayerful endurance and persistent vigilance, live our lives avoiding any kind of debts at any costs in the first place, with the gazelle intensity and the bird alertness (Prov 6:1-5). I am convinced that a truly godly life with faith pleasing unto the Lord is a holy life, an obedient life, an abundant life, and a debt-free life! Don't ever end up in a debt-end street, for a debt-end street is a dead end street.

However in the real world with countless millions of enslaved debtors, too many Christians included, how are we to ever get out and stay out of debt? How are we, as followers of Christ, to effectively demolish the devil of debt once and for all so that we can have more than enough to live on with dignity and give with liberality? Here are some time-tested and practice-proven methods of debt reduction and elimination by Dr. Andrew Liuson (2015, PP. 97-103):

Digging Your Way Out of Debt:

1. Don't pretend that the debt does not exist by ignoring it; neither run away from it. Negotiate it off with sincerity and diplomacy. Take the initiative to go sit down and talk with your creditor or your credit card company to let them know that you do sincerely intend to pay off your debt owed to them. Negotiate an amount that you can handle and let them know how you plan to carry it out regularly. If you have this humble and sincere attitude, most of your creditors will be willing to work with you as they eagerly want to get their money back.
2. Work it off with much sweat, tears and blood! He who does not learn to endure short-term pains will not live long enough to enjoy long-term gains. Thus, no pains, no gains; No sweaty sacrifices, no spectacular successes; No excesses, no successes either! No cross, no crown.
3. Scrimp it off by tightening your economic belt and cut any and all the non-essential expenditure with major sacrifices for everyone in the family involved just to survive.
4. Pray your debt off by coming to God with confession and repentance (Prov 28:13) of personal sins in wastefulness, costly hobbies and negligent attitudes, asking God for mercies and grace, and trusting God for a financial miracle of supernatural intervention and provision.

Additionally, the spiritual and practical Mrs. Jonni McCoy (PP. 42-44) offers the following seven successful steps for your debt reduction in this tough economic time. They are well worth our careful observation and more importantly, our diligent implementation:

1. Learn to live within the boundary of your income;
2. Start rethinking seriously and soberly the debts you have;
3. Make a plan to pay your debts as quickly as possible;
4. Get rid of any high-interest-rate credit cards;
5. Consolidate your bills to the lowest rate available;
6. Faithfully pay as much as you can each month – or more;

7. Turn to a reliable professional financial counselor for help if you are in debts over your head.

Establish a realistic and detailed budget, a seriously written plan with mutual agreements between husband and wife and among family members, with the absolute discipline and accountability for all the family to carry it out. List all the assets of what you own; list all the liabilities of what you owe. Snowball your debt by attacking and demolishing the credit cards with the highest interests, paying off first of all the card with the smallest balance on it, and then the second and third smallest. This will give you some encouraging small victories that will sustain you onto tackling and destroying the bigger debts as you earn more income. Discontinue the habit of buying on credit. Performing some plastic surgery with a pair of scissors on your credit cards is now an absolute necessity.

Habits become hobbies when they start costing you money, thus says a famous Jewish proverb of the simple and plain truth. Truth is often simple and plain. Radically change your habits, examine all your hobbies, and resolutely cut back on all the money-costing hobbies and all your discretionary spending; adopt and adapt to a different life style with as little expenditure as possible. Think clearly and pray earnestly before you buy anything. Make sure that you can distinguish between your legitimate needs with just the bare necessities, and human greed, and the differences between wants and desires. While the Lord does promise to supply all our need, He will not perform any miracles to gratify any of our greed!

Learn lessons from the life of the desperate "widow and oil" found in II Kings 4:2-7. Please now go to the passage and read these key verses often and be reminded of the eternal promise made to His children and summed up in I Corinthians 10:13, "And God is faithful: He will not let you be tempted beyond what you can bear … He will also provide a way out (an exit to escape) so that you can stand up under it." Indeed God is forever true to His Word. God mercifully provided a miraculous way of escape for this helpless lady and her sons. From her encounter and experience with the prophet Elisha in II Kings 4, this widow teaches us five key lessons and steps in faith and finances (Bentley, P. 46):

1. She cries out to God and the man of God for help as a sign of her dependence on God for sufficient provision and divine intervention and protection;
2. God always hears our humble cries to Him, and answers our prayers with His perfect plan, communicated by the man of God Elisha;
3. The widow has to do her part before God will do His part. This is a very crucial spiritual principle for us to remember for our daily practice in that if we desire for God to operate miraculously and mightily in our life and ministries, we must see the incentive and take the initiative to cooperate with Him, yielding to His wise and right leading, for in order to see and experience divine operation, we must do our part: demonstrating our willing obedient cooperation according to His clear and specific instruction! In this particular case of the widow and oil, she has to become a faithful steward of what she has with her two remaining assets: a little oil and a community of people willing to help her.
4. The widow, like all of us here and now, has to go and work: selling her oil to the people door to door. Notice that God did not fill her jars with cash money. Remember that God blesses and increase our efforts when we are willingly and eagerly motivated to work: putting some feet to our faith, or put our faith to our feet! How beautiful are the feet of those who go and do His bidding! Faith is not merely a static belief system; faith is an active and dynamic behavioral pattern guided and guarded, informed and inspired by the Word of God. Faith is a verb, an action word. And faith honors God and God honors the faithful by making them flourish and fruitful!
5. God provides abundance because of our obedience (Lk 5: 1-11). This formerly helpless, desperate, hopeless, and

crying widow lady now pays off all her debts, liberates her children from impending slavery, survives her uncertain future, and becomes a credible compelling and convincing testimony for His praises and glory!

Think and live like a new immigrant with diligence, frugality, and without any wastefulness or sense of entitlement. Don't blame anyone; don't compare with anyone; don't assume anything; and don't complain about anything. And don't take anything for granted. Life is never fair, and therefore don't even bother to compare, as I often say and strongly believe and teach. This is the healthy, pro-active and productive mentality of the new American. And this has been our personal philosophy, theology, history and testimony in marriage and family, faith and finances, monies and ministries for the past 30 plus years.

Think of creative innovative alternatives to increase your income and decrease your outgo as much as possible, despising not even any little things that you can find and do to generate any income. Don't ever be ashamed to apply and do the work available. Knock on doors to ask for any odd job to do; offer yourself and family for car washes, baby and house sitting, and mowing the lawns; buy and sell some small items to make money. Despise not the small beginnings. Even a journey of a thousand miles has to start with some small and slow but solid and steady baby steps. A slow but steady strategy as a financial philosophy or your "fiscalosophy" always works and succeeds! Therefore, be faithful and industrious to lay hands on the things you do with all your heart, might, discipline and diligence. The good and gracious hand of the Lord will guide and provide as you trust and obey His instructions with daily personal applications. And as we boldly apply, the Lord our Owner, and our Master will bountifully supply! The Word of the Lord is always infallible for the Lord Himself never fails!

Accept God's provision with gratitude and joy. Do not complain greedily about the things that you do not yet have; but rather be grateful to God and be content with His provision and with what you already have. The Bible teaches and assures us in I Tim 6:6 that godliness with contentment is great gain. Let your conduct be without covetousness; be content with such things as you have, for He Himself has said, 'I will never leave you or forsake you.' So we may boldly say, "The Lord is my help and I will not fear: What can man do to me?" (Heb 13:5-6).

Make sure that you will not allow any new debts to accumulate. You must make up your mind once and for all to always avoid any new debt at any cost! This is a non-negotiable principle that must never ever be violated. In order to accomplish this, you will need much time on your knees in prayerful dependence on God and in renewed determination and disciplines from God, His Word and the enabling power of His Holy Spirit. Be intentional to seek out among trusted friends with exemplary financial successes a few key accountability partners to hold you responsible. They can be from your family, church, and from your close circles of friends, and they are people you trust, respect and admire because of their proven track record of solid successes in this area of faith and finances.

Wife and husband in the context of the family as "one" in faith and finance, in spirit and in flesh, must learn to live in relational harmony with monetary agreement, and financial unity, ahead of time. United we stand and divided we fall. Let nothing be done without agreement, for a house divided against itself cannot stand. Be in unity and agreement with each other after much prayers and discussion; and be in unity with the Lord in our assignment to His Word and Spirit alignment. Two are better than one because they will have a good reward for their labor, for if one falls, the other will lift up his companion. Woe to him who is alone when he falls, for he has no one to help him up. Again, if two lie down together, they will keep warm; But how can one be arm alone? Though one may be overpowered by another, two can withstand him. And a threefold cord is not quickly or easily broken (Eccl 4:9-12).

Exercise you faith through your acts of obedience and establish a faithful practice of tithe, as it is a serious command of the Lord. No Christian can ever prosper with abundance in the biblical sense of the loaded word "Shalom" without living in obedience to His requirements of us. We must do our part before He will do His part. And when He sees faith in real serious action, the Lord will cause mighty miracles to happen. His favors of faith and finances will shift your way and in your direction. The Lord rebukes us with curses for our robbing Him with our tithes and offerings due to Him. He also and always remedies the curse with the promises of blessings if we heed His instructions. He invites us His children to try Him and test Him in this: Bring all the tithes into the storehouse of the Lord (our part of obedience), and then I will open the windows of heaven and pour our such blessings that you have no room enough to receive it... I will rebuke the devourer for your sake... and all the nations will call you blessed for you will be a delightful land (Mala 3:9-12). What a powerfully challenging and rewarding promise this is!

Remember to never ever give up! You will surely make it if you faint not. Take advantage of every available opportunity to improve yourself and apply yourself. Do not grow weary while you are doing good in sowing seed on fertile soil, for in due time, with your patience and persistence, you will reap a bumper harvest if you do not lose heart (Gal 6:9). There is always hope to those who keep the faith and who refuse to give up. As long as there is a God, there is always hope for we serve the God of Hope. All that was written in the past was written to teach us now, so that through the encouragement and the endurance of the Scriptures, we might have hope. And may the God of God fill your heart with all peace and joy as you put your trust in Him, so that you may overflow with hope by the power of the Holy Spirit that He has given you (Roman 15:4, 13). Hallelujah and Amen!

Reflections and Applications

Among all the disciplines, self-discipline is the most difficult one. But it is also the most effective and rewarding one especially in financial matters. It is not only how you make money, but more importantly how you spend your money that will finalize determine your financial situation of poverty or prosperity. I (Esther) still remember the first years I started working after high school graduation. All my salaries were automatically surrendered to my parents. After working so hard as a machinist in my village factory for six months, I was finally allowed to buy a set of clothing for the coming Chinese New Year with only $20 allowance. So I got on my bike for an hour ride to the near by city to shop for an entire day to look for the best deal for me. Though I was so hungry during the lunch hour, yet I did not spend a penny of the money on any food. I endured the temporary hunger of missing lunch for a day so as to buy the clothes I wanted, which would last me for years. I was very happy when I finally got what I wanted in spite of a grumbling stomach, enduring short term pains to enjoy the long term gains with sacrifice, determination and discipline.

In our current American culture, self indulgence and instant gratification have become rampant these days. The attitude seems to be that "I want it and I want it right now, no matter how much it costs!" If this is our attitude regarding expenditure, our pockets will soon be empty and our credit cards maxed out with no money to pay, resulting in high interests and terrible debts. If we apply just a bit of financial self discipline, it will help put us in a much better financial situation.

You might want to ask yourself the following questions:

1. Are the things I purchase absolutely necessary?
2. If so, can the cost be reduced if I'll want for a while before buying them?
3. In which way can I improve self-discipline in my personal finances?

Chapter 9

Budgeting Your Way to Balance and Bountifulness

Proverbs 20:18 --- Making plans by seeking advice; if you wage war, obtain guidance.

Proverbs 21:5 --- The plans of the diligent lead to profit as surely as haste leads to poverty.

Proverbs 22:3 --- A prudent (sensible) man sees danger and takes refuge (hides and avoid), but the simple keeps going and suffers for it (gets punished).

Proverbs 24:3 --- By wisdom a house is built, and through understanding it is established.

Proverbs 27:23-24 --- Be sure you know the condition of your flocks, give careful attention to your herds. For riches do not endure forever, and a crown is not secured for all generations.

Luke 14: 28:32 --- Suppose one of you wants to build a tower. Will he not first sit down and calculate the cost to see if he has enough money to complete it? For if he lays the foundation and is not able to finish it, everyone who sees it will ridicule him, saying, "This fellow began to build and was not able to finish." Or suppose a king is about to go to war with another king. Will he not first sit down and consider whether he is able with ten thousand men to oppose the one coming against him with twenty thousand? If he is not able, he will send a delegation while the other is still a long way off and ask for terms of peace.

I Corinthians 14: 40 --- Let all things be done decently and in order.

Knowledge is not automatically power; it is only potential power. Knowledge becomes power only when and if it is organized into definite plans of actions and directed to a definite end --- Napoleon Hill.

A budget is simply you telling your money where to go instead of you wondering where it went --- John Maxwell.

If your outgo exceeds your income, then your upkeep will be your down fall.

Always pray, plan prepare before you proceed! Better is prevention than intervention. Better building strong guardrails along the cliff than establishing emergency hospitals at the foot of the mountain.

If you are not saving money, then your budget is not working.

Some people have too much hope and too little reality check!

 Wisdom and wealth always walk and work together! They are like two sides of the same coin and you cannot have one without the other.

Be vigilant and vigorous in knowing your economic condition before you make any major financial decision and take major financial action. Provide for personal and family needs with extra surplus to help others in crisis.

One must be actively reflective in order to be proactive and effective to successfully accomplish his faith and finance objectives.

The Blessed Benefits of Budgeting

1. Budgeting as a wise biblical instruction intended for personal application, affords us the opportunity to exercise our mental, spiritual and financial knowledge and disciplines. Mere financial knowledge, according to numerous experts and research studies, only contributes to some 20% of a person's success, and the other 80% depends on the consistently disciplined way of life of the individual, in other words, his or her life style. You must know realistically and ahead of time, that budgeting is not fun; it is hard work, even frustrating and painful at times. But it is definitely worth the effort because this financial discipline will bring you much fruit later on (Heb 12:5-11). No pains, no gains; More pains, more gains!
2. Family budgeting together proves to be a wonderful tool we can use to improve and enhance marital and familial communication to care for and share with each other spiritually, relationally and materially, as the family members get to know each others in terms of their real needs, concerns, wants and desires;
3. Budgeting provides the opportunity needed for the couple to live, work and serve in harmony, unity, and agreement. It allows them to work as a team in praying and planning on how to spend their hard-earned dollars wisely and effectively. One judge lamented, saying, "Quarreling about money between the husband and the wife has been the main reason for our unprecedented divorce rate." Of the more than 50% marriages ending up in divorce in the USA, the number one reason or cause (70% approximately) given by the couples is money matters that have gone out of control for lack of budgetary disciplines due to much

rampant ignorance and/or excessive indulgence on one part or both.
4. As budgeting allows us to pray and plan carefully as to how and when and where the money is to go in full view of the necessities, essentials, and the priority, we can often make the money go further when it's well planned before hand.
5. The more we live within the budget as individuals, families, organizations and even as a nation, the more we will be able to save our way to bountiful abundance: we will have More than enough so that we can become More than conquerors in all areas of our lives and ministries.

How To Budget Your Way To Bountifulness

Developing and using a monetary budget is very important for personal financial fitness and freedom. Some people suffer financial difficulties because of pure ignorance, having no clue as to how to spend money wisely; other people have developed their budgets, but they are too unrealistic to be realized in the real world. Still others have produced a sound and solid budget, an effective spending strategy, but they lack the will power and the consistency to carry it out daily over the long haul, like people who make New Year resolutions only to forget them completely in less than a month! What a pity and shame this is. Remember that a budget is very useful only if it is put to use. A wise financial budget is futile if we promptly file it away and do nothing about it.

Having the financial knowledge and skill are good and necessary to reach financial peace and freedom, but they are not good enough because successful stewardship , as real spiritual leadership too, is much more about the will than the knowing the skill. As our Lord and Master once taught us, leading us by His personal example in John 13:15-17, that now that we know these things (principles, laws, and truths of the kingdom of God), we will be blessed and become prosperous only if and only when we actually observe, obey and do them, putting them into our daily practices! As a matter of fact, mere knowledge only puffs us up, making us feel bigheaded. But we are what we constantly do, and only when we do it, then we live it (Lk 10:28, 37 – Do it and you shall live! Go and do likewise!). Action always speaks louder than words. The results of our actions will speak for themselves and for us loud and clear, just like a fruit tree is recognized and known by its fruit.

The noted financial counselor, expert and advisor, Mr. Howard Dayton (2011, PP. 123-129) teaches that to set up a budget, all you need is to follow a three-step process preferably to be written out and followed up in a simple inexpensive notebook of accounting paper sold in most bookstores, or you can just do it on your personal computer as well:

Step One:

Begin with where you are today: by knowing thoroughly and defining accurately your current economic reality.

You are to develop your budget with your current situation by sitting down and determining "precisely" how much money you made and how much is spent. Unfortunately most people have gotten no earthly clue as to how much they are actually earning and how much they are spending. It is absolutely biblical (Prov 27:23) and essential to keep a complete and accurate financial record of every penny and dollar on a monthly basis to get a realistic picture in order to make an estimated budget. If your income is not the same from month to month, or from week to week, then make a conservative estimate of your annual income based on previous years of experiences and then divide it by 12 so as to establish a rough and general working figure for your monthly income.

Then you need to determine which expenses do not occur each month, such as real estate taxes and vacations. Estimate how much you must spend on the necessities and essentials each year and divide it again by 12 to determine a monthly cost of living. Armed with this honest information, you can proceed to complete an estimated monthly budget.

Faith and Finances

Step Two:

The solution is where you want to be: spend less than you earn.

You will be surprised and even discouraged to realize, with your estimated monthly budget in written form in front of you, the possible debt dilemma that your expenditure is in excess of your income. But take heart and do not become afraid or distressed, as this is often the case for most people who bother to develop a serious budget. To solve this problem of spending more than you make, there are really only two ways: (1). Decrease your outgo; (2). Increase your income. To balance the budget, you have to creatively set up and carry out your effective strategies with two serious cautions of Not causing any extra expenses to rise, and Not sacrificing marital and family relationships in an effort to make extra money.

An estimated realistic monthly budget should look something like this one below although it may vary from person to person, from family to family:

1. Gross Monthly Income (salary, interests, dividends and others): $ _____
2. Net Spendable Income after giving and taxes: $ _____
3. Housing Expenses (mortgage or rent, utilities, insurance, taxes and maintenance such as repairs, cleaning and supplies): $ _____
4. Total Food Expenses: $ _____
5. Transportation (Car loan, insurance, gas and oil, repair and replace): $ _____
6. Insurance (life and medical): $ _____
7. Debts (except house mortgage and car loan): $ _____
8. Recreation/entertainments (Pets, vacation, babysitting etc): $ _____
9. Clothing costs: $ _____
10. Medical bills (doctor and medicines): $ _____
11. Child care and education: $ _____

12. Miscellaneous: (personal allowances, toiletries, laundries, lawn cares, gifts for weddings, birthdays and Christmas and anniversaries, etc): $ _____
13. Savings: $ _____
14. Investments: $ _____

Income vs. Outgo:

Net Spendable Income: $ _____
Less Total Living Expenses: $ _____
Surplus or Deficit: $ _____

Ways to Reduce Personal Expenses

Before you think of creative and innovative alternatives to increase your income and decrease your outgo, you should seriously consider these following suggestions to first reduce your expenses by spending wisely and spending less:

Housing --- Rent an inexpensive apartment with few responsibilities and expenses involved on your part; buy an older and modest-size house that you can improve with your own labor; Do as much maintenance of the house as possible by yourself; lower and limit the cost of utilities in the heating, cooling, lighting and appliances. Shop around purposefully and carefully and go to garage sales and second hand stores to buy similar goods with much less costs.

Foods --- Prepare a menu for the week of home-cooked nutritious meals; try to avoid eating out; leave hungry children and spouses home while you are out shopping with your pre-determined written list; bring lunch to work; cut out the ready-to-eat foods, and reduce the use of paper products.

Transportation --- Buy the good used and smaller cars; try to get by with one car; use public transportation as much as possible; consider taking BUS # 11 (walking on your two legs!), and using a bike for local needs.

Clothing --- Make and follow a written list of yearly clothing needs; shop off-season at economic stores and garage sales;

purchase basic fashions that stay in style for a long time; buy home-washable fabrics.

Insurance, health and recreation --- Select insurance based on needs and budget; seek recommendation from capable and experienced friends to save money in house, car and health insurances; practice preventative care and proper personal hygiene; exercise regularly as good healthy habit for prevention is better than intervention; avoid expensive entertainments and plan vacation for off-season and near-home destinations.

According to Mr. Dayton (2011), there are five additional budgeting hints in balancing our budgets to gradual bountifulness:

1. Reconcile your bank statement each month;
2. Have a separate savings account to deposit a monthly amount to pay for the annual expenses such as insurance and taxes;
3. Don't just think monthly; think and calculate yearly the regularly smaller bills, for this will alarm you to the true and high costs of these seemingly inconsequential expenses when they are all added up together!
4. Control your impulse spending! Each time you begin to feel the "urge" to spend for something attractive but not planned and budgeted, you should pray and delay. As you do this, the impulse will often pass away after some days! The ability to delay the desire for instant self-gratification is a clear indication of spiritual discipline and maturity!
5. It is wise in the budget to allow for both husband and wife to have some allowances for a few legitimate personal hobbies. This will reduce possible tension and eliminate many unnecessary arguments.

Step Three:
Do not stop budgeting! Keep on keeping on.

A budget is simply a wise and disciplined plan to spend responsibly and reasonably in order to achieve a financial balance and thus to begin the savings and investing in the future. A good budget that is strictly followed through will surely get you out of debts and keep you out of any debts, which is the very first step to financial peace and prosperity, financial fitness and freedom! Budgeting is not easy and it is no fun; it is hard work that requires teamwork and serious efforts, but it is certainly worth it! Budgeting saves you thousands of dollars over the year, and helps you demolish old debts and avoid new debts! There are no short cuts in money matters, and the so-called short cuts never pay off in a long run! Be encouraged, inspired and empowered by the Word of God and these wonderful practical principles for you today. You can do it if you put your heart to it; and you will make it if you develop this discipline as a real disciple of Jesus. Start with you, start here and now, and start with the small, for a thousand mile journey must begin with the first step, thus says the Chinese proverb. This is known as the Law of the Process. Quality product comes only from the necessary and even strenuous process. No one can launch out with giant leaps if she or he does not commence with solid little baby steps. Starting with baby steps and small wins, you will feel victorious and gradually become prosperous for the glory of God and the cause of Christ. Patience and perseverance pay plentifully.

Lo, money is always plentiful for those who understand the simple rules of its acquisition, thus says the fascinating and intriguing sage of old, *The Richest Man in Babylon* (Clason, 1955). Just as a heavy and full purse causes a light heart, so a lean and light purse causes a heavy heart of worries, anxieties and burden. According to George S. Clason, there are 7 basic cures that will guide us away from the stringencies of a lean and mean purse. These seven universal and unchangeable laws of financial abundance, like the law of gravity, have proven themselves to be the sure keys to a full, fat and bulging purse, a larger bank balance and a gratifying financial progress and a life with much more abundance:

1. Start thy purse to fattening by strictly saving a minimum of 10% of your earning;
2. Control thy expenditure with a strong budget, determinedly denying any desire for instant gratification;

3. Make thy gold multiply by investing your money and putting it to labor and reproduce itself in kind for you;
4. Guard thy treasure from loss by always securing and protecting your principal. Invest only where your principal is safe, where it may be reclaimed if desirable and where you will not fail to collect a fair rental or return. Consult with wise and experienced people.
5. Make of thy dwelling a profitable investment. Many blessings will come to you as you own your own house.
6. Insure a future income by investing in land and houses to provide in abundance for the needs of growing age and for the protection and provision of the family.
7. Increase thy ability to earn by developing strong and definite desires and by studying and cultivating yourself to be wiser, more skillful and thus more useful to make a continuous profits with continuous services.

The Five Laws of Gold

If you will give the regular people a choice of either wisdom or gold, what do you think they will do? They will totally ignore your wisdom, and immediately grab the gold you offer and waste it in a short amount of time. Soon enough they will cry out again because they have no more gold. This is unfortunately the human nature in full display for the majority of the people. Remember that wisdom and wealth always walk and work together! Gold is plenty and is reserved for those who know these five laws of gold concerning its nature and who will abide by these universal golden rules (Clason, P. 63). Let's study them and apply them:

1. Gold comes gladly with increasing quantity to him who will put no less than 10% of his earnings to create an estate for his future and that of his family;
2. Gold labors diligently and contentedly for the wise owner who finds for it profitable employment, multiplying even as the flocks of the field;

3. Gold clings to the protection of the cautious owner who invests it under the advice of men wise in its handling;
4. Gold slips away from the man who invests it in businesses or purposes with which he is not familiar or which are not approved by those skilled in its keep;
5. Gold flees the man who would force it to impossible earnings or who follows the alluring advice of tricksters and schemers or who trusts it to his own inexperience and romantic desires in investment.

Reflections and Applications

Now you have gained some fundamental knowledge on your financial planning through establishing and living by a budget. However, while knowing is good, it is not good enough. What is needed is the consistent and disciplined application of the knowledge to our daily lives, which will lead to real change and powerful transformation when the rubber meets the road. As the saying goes, the test of the pudding is in the eating.

RecentLy, I have been trying to learn fishing. I have gained lots of knowledge and information through reading related articles on the websites and watching videos on fishing, learning the habits of the fish, the current of the river, casting the lines, selecting different lures for different fishes, and the timing for fishing. Yet in spite of the tremendous amount of knowledge, I still have to go out and try out the effectiveness of different methods. I still have to practice to figure out the best lures for certain fishes in certain locations and at the appropriate time in order to be fruitful and effective. In the same way, we must test and approve the validity of financial concepts in our own lives through real practices before we can become successful. We learn by doing for it is in doing that we are actually learning something. Go and do likewise.

Here are a few questions to consider:

1. Have you ever budgeted your personal finance that has produced a positive result?

2. What useful insights have you learned from your practices with both failures and successes?
3. With what you've learned and experienced so far, how can you further improve your own budget that will be fitting and adaptable to your financial well-being?

Chapter 10

Put Your Money to Work for You: Saving and Investing

Proverbs 6:6-8 --- Go to the ant, you sluggards; consider its ways and be wise! It has no commander, no overseer or ruler, yet it stores its provisions in summer and gathers its food at harvest.

Proverbs 12:15 --- The way of a fool is right in his own eyes, but a wise man listens to advice.

Proverbs 13:20 --- He who walks with the wise grows wise, but a companion of fools suffers harm.

Proverbs 15:22 --- Plans fail for lack of counsel, but with many advisors they succeed.

Proverbs 19:2 --- It is not good to have zeal without knowledge, not to be hasty and miss the way.

Proverbs 21:20 --- In the house of the wise are stores of choice food and oil, but a foolish man devours all he has.

Proverbs 24:27 --- Prepare your work outside and make it ready for the field; afterward, then, build your house.

Proverbs 30: 24-25 --- Four things on earth are small, yet they are extremely wise: ants are creatures of little strength, yet they store up their food in the summer.

Matt 25: 26-27 --- His master replied, "You wicked, lazy servant! ... Well then, you should have put my money on deposit with the bankers, so that when I returned I would have received it back with interest." — Jesus Christ

Compound interest is the eighth wonder of the world. He who understands it, earns it ... he who doesn't, pays it. Compound interest is the most powerful force in the universe. Compound interest is the greatest mathematical discovery of all time --- Albert Einstein

Fools can make money. It takes a wise man to know how to spend it --- English proverb.

Want to safely double your money? Fold it over once and put it in your pocket.

The greatest use of life is to spend it for something that will outlast it --- William James.

Without a doubt our Christian faith in the infallible, authoritative and powerful Word of God informs and inspires us to get actively involved in seeking good and Godly advice on money matters, always plan ahead, always work hard to make all the money we can, save all the money we can, invest with diversification, and make our money make more money with maximization and multiplication so as to magnify the Lord with compassion for the needy and generosity for His cause and missions on earth. From the very beginning of the Holy Scriptures, we have been commanded of the Lord to "be fruitful and multiply", to increase and subdue for the glory of the Lord (Gen 1:28). By His sufficient grace, we as the followers of Christ, must become more faithful, fearless and forceful so as to flourish and be more fruitful and profitable with our high calling for His higher purposes and greater glory. To be sure, this is not a mere and random suggestion for some philosophical or theological contemplation; rather it is a loud and clear divine command and commission from our Creator, Owner, Master and Lord to go forth and bear fruit with bold action! This is also our joy, honor, supreme privilege and solemn obligation.

As we go all out to labor hard and work smart, the Lord is pleased with both our diligence and intelligence and bountifully rewards us with more income. And with the money we honestly make, we take care of bills and family needs here and now. However, we are not only to make money, we are urged to plan ahead and save money for a rainy day and even to leave a good inheritance to our children and our grandchildren, as it is the biblically wise thing to do. Proverbs13:22 A good man leaves an inheritance for his children's children, but a sinner's wealth is stored up for the righteous.   With our debt-free living and our sufficient savings in place, we are then properly positioned and plentifully prepared to continue our abundant life even in the events of illness, accidents, temporary unemployment, disability, and old age.

As the righteous of God, we are to live by faith just as we are saved by faith in Jesus Christ the Lord. But the Holy Bible also commands us to put our faith to our feet, or to put feet to our faith, for faith without work, or deeds, or action, is dead, and can become deadly hypocrisy! We are commanded and go and learn from the tiny little ants (Prov 6:6-8). Joseph provides us an excellent example too of saving and investing for the future in Genesis 41. We are convinced that in our culture of alluring consumerism and wasteful materialism, most of us spend way too much more than we make, resulting in deep financial troubles as people are drowning in debts and even resulting personal bankruptcies. We as the children of God must dare to be different in order to make a real difference as light and salt for Jesus by cultivating and developing a different spirit if we ever hope to make a significant impact on the world. Instead of being passive and impulsive consumers and careless and reckless spenders, we must obey the Word and Godly counsel to become active and creative conservers, strict savers, and wise contributors. The wise always work hard, make, save, give and enjoy money as a blessing and a favor of the Lord who gives them the ability and power to get wealth (Deut 8:18), just like the one described succinctly in Proverbs 21:20 that declares In the house of the wise are stores of choice food and oil, but a foolish man devours all he has! Here is one we really love and daily experience: Proverbs 10:22 The blessing of the LORD brings wealth, and he adds no trouble (sorrow or toil) to it.

Wisdom and wealth always walk and work together to accomplish a higher purpose. The wealthy have all kinds of treasures in their nice houses because they are very wise and disciplined in saving up money and strategically investing money to make it grow. The Rev. Tom Rosen gives us 8 nice tips on saving money from the wisdom of the Word (The Wisdom of Saving --- www.ministry127.com). Let us study these sound instructions for our daily applications:

1. Begin by making savings a priority for yourself and your household budget;
2. Honestly and thoroughly examine your financial condition with a tighter budget so as to recapture and redirect your resources towards savings;
3. Commit with strict discipline to set a dollar amount to save and invest per month after your tithes and offering to the Lord;
4. Build up a cushion of cash saving before investing. This cash saving should cover 3-6 months of family expenses, starting with $1000 set aside.
5. Make your saving or investing deposits automatic. It's not likely for you to save and invest monthly if you have to think and decides.
6. Get good Godly counsel on how to save and invest securely and profitably the money that the Lord has entrusted you as His steward;
7. Diversify your investments. Don't put all your eggs in one basket, as the good ole cliché says it right. The wise and wealthy King Solomon did not put all his treasured goods

on one ship, but on many different trade ships, declaring that we need to divide our portion to seven, and even to eight. Why? For you do not know what evil might be coming on the earth (Eccl 11:2). God blessed King Solomon with wisdom, honor and riches as everything his hands touched powerfully prospered. Solomon was both a marvelous saver and perhaps the best investor the ancient world had ever known at the time.

8. Continue investing for a long time, like the faithful and profitable steward in Matthew 25. Develop self-control which is an essential fruit of the Holy Spirit in our lives. . Don't ever lose heart or give up. Just keep going onward and forward u distracted and uninterrupted. And you will surely accumulate and prosper after many days (Eccl 11:1).

If there is one more thing to be said of the divine wisdom of saving and investing from Solomon the King, it has to be his emphasis on honest money making and ethical investing in the fear of the Lord, for the fear of the Lord is the beginning of wisdom and the knowledge of the Holy One is understanding (Prov 9:10). Solomon has this final royal advice to offer us in Ecclesiastes 12: 13-14, "Now all has been heard; here is the conclusion of the matter: Fear God and keep His commandments, for this is the whole duty of man. For God will bring every deed into judgment, including every hidden thing, whether it is good or evil." What wonderful instructions on our spirituality in view of His eternity, and what marvelous life lessons on Scriptural stewardship of honesty, duty, industry, and accountability which is the foundation of integrity. As Hebrew 4:13 warns us all kingdom managers, "Nothing in all creation is hidden from God's sight. Everything is uncovered and laid bare before Him to Whom we must give account.".

Never depend on just one single income. Make money from a variety of income streams. The word "monies" means financial resources from various sources. Just as you do not put all your investment eggs into one basket for security and growth, you try to make monies from many different areas and arenas of life: regular job and salary, more speaking engagements, teaching extra courses in another location, writing a few books to sell, land purchases and rental properties, and investing in stocks and mutual funds with professional assistance. In this one, in case one stream of your income becomes shallow and even dry up, you will always have other income streams flowing continuously your way with no worries. Diversification is both incoming and investments is very important in the protection of your basic principal and the expansion of your investment capital, as King Solomon and other financial experts wisely teach us. Ecclesiastes 11:2 "Give portions to seven, yes to eight, for you do not know what disaster may come upon the land." To do all this well, one must make serious efforts to constantly sharpen his saw and continuously strengthen his skills to be proactive and useful and thus productive and profitable.

An old saying goes, "money talks." We believe money also walks. Along with financial affluence, will come proportional influence, as affluence produces influence in all senses of the words. The rich have many friends for many reasons as the law of attraction is at work for them. But when the poor speak, no one is listening because no one wants to listen to a powerless poor person who unfortunately has little to nothing to offer. Christian financial counselor and wise spiritual advisor, Mr. Larry Burkett (1993, PP. 233-237), was once asked a very penetrating question, "Why should we help rich people get richer?" His answer: teaching Christians to invest their surplus resources wisely and properly is just as necessary and important as teaching them to budget. Christians who are working diligently, saving aggressively and investing wisely can multiply their resources so as to give more for Kingdom causes of The Lord Jesus with more impact to make for Christ sake. How can one give if he or she does not have?

The Bible is not at all against savings, surpluses and prosperity. On the contrary, saving and investing require much wisdom and intentional strategy, and they are signs of intelligence plus diligence, and the lack of them for the believers are indication of slothfulness and foolishness. The legitimate reasons for savings and investing are to first fulfill our family responsibilities; and second, it is in preparation for more giving to further the work of God. The two key words to remember to watch out for ourselves in the process is our attitude (Lk 16:10-11) and our spirit of contentment (I Tim 6:6). We must also maintain and hold the right priority as we are blessed with more and more prosperity (Matt 6:66, Lk 16:13) to put God and His missions first, to serve God with money and not to be mastered by the money in our service to the Lord. Mr. Burkett warns Christians with four "illegitimate reasons" for investment:

1. Pride---the desires to be elevated by others because of one's material achievements. We must never fix our hope on the uncertainty of riches and thus become conceited (I Tim 6:17).
2. Greed---the insatiable desire to have more continually and the demands for only the best (I Tim 6:9).
3. Envy--- the desire to achieve based on the observation of other people's successes (Ps 73:3).
4. Ignorance---lack of discernment by following the counsel of the misguided people. Proverbs 14:7 teaches us to "leave the presence of a fool, or you will not discern words of knowledge."

The Kingdom of God, declares the Lord Jesus, advances by force, both spiritual and financial as it takes monies, lots of monies to carry our the missions ministries all over the world from local to global (the glocalization of the Great Commissions). Let us once and for all get rid of the scarcity philosophy and the poverty mentalities as a foolish measure of pseudo-spirituality that is unscriptural. Let us make all the money we can make, save all the money we can save, invest all the money we can invest, and give all the money we can give for the poor and the needy, and for the proclamation of the good news of the Kingdom of God around the whole world until all have heard. Then the end shall come as Jesus the Lord will return for the second time in glory, power and majesty (Matt 24:14). Let us courageously rise up to embrace the marvelous Master, experience the magnificent Message and expand the mighty missions as the Lord had taught the disciples on the road to Emmaus (Lk 24:13-49) to be whom God has created us to be, to go where the Holy Spirit directs us to go, and to do exactly what the Lord Jesus has commanded and commissioned us to do (Eph 2:10), the more the better! We are God's workmanship, created in Christ Jesus to do good works, which God has prepared in advance for us to do. WE are what we do, and do it, you will live. And the more we do, the bolder and better, brighter and bigger we become, spiritually and financially!

According to the wise motivational and financial Guru Mr. Napoleon Hill (PP. 131-138), saving money is obviously one of the essentials for success, and saving money is solely a matter of habit. It is literally true that as a creature of habit, the man through the Law of Habit, shapes his own personality. Through repetition, any act indulged in a few times, will become a habit, and the mind appears to be nothing more than a mass of motivating forces growing out of our daily habits. We are victims or victors of our own habits of thinking and talking poverty and prosperity. In order to save and invest to achieve abundance, these five key steps have to be resolutely taken:

1. Set up in your mind a definite description of that which you want, including the amount of money you intend to earn through the Law of Definite Chief Aim. This mental process will help you destroy the poverty consciousness and set up the prosperity consciousness.
2. Practice the Law of Habit for developing and deploying money earning strategies with the help of the Law of Imagination.
3. Utilize the Law of Attraction – like attracts like. If you really want to be positive, productive, and prosperous, then be intentional and be proactive to go out of your way to seek

out people who are positive, productive and prosperous. If you walk with the wise and wealthy, you will become wise and wealthy, most likely, because stuff does jhave a tendency to rub off on you gradually and naturally (Prov 13:20).
4. Develop a pleasing personality in working harmoniously with others. Connectivity unleashes creativity. And cooperation and collaboration are the sure foundation for wealth creation!
5. Exercise and live the extra-mile principle, doing more and better than what you are asked or told, with great enthusiasm and with no expectation of getting paid for doing it. To lead is to exceed with speed before you can succeed!

Compounding Interest

10 Reasons Why Compounding Interest is the 8th Wonder of the World(AndrewSather,April 23, 2014 @www.einvestingforbeginners.com)

The words "compound interest" are two of the most powerful in the investing world since the ancient of times as it allows you to make your money make more money for you. As a simple definition, compounding interest is basically the ability to grow an investment by reinvesting the earnings along with the original investment. It works powerfully over time regardless of your culture, gender or color. It affects everyone the same as the time goes on. Here are the reasons:

1. Compounding interest is the greatest equalizer in that we all share the same universal commodity together, and it is called "time". Time is the only thing we have in common and we are all equals before time.
2. Compounding interest utilizes momentum. A small piece of snow can become an avalanche as it snowballs down hill over time to become bigger and unstoppably more powerful. This is the same with your money saving, investing and wealth accumulating. The work you do at the

beginning may be very tiring and seemingly insignificant, but once your wealth snowballs, your wealth literally and naturally attracts more wealth. Just as the snowball attracts much more snow to be massive, so you always attract into your life the people, ideas, and resources in harmony with your dominant thoughts and values (known as the Law of Attraction). And just as a snowball compounds and grows bigger and bigger, so will your saving and investing become more and more over time with consistency.

3. Compounding interest can and will create millionaires from average people if they will invest consistently over a long time span of 20, 30, and even 40 years! This obviously takes lots of personal foresight and endurance, which separates the ordinary from the extraordinary.

4. Compounding interest teaches you patience. It at its core is best served by conservative investing, not trendy or speculative investing. You will not see results over night; but you will be amazed at its results over time! Therefore, develop and grow the virtue patience for patience always pays off generously over a long run. Don't run after "easy money" and don't fall for the "get-rich-quick" schemes. Seek professional advice and Start as earlier as possible with a Roth IRA and/or some good mutual funds with solid performance records over many years.

5. Compounding interest lets you sleep well at night. What do the wisest and wealthiest investors have in common? They are always smiling! Why? Because time has become their best ally and they are making money every second of the day. The world famous investment Guru Mr Warren Buffet once said that, "I always knew I was going to be rich, so I was never in a hurry to."

6. Compounding interest is your friend if you are poor. Poor and young people have the biggest advantage and that is time! Only time will tell if you are smart enough today to put some money to work for you.

7. Compounding interest teaches and rewards discipline. A healthy and disciplined habit is a good productive habit. Invest the same amount every month, and there is a financial and business term for it --- Dollar Cost Averaging. Why? Because by doing this, you automatically buy less when the market is up, and buy more when the market is down. It's classic buy low, sell high. By doing this, you also resist being greedy when everyone else is greedy, which results in losses.
8. Compounding interests separates the rich from the broke. No wonder the famous and great scientist Albert Einstein said that, "Compound interest is the eighth wonder of the world. He who understands it, earns it... he who doesn't, pays it." Your time is an invaluable resource for you. Make compound interest work for you and not against you, by investing to earn interests for yourself, and not by borrowing to pay interests to your creditors! We are all creatures of habits, and your habits can make you or break you, all depending on what they are. It is the habits that you live with which define your wealth. If your spending habits cause you to fight against interest, you are going to fight that fight the rest of your life and you will never be rich. However, if your habits create interests for you, then you can just sit back and relax, for your compound interest is working for you to make you rich some day!
9. Compounding interest can save our kids' generation. There is such a disregard in our culture these days for the future. There are way too many people who live with a mindset of scarcity and poverty instead of abundance and prosperity. Approximately 70% of Americans are actually living from paycheck to paycheck. If we take serious responsibilities for our finances with all the wisdom available, we will all kick our debt habits, achieve financial freedom, and build wealth for our family and future generations. Let us become wise, mature, disciplined and responsible to take this eighth wonder of the world seriously and do something great with it!

10. Many people fortunately do understand compounding interests, and they are earning and winning too. Lets learn from them so that we all can grow wise and wealthy.

The noted Christian financial counselor Mr. Ron Blue (PP. 188-196, 2016) gives such sound and solid advice in an effort of assisting us to master our money in the area of saving and investing with the 5 sequential investment strategies:

1. Eliminate all your high-interest and short-term debts before you even think of savings and investing.
2. Keep at least 3-6 months' living expenses in a money market fund or in a savings account. This positive cash flow is required before investing.
3. Put savings for major purchases in a money market fund, CD, or treasury.
4. Diversify your savings and investments to meet long-term goals in money market funds, CD, treasuries mutual funds, real estates, bonds and equities. This is a time-tested rule of investment, "Never put all your eggs in one basket!" Consult reliable experts in the area and learn from those who are already proven successful.
5. Use your investment dollars to complete long-term goals such as starting your own business, extra giving or paying off mortgage.

Additionally, according to Mr. Blue, as Christ followers, we must pay close attention to these biblical principles of sound mind investing:

1. Don't presume upon the future (James 4:13-15).
2. Avoid speculation and hasty investment decisions, especially those motivated by greed or fear (Prov 13:11, 28:20, 22).
3. Never cosign (Prov 11:15, 17:18, 22:26-27).
4. Evaluate the risk of an investment (Lk 14:28)
5. Avoid investments that cause anxiety (Matt 6:31).

6. Be in unity with your spouse (Eccl 4:9-12).
7. Avoid high-leverage situations ((Prov 22:7).
8. Avoid deceits from others or from self (Prov 11:18).
9. Tithe from your investment gains (Pro 3:9-10).

Reflections and Applications

Out of hard work and savings, we can build up surpluses, having taken care of life's basic necessities of life. We should invest our surplus where it can grow, which is to use money to make more money. I still remember that after we have bought our first house with cash with basic family necessities taken care of, we began to think how to invest and create an income for the family. At that time, our two las Christina and Lucinda were very small and I had to stay home to take care of them while my husband traveled and ministered all over. Talking with others we have learned that the real estate was one of the good sources for good investment. I have been always good at handy work and can repair most everything. So we went out and searched and bought our first rental house under $50,000. One week later we rented out for $500 a month for many years to generate a family income. Investments must bring returns!

And this financial trend and investment strategy continued successfully with several more houses paid for and rented all with the surplus income, fully utilizing the money to make more money by hard work, wisdom, and being responsible and dealing with all kinds of maintenance issues and people problems. Through perseverance and consistency and the favors of the Lord, we have been truly blessed and have learned a lot about life about the good, the bad and the ugly in terms of human relationships, trustworthiness, money matters, the issues of law and justice, mercy and compassion. We are so thankful and blessed. Praise the Lord Jesus!

Faith and Finances

Here are a few questions for you to ask yourself:

1. In which way can I improve my savings and build up my surplus under my current situation?
2. What kind of investment opportunities do I have in front of me that I can fully utilize to increase my income?

Chapter 11

Caring and Sharing, Loving and Giving

John 3:16 --- For God so LOVED the world that He GAVE His only begotten son that whosoever believes in Him, shall not perish, but have ever-lasting life.

Our Creator God is such a Loving and Giving God, and we are created in His image and we carry His nature. Therefore, we, like Him, must be love and give too.

Galatians 2:20 --- I have been crucified with Christ and I no longer live, but Christ lives in me. The life I live in the body, I live by faith in the Son of God, who LOVED me and GAVE Himself for me.

Ephesians 5:25 --- Husbands, LOVE your wives, just as Christ LOVED the church and GAVE Himself up for her.

Love and Give --- There is a definitive correlation between loving and giving. One can give without loving, but no one can love without giving, for God so loved that He gave!

The path to authentic and abundant living is generous giving!

God's work done in God's way will never lack God's supply. — Hudson Taylor

Faith and Finances

Matt 10:8 --- Freely you have received. Freely give.

Acts 20:35 --- It is more blessed to give than receive (Jesus Christ).

Luke 6:38 --- Give, and it will be given to you. A good measure, press down, shaken together and running over, will be poured into your lap. For with the measure you use, it will be measured to you --- Jesus Christ.

II Corinthians 9:6,8 --- Remember this: Whoever sows sparingly will also reap sparingly, and whoever sows generously will also reap generously... And God is able to make all grace abound to you, so that in all things at all times, having all that you need, you will abound in every good work (the law of the harvest and the law of reciprocity).

I Timothy 6:17-19 --- Command those who are rich in this present world not to be arrogant, not to put their hope in wealth, which is so uncertain, but to put their hope in God, who richly provides us with everything for our enjoyment. Command them to do good, to be rich in good deeds, and to be generous and willing to share. In this way they will lay up treasure for themselves as a firm foundation for the coming age, so that they may take hold of the life that is truly life.

We must first give before we get. Don't live beyond your means --- rather Give beyond your means --- Rabbi Daniel Lapin.

If you want to be rich, give; If you want to be poor, grasp; If you want abundance, scatter; If you want to be needy, hoard! --- Anonymous.

Dare, Care, and Share --- Sharing is caring, for if we care, we will share. When we share, we show that we care. Let's dare to share to demonstrate our care.

Loving and Giving

The first gift of LOVING is actually listening. Active listening is GIVING full attention to someone; for we have not learned to love until we have learned to listen.

Christianity is not just a religion about Christ; it is a deeply personal, and daily intimate relationship with Christ. And Jesus Christ has set up an example to emulate in that He cared for us and shared with us His very life, and He loved us so much that He gave His life on the cross as a ransom for our iniquities. Rom 5:8 summarizes precisely and declares forcefully this close correlation between the caring, loving nature of God and the sharing, giving actions of God, "But God demonstrated his own love for us in this: While we were still sinners, Christ died for us." Indeed just as our Lord said and did, greater love has no one than this, that a person is willing to lay down his very own life for his friends (Jh 15:13). As Christians, we have this command from our Lord Himself to love one another sincerely and unconditionally, just as He has loved us. Loving and giving, as has been demonstrated, are the two sides of the same coin, so to speak, and this Christian love is not just in kind words or giving money only. According to the famous Christian psychologist and counselor Dr. Gary Chapman (*The 5 Love Languages,* 1995), love actually speaks five different languages of giving:

1. Giving words of affirmation. This can be both written and spoken words that are not hard, harsh or critical, but affirming, encouraging and complimenting the listener. One of our all time favorites in this regard is found in Proverbs 25:11 --- a word aptly and fitly spoken is like apples of gold in settings of silver. How beautiful and uplifting this word picture is!
2. Giving quality time. We show our love by sharing time together: running errands, taking trips, doing things together, sitting and walking and talking with each other in quiet places one-to-one with undivided attention and without any interruption.

3. Giving gifts. Love not only entails the giving of our time, but also giving some special gifts to others in special needs and on special occasions. Giving material and monetary gifts to someone with a pleasant and sincere smile is a loving service in style! It is the most visible and tangible way to shine the light and show the love and share the life of Christ!
4. Giving service. Anyone can be truly great in the eyes of our Lord, if he or she is willing and eager to humbly serve, for true greatness in found in humble quality service as exemplified by Jesus Christ through His humble servant leadership of trading His titles for the towels in John 13. The truth of the matter for us is that only very few t of us will most likely be able to do great things in this life, but equally true is that all of us can do small things with great love! The book of Acts is not a book of mere talks. It's a book full of wise and bold actions which speak louder and are more convicting and compelling than eloquent declaration, because they are love in real demonstrations. Acts of kindness always open eyes of blindness. Acts of services such as assisting with house chores, helping out in various projects, and doing something for someone in needs always go a long way. These acts of kind loving services for others with no expectation for anything in return are indications and authentications of our genuine and dynamic faith (James 2:14-17).
5. Giving proper physical touches such as a handshake, a hug, a pat on the back, the laying on of hands in prayers, and even just sitting closely together with sympathetic and pleasant facial expressions. These special loving touches give the receiver joy, peace and encouragement and appreciation as they communicate help, hope and healing.

For the real disciple of Christ, the decision to give financially must be rooted in the attributes of our generous God and out of our intimate relationship with Him. In order to cheerfully, sacrificially and generously give unto the work of the Lord, we must learn from the Macedonian Christians who "gave themselves first to the Lord, and then to us in keeping with God's will", thus declares the apostle Paul in II Cor 8:5 as a key spiritual stewardship principle. When we have both realized and internalized the truth of Christian stewardship with its first two fundamental principles that God is the sovereign owner of everything we are and all we have (including our very own lives), and that we are just managers of God's properties and businesses, then it becomes easier for us to give financially and share resources wisely and generously. Any serious and real disciple of Christ committed to the cause of Christ will regularly (weekly or monthly) give a portion of his income (a tithe, a minimum of 10%) for the advancement and furtherance of the Gospel of the Grace of God! Paul clearly and correctly instructs us followers of Christ with the central truth in I Tim 6 that we did not bring anything into this world and when we die, we will surely be able to take nothing out of this world. Therefore, we must become grateful for, and content with, all of God's provision and wonderful gifts of His generosity, and learn to care for others compassionately and give cheerfully and liberally to the cause of Christ both locally and globally.

Here are ten essential and Scriptural principles and truths concerning giving in the context of wise spiritual stewardship:

1. God expects and requires us to give Him a portion from our first fruit. Proverbs 3:9-10 are both a premise and a promise (much like Prov 3:5-6), commanding us that we are to honor the Lord with our wealth and from the first of all our produce (income); so that our barns will be filled with plenty and our vats will overflow with new wine. As with all the other spiritual laws and principles found in the Bible, the Lord shall surely do His part if and when we do our part (read II Chro 7:14 & Matt 24:14). If we desire to receive His divine promises, we must be diligent and obedient to fulfill the necessary premises. Our very first and our best truly belongs to God our ultimate Provider and Protector,

Faith and Finances

as our thanksgiving offering unto Him Who has given us so much! Jesus did not say, "If you give", but repeatedly and emphatically said that "When you give…" (Matt 6:2-4). Giving is expected of us, and it is not a matter of "if", but a matter of when, how and how much.

2. God expects us to give liberally, joyfully and cheerfully, and not grudgingly or under pressure, coercion, manipulation or compulsion (II Cor 9:7). Let us give freely to His cause for He has freely given us all things (Matt 10:8), including His very own life on the cross to forgive our sins and to purchase our very redemption as children of God! Greater love has no one than this, that one lay down his life for his friends (Jh 15:13). And that was precisely what our Lord Jesus said and did with His life for you and me.

3. God expects us to give for the right reason and with the right motive of the heart (Matt 6:1). I believe that God is more concerned about our attitude and motive of giving than the amount of our gift. We love Him because He first loved us, and we give because God our Lord has given us so much and so abundantly already. When we give, we seek His pleasure and for His praises, and not man's approval or applause. We give for the glory off God and for the good of His people.

4. God expects us to give willingly and proportionately, in accordance with our means, for no one can give what she or he does not have. II Cor 8: 12 says that, "For if willingness is there, the gift is acceptable for what one has, not according to what he does not have." For everyone to whom much is given, much shall be also required from him. And to whom much has been committed, of him they will ask the more (Lk 12:48). The message is very clear here in that God has given us so many possessions, not just to improve our standard of living, but to enhance our level of giving. We are not merely to use it for our own enjoyment, but also for the benefit of the needy and the cause of Jesus around us and around the world.

Loving and Giving

5. God expects us to give generously, not with equal amount, but with equal sacrifice. Our desire is not that others might be relieved while you are hard pressed, but that there might be equality… your plenty will supply what they need so that in turn their plenty will supply what you need. Then there will be equality, as it is written 'he that gathered much did not have too much, and he that gathered little did not have too little.' (II Cor 8:13-14, Ex 16:18).
6. God expects us to carry out planned and systematic giving, with a clear purpose for the gift given or the offering to be collected. To help the Jerusalem churches in need of support, Paul wrote the following clear instruction to the Corinthian church in I Cor 16:1-2. "Now about the collection for God's people: Do what I told the Galatian churches to do. On the first day of every week, each one of you should set aside a sum of money in keeping with his income, saving it up, so that when I come, no collection will have to be made. Everyone should give what he has already determined or decided in his heart to give.
7. God expects our giving as a reasonable and spiritual act of worship to God. We give to the Lord not just because of what He has done and will do for us, but more importantly because of Whom He is. He is faithful and wonderful. He is compassionate and merciful. In Him we have found love, joy, peace, purpose and prosperity. He alone is worthy! He is worthy of all our praises, and giving back to Him materially to His cause of benevolence and missions what He has already given to us is a visible and tangible act of sincere gratitude and worship. "You will be made rich in every way so that you can be generous on every occasion, and through us your generosity will result in thanksgiving to God." (II Cor 9:11).
8. God expects us to give in light of the incarnation of Christ. Since we have experienced the grace and love of our generous Lord Jesus Christ that though he was rich, yet for

our sake He has become poor, so that through His poverty we might become rich (II Cor 8:9). What profound theology! The Lord Jesus has set us a concrete and compelling example of loving and giving, of caring and sharing. We must follow suite and become more like Him.

9. God expects us to first give before we expect to receive. Luke 6:38 states this truth crystal clear with the promised blessing of abundance because of faith and obedience. Jesus commands us to, "Give, and it will be given to you. A good measure, pressed down, shaken together and running over, will be poured into your lap. For with the measure you use, it will be measured to you." Wow, what a wonderful instruction is this, and how precious, penetrating, piercing and peerlessly powerful it is for us to know and follow! And we will be blessed if we do. Don't live beyond your means, but do give beyond your means. We have personally experienced many times in many places all over the world that as we passionately and obediently pour out into others both spiritually and financially, the Lord has never once failed to pour back into us with MORE THAN ENOUGH so that we can live and serve abundantly and victoriously as MORE THAN CONQUERORS! Please study and meditate on the famous poem The Chosen Vessel in the last chapter of the book.

10. God expects us to experientially and relationally know that indeed as the Lord Jesus Himself teaches us, ""For it is more blessed to give than to receive." (Acts 20:35). And through the compelling example of the Apostle Paul, we also see that giving is not just financial, but also psychological, emotional and relational. If we truly love, we can't help but give; and as we give, we are more blessed of God in all areas of our lives as shining witnesses for the glory of Jesus for all to see (Matt 5:16).

In our Christian giving, we must always pay close attention to the motive of our heart behind the gifts. Our attitude about our giving is actually must more important to the Lord than the act and the amount we give unto the Lord, just as our attitude in life and ministries for the Lord is much more crucial and essential than our activities and accomplishments for the Lord. We give willingly, cheerfully, liberally and even sacrificially as unto the Lord, and not to please, impress, appease or manipulate anyone, but as our sincere gratitude to the Lord and our genuine love for others.

According to the *NIV Stewardship Study Bible* (P. 664), we are to establish a pattern of generosity with these 8 P words: priority, privacy, promptness, premeditated, periodic, personal, prompted heart and pride-less spirit. Additionally, there are at last four acid tests from the Lord about our giving:

1. Giving is a test of our faith (James 2:17). Faith by itself, if not accompanied by action, is dead.
2. Giving is a test of our love for God (I Jh 3:17). If anyone has material possessions and sees his brother in need but has no compassionate action on him, how can the love of God be in him?
3. Giving is a test of our love for our neighbors (Matt 9:35-38).
4. Giving is a test of the priority of His Lordship in our life. The ultimate challenging test of the Lord Jesus to the rich young ruler is found in Matthew 19:21-22. Unfortunately this young man failed the Jesus Lordship Test very miserably. "If you want to be perfect, go sell your possessions and give to the poor, and you will have treasure in heaven. Then come, follow me." When the young man heard this, he went away sad, because he had great wealth. He was a worshipper of wealth and gold, and not of God!

Now that we have examined and learned the biblical truths and principles of why, what and how to give, giving God's way, we must also become aware of people giving in the wrong way against the teachings of the Scripture. God's work must be done God's way before we can expect God's prolific provision and sufficient supplies.

In the same way, God's money must be managed God's way before we can receive more blessings from God Himself. According to Pastor Steve J. Cole, (Lesson 5: Giving God's Way, www.bible,org), Christians must be warned against six wrong motives of giving. Let's look at them one by one:

1. Pride. You are giving for the wrong reason if you intend to use your gifts to get honor and praises from people for your "great" generosity, trying to make a name for yourself. Our giving is to be done in secret before the Lord and He will reward us (Matt 6:1-4). Thus putting up a plaque and naming some buildings in honor of donors violate this principle and can cause intoxicating pride.
2. Greed. Many have wrongly interpreted the teaching of Luke 6:38 with the greedy intention that they are entitled to get much more because they have given. Jesus is simply stating the principle of generosity and reciprocity, not for us to twist it to satisfy or gratify our own greedy desires.
3. Guilt. If someone feels guilty for having so much, and that guilt drives him to give, then it is wrong and very unhealthy.
4. Pressure. We are not to give "under compulsion" (II Cor 9:7) or emotional manipulation, and sensation appeals. Don't respond compulsively to high-pressure tactics from some Christian fundraisers.
5. Gimmicks. This is a blending of both greed and pressure. It is an appeal to the fleshly desire under pressure, to get more in return. This practice is opposed to the scriptural giving, highly manipulative and even deceptive. It must be avoided and exposed.
6. Power. Believe it or not, affluence is influence and money is power. Common is the phenomenon of some worldly donors who threaten the church and ministries that if you don't do what they want done, they will take their large gifts elsewhere. This is the way of politics, and it is not how God's church should operate. It is wrong to show favoritism

and preference to the wealthy as James teaches (2:1-9); and it is very sinful to use your money to buy power, position, influence and authority as is shown in Acts 8:18-24 in the case of Simon the Sorcerer who wanted to bribe the apostles to buy the Spirit's power and gift. He was severely rebuked and condemned by Saint Peter for such an evil intention and action. "May your money perish with you because you thought you could buy the gift of God with money. You have no part or share in this ministry because your heart is not right before God. Repent of this wickedness and pray to God … for I see that you are full of bitterness and captive to sin." Wow and Woe! That is severe and intense indeed. In my (HY) humble and simple interpretation of "May your money perish with you", it means "Take your money and go to hell!" What a timely warning to us all!

Reflections and Applications

In life there are basically five S's that most of us must go through as a necessary process: Struggle, Survival, Success, Significance, and Surrender. Through our struggles of different kinds depending on the levels of life's difficulties, we get to survive. Having sufficiently survived, the human spirits further strive for successes. After achieving a certain measure of successes through both human intelligence and diligence, we begin to develop a sense of emptiness in spite of material and positional achievements. We start to search for the real meaning and true purpose and spiritual significance of life from the ordinary to extraordinary. We begin the process of sharing, caring, loving and giving as an important way to achieve some significance out of our sufficiency and abundance with a willing, able, and joyful heart. Indeed it is more blessed to be able to give than to receive. And we can not give what we do not have. Eventually the truly spiritual come to the last stage of Surrender and Submission to the perfect will of the Creator God to experience the ultimate joy, satisfaction and complete fulfillment of the human life. "It is well with my soul!"

Faith and Finances

When I (Esther) was in middle school, I always had the desire to have two ink pens, one black and one red. I only possessed one for my daily use. One day we had a school competition and talent show, and I won the first place. The price was a notebook and an ink pen. I was so overjoyed that I finally could fulfill the desire of my heart of having 2 ink pens. I was from a large family with six siblings. Life was hard. One of my young brothers just lost his own pen and when he learned about my ink pens, he cried out to my mother with the request of "either buying me a new one or making my sister give me one!" So my mother forced me to give up my new pen to him. In spite of my strong protests against the demand, explaining and insisting that this was my Reward Pen I earned from the school competition and it did not cost any family money, my mother still made me give up my new pen to him, causing me to cry over the childhood incident for several days. I did give my new pen to him, grudgingly, tearfully, and helplessly with a lot of resentments and hopelessness. Even though this was one way to give, yet I know that it was not the proper or good way to give.

In my impoverished little village, there lived my (Hong) grandfather who was kind and generous to others in spite of his own family poverty. He had a wife with 7 hungry kids, with barely enough food or clothing for his own family. But when he saw a neighbor more poor than him, he just took a blanket from his little mud house and gave it joyfully to the poor man. This, however, caused a major conflict in the family for years to come. His wife and kids became very resentful and angry with him, and his act of charity really was taken from their bare necessities and even abject poverty. This is another way to give: giving out of personal compassion but sacrificing the family needs, giving out of joyful heart but neglecting one's own responsibilities. It is a great blessing when we are able to give out of the abundance we have and from the heart of joy. That is the great way to give: blessed to be a blessing!

Loving and Giving

Here are a few questions for your consideration:

1. What was the true condition of my heart when I was giving?
2. What were the results of my giving in terms of myself, my family and my little beneficiary?
3. What is your attitude toward giving, and why?

Chapter 12

Monies and Ministries
A Relational Approach to Fundraising
For Kingdom Services

Malachi 3:9-10 --- You are cursed with a curse, for you have robbed Me (in tithes and offerings), even this whole nation. Bring all the tithes into the storehouse, that there may be food in my house. And try (test) Me now in this, says the Lord of hosts, if I will not open for you windows of heaven and pour out for you such blessing that there will not be room enough to receive it.

Luke 6:38 --- Give, and it will be given to you: good measure, pressed down, shaken together, running over will be put into your bosom. For with the same measure you use, it will be measured back to you. --- Jesus of Nazareth

Luke 8:1-3 --- Now it came to pass, afterward, that He (Jesus) went through every city and village, preaching and bringing the glad tidings of the kingdom of God. And the twelve were with Him, and certain women, Mary called Magdalene... Joanna...Susanna, and many others provided for Him from their substance.

Romans 15:24 --- I plan to do so when I go to Spain. I hope to visit you while passing through and to have you assist me on my journey there, after I have enjoyed your company for a while.

Philippians 4: 15-19 --- Now you Philippians know also that in the beginning of the gospel, when I departed from Macedonia, no church shared with me concerning giving and receiving but you only. Even in Thessalonica you sent aid once and again for my necessities. Not that I seek the gift, but I seek the fruit that abounds to your account. Indeed I have all and abound. I am full, having received from Epaphroditus the things sent from you, a sweet smelling aroma, an acceptable sacrifice, well pleasing to God. And my God shall supply all your need according to His riches in glory by Christ Jesus.

I have never met a man who has given me as much trouble as myself --- D. L. Moody.

The number one enemy of deputation is ME. The number one enemy of fundraising is ME --- William P. Dillon.

God's work, done in God's way, will never lack God's supply --- Hudson Taylor.

The Yang Fiscalosophy: Trust deficiency results in financial delinquency. Five T-Factors are required in our request for trust which is the law of the solid ground and the cornerstone of all meaningful human relationships: Truth, Transparency, Track-record, Tests, and Time. People will financially travel with you if they can spiritually and relationally trust in you!

Fund raising in its final analysis is people raising, and i's friend raising! The more friends you raise, the more funds you will have. The fewer friends you have, the fewer funds you will have. No friends, no funds. Monies follow ministries in the same way that finances follow faith. They work proportionally with each other.

Without a doubt, one of the major challenges and obstacles for any type of ministries we all at times face, is the issue of funding an finances: how we are to go about funding the ministries that God has clearly called us to carry out. For all the Christians who are working to advance the missions and the causes of the kingdom of God both locally and globally, this chapter is crucial for you. It does not matter whether you are full time or part time, career missionary in a foreign country, or planning to carry out short-term missions projects and trips, this chapter, as a valuable resource will definitely encourage you spiritually, equip you practically, and empower you strategically to lay out a biblical foundation and a practice-proven methodology for funding the ministries by overcoming several negative factors that often hinder and hurt your progress.

We are convinced, with 30 some years I. Both intensive and extensive missions and ministries the world over, that one of the major reasons that fundraisers for the ministries are too often frightened and discouraged is because they have not been given proper and sufficient teaching and effective training regarding the biblical and spiritual ways of dealing with monies and ministries. Way too many churches, missions organizations and their missionary accounts, including many of our good friends and colleagues, are financially depleted and they are broke, constantly living from paycheck to paycheck, just as 7 out of 10 fellow Americans do. The main reason or cause for all this is because our thoughts, ideas, values, and experiences with finances have been formed and shaped by our dominant American culture, and the way people have been raised in their families. Much of the American values and ways are far from being biblical or spiritual; in fact, they are quite casual, cultural, carnal, and even consequentially calamitous and catastrophic, as we have firsthand and personally witnessed too much and too often with too many.

Therefore, coming from a drastically different background and culture, and more importantly based on our 30 plus years of keen observation, active participation and serious application in life and ministries, Dr. Esther Yang and I, the "dynamic duo" as we have been often referred to by many all over the nations, we are eager to help you and will offer you Scriptural instructions, personal reflections and conclusions with your anticipated applications as to what, how and most importantly, why we must fund raise. We promise you that these powerful principles will work profitably and prolifically for you only if and only when you habitually put them into your personal practice constantly and consistently.

Accumulated Advantages of Fund Raising:

1. Fundraising is actually faith building in that it activates and energizes and thus develops our faith and causes it to grow healthier and mightier. Faith is like a muscle: the more we exercise it and use it, the stronger it gets!
2. Fundraising, if carried out spiritually and appropriately, is God's way of proving Himself to us and as a credible witness to many others that He is more than willing and able to supply all our needs according to the glorious riches in Christ Jesus (Phil 4:19, Eph 3:20). Therefore by His sufficient grace and for His eternal glory, we can do all things and become more than conquerors in all things through Christ Jesus Who loves strengthens us Phil 4:13, Rom 8:37).
3. Fundraising teaches us to humble ourselves to get down on own knees to cry out to God and listen to God's still and small voice, and learn to apply His Word His way to finish His work! It teaches us to develop our spiritual virtues of dependence on, confidence in, and obedience to His will and His call.
4. Fundraising allows us the unique opportunity to educate, inspire, recruit and enlist many people to be involved in the heartbeat of God: Missions. Indeed fundraising is people raising, it is friends raising. If you take a intentional and highly relational approach to fund raising, connecting with people head to head and heart to heart, God will graciously and generously send a wonderful army of prayer warriors and financial sponsors to help you fulfill your call: making the Great Commission a Great Completion.

According to the Rev. William P. Dillon (PP. 17-19), the foremost expert and authority in the area of people raising and the ministry of deputation, there are at least six benefits from raising financial support:

1. It attracts a base of prayer support from potential and prospective donors;
2. It stretches the faith of the fund raiser as fundraising is one of the most personally maturing and spiritual fulfilling ventures of life;
3. It stimulates and encourages enthusiasm, vision and dedication in the body of Christ for their involvement in the kingdom work. This is accomplished through the fund-seeking missionary who is an incarnate model for missions, who becomes a mobilizer for the work of the Lord, and who serves as a minister for missions and ministries.
4. It broadens the base of financial support for you and your organization as He connects you to more and more supporters with more open doors of opportunities for the ministries of multiplication;
5. It develops you as a person as you learn how to work with various people, how to adapt under difficult circumstances, and how to use time, tact, and talent with poise, polish and proficiency to your best advantage. As you experience God's limitlessness in spite of your limits, you know that deputation is not a punishment of God, but a privilege from God.
6. It stimulates fellowship among other believers, and this caring and sharing fellowship is very enriching, uplifting and rewarding for those who have experienced it personally, like us, many times and in many places.

Developing a Positive Attitude and Reach a Productive Altitude

Do you know what is the smallest thing in all of us us that makes the biggest difference in the world? It is not our intellect; it is not emotion; it is not our education; it is not our social position. It is our attitude. Our attitude is the smallest thing that often makes the biggest difference for us in all areas of our life, even and especially in raising money for the worthy causes and missions ministries. An attitude of gratitude will raise our altitude with fortitude. Attitude determines also our aptitude, latitude and longitude. ATTITUDE to me as an acronym means, "Always Take The Initiative To Unselfishly Display Enthusiasm", for we have discovered through proven practice of many years that people like to support those who are passionate about their calling and their missions. Passion is like contagion and infection in a healthy and positive sense because it touches people and moves them to action as they want to be a part of the work by praying for you and investing in you. Enthusiasm is exciting, and it excites people to do something about what they are excited about. Part of this has to do with the fundraiser's calling and personality, and a larger part of it, if it is genuine, comes from the anointing of the Holy Spirit.

It has been tested positive and proven true that positive thinking leads to passionate living which in turn causes productive harvesting. Scripture emphatically teaches that as a man thinks in his heart, so is he (Prov 23:7). And as the mind goes, the man follows. Our life then, is a product of our mind. Therefore change your thoughts, and you will change your life (Rom 12:2). This is the spiritual power that comes from positive thinking. According to an excellent online article by Mr. Larry Alton (www.success.com), there are 7 practical ways one can employ and utilize to prioritize our mental wellbeing and achieve a positive mindset:

1. Start your day with positive affirmative declarations, because how you start the morning sets the tone for the rest of the day. I quote Ps 118:24 and sing the song early every day that "This is the day the Lord has made, and I will rejoice and be glad in it!" The Bible contains more positive and affirmative declarations than any other book I know, because it is the powerful promises of a loving and caring God for His children.
2. Focus on the good things, no matter how small and seemingly insignificant they are. In the end they all add up together to form a positive power and productive energy.

3. Find humor in bad situations. In other words, don't take yourself too seriously for God's sake! Be humorous and make fun of yourself.
4. Turn your failures into your life lessons that prepare you for future successes. Failures are seldom fatal and they are never final. They can be your friends if you learn from them. No wonder the Chinese proverb says that failure is the mother of success. Sir Winston Churchill once famously declared from many personal trials and experiences in life that success is "the ability to go from failure to failure without ever losing your enthusiasm." What a special secret of success that's readily applicable to all areas of life, be it spiritual, psychological, relational, emotional and financial!
5. Transform your negative self-talk into positive self-talk. One of my favorites is "Satan had me bound, BUT Jesus set me free!" "Once I was lost but now I'm found; once I was blind but now I can see." "One I was a desperate and hopeless atheistic communist, but now I am saved, sanctified and saturated by the Holy Spirit as a child of God and a minister of the Gospel of God's grace!" Genesis 50:20 records Joseph as saying this amazingly positive spiritual truth to his sorry and evil brothers, "You meant it for evil against me, but God meant it for good to save many people's lives".
6. Focus on the present. Live one day at a time and don't worry about the future or the things beyond your control. Jesus makes this clear in His sermon n the Mount especially in Matt 6:25-34 as you study it.
7. Find and surround yourself with positive friends, inspiring mentors, and uplifting co-workers. Their positive outlook on life, positive stories of successes and their positive affirmation will positively affect you! And this spiritual positivity will surely propel much productivity and profitability your way for His greater purpose and higher glory!

I strongly believe and actively live my life according to this personal faith and thus heart attitude: Living a life that really matters, with no regret, no retreat, no reserve, and no retirement; Rather live your life with conviction, clarity, contentment, compassion, confidence, commitment and most importantly, courage, for courage is the mother of all virtues. Without courage, there is no virtue! When you become fearless, then your life and ministry become limitless! Be always joyfully grateful and never ever be greedy; be content with godliness and never be covetous; be active and not passive; be positive and not negative; be passionate and not pathetic; be optimistic and not pessimistic. Be faithful, forceful and fruitful, and do not be fearful and thus fruitless.

In raising ministerial and missions support to do the work of God and to finish the mission of God for our lives, we must always pay close attention to and ascertain our own pure heart motive and our spiritual attitude. A scriptural perspective and kingdom priority have to be well established. Requesting funds from Christians individually and from churches corporately is not only permissible, it is totally biblical and practical. While the Lord can and has provided for many with miracles, yet He expects most of us most of the time to go out and work hard with the mentality of positivity and a skillful strategy to cultivate people relationships and special friendships that in turn will contribute to our support. One must overcome the erroneous and negative thoughts that fundraising is just a necessary evil, and even a dirty job that has to be done as one goes around begging people for money. Also the defeatist and fatalist and pessimistic attitudes such as, "I'm just not good at this money thing, and I just can't do it!" or "I feel so guilty asking people for money even for ministries. I am so embarrassed by, and ashamed of it." Or "Money is just a filthy lucre." All of these must be gotten rid of from the inside out before one can be passionate and powerful, proactive and productive in what she or he does.

Fundraising is, once again, people raising; fundraising is friends raising, and fundraising is the connection and the formation of strategic kingdom relationships to accomplish the kingdom mandates Jesus gives us. Fundraising is both the will of God and the call from God for all of us who love God and who are called according to His purpose: go into all nations to win souls and make disciples, announcing the good news of the kingdom of heaven until all have heard and have had a chance to make a decision for their eternal destiny. Raising God's people through trustworthy relationships to obtain the resources God has given to do His will and to finish His work (John 4:34-35) with a sense of personal urgency is absolutely scriptural and thus profoundly spiritual. It is not a human punishment; rather it is a divine assignment that requires our human alignment, especially attitude alignment. It is an honor, and a special privilege to seek out partners with the opportunity to actively and generously invest, not just passively or compulsively contribute, in the greatest thing on earth: the mission of God. It is a great ministry of joyful service unto the Lord. Let us serve the Lord and His purpose with gladness (Ps 100:2). Sincere service with a sunny smile has always been our special spiritual style! It has certainly worked for us for over 30 years, and it will surely work for you as you apply yourself daily and diligently.

According to Mr. Dillon (PP. 57-58), of all the methodologies and strategies available, two of the most essential and crucial principles must be repeatedly instructed and seriously applied in order for your fundraising to be effective and fruitful for the glory of the Lord:

1. Relationship! People give to people. People give to people they know. People give to people they know and trust. People give to people they know, trust, and care for! Therefore, start intentionally developing key relationships with caring people that the Lord has already brought you across your path. Many people make the mistake and thus become unfruitful because they assume that because they are called to the ministries, other Christians will naturally or automatically want to support them. We believe that since fundraising is indeed people raising and that fundraising is a serious spiritual ministry, we must sincerely love, value and minister to the people and touch their hearts before ever asking for their hands. And once the relationship is

established with the people, then funds will coming your way maybe slowly but steadily. A slow but steady strategy always succeeds. Remember to strengthen the hands that bless you with all the 5 love languages, and never ever cut the hands that feed you.
2. Be both personal and practical. This second key to raising funds successfully is for you to personally contact people you know in the most personal and practical way possible. Studies have proven time and again that the most effective form of communication is one-on-one. Fundraising forms diminish in effectiveness as they become increasing impersonal. So be relational, personal and practical. Don't use impersonal tools of communication for fundraising such as random advertising, impersonal letters, and mass mailings. Avoid "the shotgun approach" to fundraising by rushing off to everyone in every direction, wasting too much precious time, energy and limited resources, randomly contacting people who don't know you, trust you, or care about you.

As you intentionally and systematically go to the people whom you target, the people whom you know, who know, trust and care about you, meetings people one-on-one and in small groups, you will strengthen old friendships and also make new contacts. And as you keep on experiencing God working in and through you with enhanced communication and relationship skills, people will respond to partner with you through their spiritual prayers and financial supports. The apostle John (II Jn 1:12) is quite revealing and instructive when he insists on visiting and talking with the people "face to face, so that our joy may be complete." Nothing can replace that personal and relational touch in all areas of ministries especially when one needs to raise the support to do His missions. This biblical and effective strategy of going to people personally, Mr. Dillon (P. 62) assuredly tells us, will work for all of us as we follow these following twelve steps:

1. Begin with your home church.
2. Determine prayerfully and strategically to whom you will go for funds.
3. Record, catalog, and prioritize your prospects.
4. Get the word out. Word of mouth is often the best advertising.
5. Make appointments.
6. Conduct the visit.
7. Track your funds.
8. Say thank you.
9. Conduct a phone appointment.
10. Expand your contacts.
11. Cultivate your donors.
12. Re-solicit funds.

Beating the Spirit of FEAR
(False Expectations Appearing Real)

II Tim 1:7 – "For God has not given us a spirit of fear, but a spirit of power, love and sound mind."

As you look around you, you will realize that there are so many people paralyzed in life with all kinds of fears. No wonder the Holy Bible declares 365 times "Fear Not!" or "Don't be afraid!" as we daily deal with the fear factor. As a matter of fact, one verse alone in Ezekiel 2:6 speaks three times repeatedly with "Fear Not". When you by faith identify and confront the fear fact in the presence and power of the Lord along with the promises of the Word of God, your fear will diminish. As you become more and more fearless, your life and ministry become more and more limitless!

Fear is real in every aspect and area of life in our fallen and sinful world, even, perhaps especially in the deputation ministry of people raising and fund raising in the context of complex and complicated relationships. According to Mr. Dillon (PP. 37-43), our human fears while living in this world can be reduced and diminished, but they cannot be totally and completely eliminated, not in this life. Many of the fundraiser fears come from negative emotions and false beliefs. Such things as shame, guilt, feelings of embarrassment, and unworthiness must be clearly identified and dealt with by replacing these emotions with solid Scriptural instructions with emphasis on role-play and practice. Inaccurate, illogical, irrational and erroneous beliefs about personal worth, money, possession, giving, relational needs for performance-based approval, fear of failure, uncertainty of future, the infection of perfection and others' rejection and other low self-esteem issues must be thoroughly corrected and re-directed by the Word of God. Selfishness and self-doubt must be exposed and eliminated, repealed and replaced and reprogrammed by the principles and truths of the Holy Scripture. What really matters is not what others say or expect from us; neither does it matter what and how we think or feel about ourselves; what really ultimately matters is what God says about us! Our identity and integrity, our values and worth, which matter for eternity, are all hidden and secured for us in the Lord Jesus Christ. He will never leave you or forsake it. He will never fail you or forget you. Jesus will be with you always by the power of His infallible Word and by the presence of His powerful Spirit. So be strong and very courageous, trust deeply and obey completely the Lord. Then you will be a fabulously faithful and fantastically fruitful fundraiser to be blessed and used of the Lord! You will be a shining testimony and compelling witness for the Lord and an excellent example for all to emulate!

I Samuel 30:6 gives us a spiritually powerful and historically factual declaration in the midst of horrific devastation and destruction, "But David strengthened (encouraged) himself in the Lord his God." King David, the greatest leader of all Israel, always obtained, maintained and sustained an intimate personal and spiritual relationship with "the Lord his God", and this personal intimacy is the key to his spiritual victory. David, as all his other mighty warriors who lost everything and who wanted to stone him, was admittedly very afraid of both the Philistines and the Amalekites. But a careful and prayerful study of Psalm 56 reveals the five secret sources of his spiritual stamina, strength and successes in overcoming fear by five effective methods of maximizing his faith and minimizing his fear. Please read these 13 verses carefully and prayerfully below on your own, and then discover the following principles of truth so as to actively and aggressively apply to your own life and ministry of multiplication:

Psalm56:1 Be merciful to me, O God, for men hotly pursue me; all day long they press their attack.56:2 My slanderers pursue me all day long; many are attacking me in their pride.56:3 When I am afraid, I will trust in you.56:4 In God, whose word I praise, in God I trust; I will not be afraid. What can mortal man do to me?56:5 All day long they twist my words; they are always plotting to harm me.56:6 They conspire, they lurk, they watch my steps, eager to take my life.56:7 On no account let them escape; in your anger, O God, bring down the nations.56:8 Record my lament; list my tears on your scroll - are they not in your record?56:9 Then my enemies will turn back when I call for help. By this I will know that God is for me.56:10 In God, whose word I praise, in the LORD , whose word I praise-56:11 in God I trust; I will not be afraid. What can man do to me?56:12 I am under vows to you, O God; I will present my thank offerings to you.56:13 For you have delivered me from death and my feet from stumbling, that I may walk before God in the light of life.

1. Fervent prayers to God (V. 1). David poured out his heart in tears before God, crying out to the Lord for mercy and deliverance in the face of evil with the dangerous attacks of the enemies. As his prayers went up to God, God sent His power down to him. More prayer, more power; little prayer, little power; and no prayer, no power. That is the infallible spiritual truth of the Christian walk, which is best done on our knees in daily prayers.
2. Put you trust in God and in the precious, peerless and powerful Word of God. (VV. 3, 4, 11)). David declared that when he was admittedly afraid, he would trust in God; and when he put his trust in God and in the powerful Word of God, his faith increased and he was no longer fearful of what

mortal man could do to him. The deeper our trust level, the lower our fear level. This also reminds me of the well-known passage in Isaiah 26:3-4, "You will keep in perfect peace him whose mind is stayed on You, because he trusts in You. Trust in the Lord forever, for in Yah, the Lord, is everlasting strength." The more our mind is focused on the source of our peace, the Prince of Peace Jesus the Lord, the more we will experience the perfect peace. The deeper our trust in the Lord, the greater will be His strength for us to overcome the enemy and all the fears that the devil throws at us like the fiery darts. You will overcome by faith in Christ Jesus in spite of the fear and troubles (Jh 16:33) just as King David did.

3. Start praising God for His faithfulness and goodness, and for all the wonderful promises He has made to His people (VV. 4, 10, 12). Praise, praise and more praises. Praise the Lord for Who He is and praise the Lord for what He has done. As the sweet psalmist of Israel, David was always keen on singing the praises of the Lord, for He understood the secret truth of Ps 22: 3 that the Lord of Israel is holy and the Lord inhabits and is enthroned by, the praises of His people. Just as the power of God comes down through our prayers going up, His holy and mighty presence comes down upon us like a refreshing and energizing shower, as our whole-heartedly passionate praises go up to Him. More praise from us, more presence from Him. And in His presence, is there the fullness of joy (Ps 16:11), and this joy of the Lord is our strength (Neh 8:10). These are also His blessed assurance for us that in the midst of the trying circumstance, there is the joy unspeakable and it's full of glory. His presence makes the greatest difference in our life and ministries. That still and small voice from within will let you know that this too shall pass and that it will be well with my soul.

4. Remember what the Lord has done for you in the past, and remind Him that you are on this mission for Him (VV. 8, 13).

David knew well that it was the Lord who had delivered him before, and the Lord will certainly deliver him again from the snare of death of his prideful enemies. The Lord has been our help in the past, and the Lord alone is our hope for the future. The fact that "Christ in you is the hope of glory" will give you sufficient encouragement and empowerment with all joy and peace both now and forevermore (Rom 15:4, 13, Col 1:27). This blessed assurance will enable you with enough endurance to win the final victory. You shall live and not die, and you shall bring forth thanksgiving testimony to His glory as you walk before God in the light of life. The Lord is declaring to you right now, "Don't be afraid; only believe. For I know the plans I have for you, plans to prosper you and not harm you, plan to give you hope and a future!" (Marl 5:36, Jer 29:11).

5. Know and live the central truth of Verse 9 which has been powerful repeated and emphasized by the fearless apostle Paul in Romans 8:31 (If God be for us, who then can be against us?), "For this I know that God is for me" when I call for help. And if God is for us, nobody and nothing can overcome us or stop us from doing His work and finishing His mission assigned to our lives. One person with God on his or her side is an absolute majority, for greater is He who lives in us than he that's of the world, and anyone born of this God shall overcome the world. This is the victory that has overcome the world, even by faith (I Jh 4:4, 5:4). The more we are faithful to the Lord, the more we become fearless of man and the circumstances. Your life becomes limitless as you through Christ by faith become more and more fearless!

One method that will diminish fear is the living reminder to yourself that this ministry of fundraising is really not about you. It is all about Jesus, and you are doing it for Jesus and not for yourself. This spiritual thinking and personal conviction will greatly reduce and effectively weaken the fear factor. The bottom line is that you are not begging or asking money for yourself or pressuring or manipulating people in any way to give. As you spell out your vision with passion and clarity of presentation, you are simply and boldly giving the people of God a unique and important opportunity to invest and partner with you in God's divine and eternal program. This key perspective will take the focus away from you and puts it back on giving people the opportunity for kingdom partnership. Remind the body of Christ what the Lord Jesus Christ said that it is more blessed to give than to receive (Acts 20:35). Remember that as much as your need their supports, your donors have a greater need to give than you have to receive. Be absolutely convinced deep down in your heart that there is plenty of resources out there, more than enough in super abundance to meet all the ministry needs, and people are just looking for worthy causes and trustworthy people to partner with and invest in. May God give you the special favors to be the one they like, know, trust, care about, and partner with. Educate the people of God, your prospects and donors with the six keys of the Treasure Principle outlined by the Rev Randy Alcorn in his book (2008, PP. 121-131):

1. God owns everything. God has entrusted us His stewards to manage His businesses and assets.
2. My heart always goes where I put God's money. Where your treasure is, there, will also your heart be.
3. Heaven is my "better country" and this world or earth is not my home (Heb 11:16).
4. We should live for the line and not the dot. The dot is the here and now on earth, but the line extends forever into eternity. Live with God's eternal kingdom perspective.
5. Giving is the only antidote to materialism as it is our joyful surrender to our Master and His greater agenda. It dethrones me and exalts Jesus. Generous and especially sacrificial giving can and will defeat the spirit of greed.
6. God prospers me not to raise my standard of living but to raise my standard of giving. God gives us more than enough so that we can give generously to Him and His causes.

Beating the Negative Spirit in Fundraising

While positivity propels you to passion, productivity and profitability, nagging negativity, on the other hand, navigates you nowhere. Negative thing can and will lead you down a road of no return. Negative thinking affects negatively every aspect of fundraising, rendering the ministry efforts futile and fruitless. Sow a word, you will reap a thought; sow a thought, you will reap an act; sow an act, you will reap a habit; and sow a habit, you will reap a destiny. How true and accurate is this ancient Chinese proverb! This of course all depends on the type of seed sown and grown inside of us. Fill your heart and mind daily with a special dosage of the promises of God's Word that is always promising, prophetic, positive and productive for our lives and ministries. Negativity alienates key relationships which in turn weaken your deputation, resulting in the work of the Lord suffering major losses. This is true because (Dillon, P. 51):

1. Negative thinking produces negative thoughts;
2. Negative thoughts produce negative actions;
3. Negative actions productive negative results.

Beating the Pessimistic Spirit in Fundraising

Pessimism produces pathetic poverty and powerlessness. One cannot be a real disciple of the Lord Christ who lives in him as the "hope of glory" if she or he is chronically pessimistic about everything especially the future. Don't be a pessimist because a pessimist sees only all the obstacles in any given opportunity while the optimist sees all the opportunities in spite of the oppositions and obstacles. Believe in the promises of the Word of God and live them out daily, and you will see the brighter sides of all things in His marvelous light despite the present darkness. That's what true faith is all about: Faith is seeing light with your heart when all your eyes see is darkness. Faith doesn't doubt in the dark what the Lord has already shown you in the light. Don't be discouraged or become pessimistic by your incapacity to dispel darkness from the world;

rather, light your little candle, step bold forward and let it shine for Jesus! Your future is not gloom and doom; your future is as bright and hopeful as the promises of your God who is your help, healing and hope. You must renew your mind by the transforming power of the Word and be filled and refilled by the Spirit so that you will be positive and proactive in order to be highly productive in your ministry of deputation for Jesus cause and His glory. Therefore, take heart, keep calm and carry on the mission the Lord has entrusted and placed in your heart and life.

Beating the Passive Spirit in Fundraising

Make up your mind to always be active and proactive, and never be passive. Passivity propels painful powerlessness that further results in poverty. Nothing is more painful than poverty, as the good ole Jewish proverb goes. In order to be effective, you must be constantly reflective and active. Have faith in the Lord and the Word of God; surround yourself with the joyful, caring and strong fellow believers; ask the Lord to send you and fill you with the Holy Spirit of power and boldness so that you can receive a fresh spiritual perspective, see the innovative alternative, desire the incentive and take the necessary initiative to reach your objective. Remember to always delight yourself in the Lord (doing everything and anything in your power by faith with obedience to please the Lord), and He will give you the desire of your heart (Ps 37:4). Start with you, here and now; and start small, for you cant not launch out with giant leaps if you don't begin with small but solid baby steps. And despise not the small beginning as there would be no mighty Mississippi River without the small Lake Itasca .

Do not assume
for it will make an "Ass" out of "u" and "me" ---
thus "Assume"

Jesus teaches us to be humble, sensitive and not be presumptuous. In one of His parables about an invitation to eat at a banquet, He says that we should take the least important and the most obscure seat available in the house or around the table. If you assume, out of personal ignorance and/or self-importance to take a prominent seat at the head of the table that's reserved for someone else like a real VIP, what a shame and dishonor it will be when you are asked to move to a little stool at the corner, in front of all the others! In the same way, don't assume that you will be fully taken care of with appointments, a certain amount of income and nice accommodations. You might be utterly humiliated and disappointed if you do. But you are gentle, humble, sensitive, and adaptive in fundraising with an eager spirit to share and a passionate heart to serve, you will be pleasantly surprised at what the Lord has in store for you out of His supernatural abundance. Learn to live by faith and not be sight, feeling or foolish and greedy assumptions like the idle workers in the Lords vineyard (Matt 20). Learn to be content in all circumstances, and be obedient to the Holy Spirit guidance at all times.

Do Not Compare with Anyone: Looking unto Jesus

Life is never fair, therefore don't even bother to complain or compare. Comparison is completely carnal, as it arouses either pride or jealousy. Comparison also causes hard and harsh criticism and even all-out condemnation from without as one is filled with cynicism from within. Additionally, carnal compassion chokes out every bit of our spiritual conviction and Christian contentment. Instead of comparing occasionally with others in stature and in status, be it social, educational, economical, always be gratefully focused on the Lord, looking unto Jesus the Author and Finisher of your faith, and the provider and protector of our finances and fruit. Be content with what God has already given. They that are content are very thankful. After we have faithfully done everything the Lord has called us to do, we will be assured of the voice of the Master, calling us out, "Well done , thy good and faithful servant! Enter into the joy of your Lord". Godliness is contentment, and Godliness with contentment is great gain (I Tim 6:6).

God's Work, Done God's Way, Will Never Lack God's Supplies --- Hudson Taylor

How God Funded His Ministries in the Bible, and Still Does Today

One thing that stands out for sure from the studies of the Bible is that the Holy Scriptures are not silent on money matters, nor quiet about how to finance and fund the ministries. In order to clearly understand and really know the will, the ways and the work of God, it is very important that we delve deeply into the Word of God and learn and adopt the values and the perspectives from His Word. As fallen and thus imperfect children of God saved by His grace, if not prayerful and careful, we tend to do God's work, man's way before we even realize it. Stewards with an unrighteous motive (Luke 16, the parable of the unjust manager) can easily do all the right things for all the wrong reasons, with all sorts of internal rationalizations and external justifications that are offensive to God. But if we understand and apply God's kingdom perspective with our humility and purity of heart and active obedience of life, it will give us the confidence to live in divine guidance, spiritual significance, and financial abundance. As a result, we will be enlisting and recruiting many others to partner with us for the higher purpose of expanding His Mission in this lost and dying world. Ultimately our God Jehovah Jireh, is in charge of providing for all the need of His people beyond any strategies or structures of our own, as we go about His business. "And my God shall supply all your need according to the riches of His glory in Christ Jesus." (Phil 4:19).

Here are several key biblical ways that God employed and still uses to fund and finance His missions and ministries through our obedience to His call:

1. God supplies our needs for His ministries miraculously and supernaturally (II Kings 4:1-7 Elisha, the widow and the oil, Ex 16:13-17 quail/manna, I Kings 17:1-7 the raven). The Lord works in mysterious and miraculous ways His wonders to perform so we can have more fervent faith in following Him faithfully and serving Him joyfully.

2. God supplies our needs for His ministries by wisely setting up an established workable structure in place (Num 18:21-24, II Chro 31:4, Deut 14:22-29). God called on Israel as a nation to support the Levites and the priests who were "full time" in the ministries; and He still commands His people the followers today to pay the tithes monthly to support the work and workers in the churches. He further warns and rebukes with severe consequences for knowingly and willfully disobeying the tithing system, and promises to reward abundantly those who are obedience in Malachi 3.
3. God supplies our needs for His ministries by giving us the smarts, stamina and the skills to make money with our professions (Acts 18:1-5). As a successful tentmaker, the apostle Paul further declares this deeper truth than mere self-support, referring to himself that, "Yes, you yourselves know that these hands have provided for my necessities, and for those who were with me. I have shown you in every way, that by laboring like this, that you must support the weak. And remember the words of the Lord Jesus, that He said, 'It is more blessed to give than to receive.'" (Acts 20:34-35). As we have privileged to serve the Lord passionately in many countries over so many years, we have known and seen wonderful ministers and missionaries who find good employments with their God-given talents in different settings, with the central objective of carrying out evangelism, discipleship, and church planting. This is currently known by the acronym BAM: Business AS Missions. It is very effective and fruitful in all places, but absolutely necessary especially in hostile territories and countries where the Gospel of Christ is forbidden to be preached legally and openly.
4. God supplies our needs for His ministries through our personal appeals to churches and individuals who share our values, vision and passion ((Rom 15:20-24, Phil 4:17-19) as the Great Commission Christians.
5. God supplies our needs for His ministries indirectly through a third party (Acts 11:27-30, Philemon).

6. God supplies our needs for His ministries through church sponsorship (Phil 4:10-20). This is a most common way nowadays as the church decides to adopt a missionary or a missions project for a certain period of time to accomplish a specific purpose.
7. God supplies our needs for His ministries through the faith communities like a special Christian gathering (Acts 4:32-5:11) and informal and irregular Christian fellowship meetings.
8. God supplies our needs for His ministries by touching hearts of the leaders and authorities inside and even outside the church (Neh 2:1-8) with His favors of provision. Vision enables and secures provision, and provision follows the God-given vision. The Lord is the One who makes the connection between vision and provision so that we can go and do and finish His missions. Nehemiah received all he needed because of "the good hand of my God upon me." The one thing we have learned in all these years of serving the Lord in missions is that if you will be clear in seeing God's vision and be crazy bold in doing His mission, you will obtain His provision! God will touch and move people to supply all you need both naturally and supernaturally. This principle of truth has never failed!

Before You Decide, Secure A Guide:
Coaching in Fundraising

According to Merriam-Webster online dictionary (www.merriam-webster.com), the word "coaching" is defined as "training intensively, by instruction and demonstration", and the coach is the person who is a "private tutor, the one who instructs and trains" with demonstration and example. Just as intentional responsibility produces personal and spiritual maturity, so only strict and serious accountability will ensure a life of high integrity, which is extremely critical for money matters and fund-raisers. According to Mr. William P. Dillon (PP. 191-194), the noted Christian fundraising coach who trains prospective ministers and missionaries with Biblical principles and wonderful role-plays, the accountability aspect of coaching is a crucial part of the coach's role in training in that he is someone that make you do what you do not want to do. This immediately remind me of our Lord Jesus Christ, the Master Coach of our life who spoke in no uncertain term to Peter in John 21:18, "I tell you the truth, when you were younger you dressed yourself and went to where you wanted; but when you are old, you will stretch out your hands, and someone else will dress you and lead you where you do not want to go." Wow, how revealing is this kind of coaching!

Fundraising is not always fun, and raising money has never been easy for most people. This is especially true of new comers in the deputation ministries. Good missionaries we know have all experienced fear, anxiety, traveling long distances with little fund to show for it, and thus they become discouraged, frustrated, even doubtful of their call, they eventually quit. How sad this reality is. But praise the Lord for the good news that with spiritual strategies, and effective coaching in fund raising and relational skills, all of these aggravation, irritation and frustration of dragged-out time and energy can be gradually reduced and prevented with a good coach. As the good ole cliché goes, "Where there is a will, there is a way", especially when it is clear the will of God for you. In fundraising as people raising, there are two major roles the coach plays for the fundraisers: first the coach praises you for what you are doing right, and second the coach critiques you on what could be improved. The coach then is your visible and tangible "accountability partner" to ensure you of the correct and effective path to reaching your financial goal. And if you really want to be fruitful and successful in going through all the four key ingredients in fund raising, namely, (1). Selecting the contact names, (2). Securing the appointments, (3). Actually visiting and speaking with the people you have appointments with, and (4). Following up with reports both problems and progress in your ministries, prayer requests and praise reports, you must have a coach whom you respect and admire because of the good profile and solid track record she or he possesses (Dillon, P. 192):

1. Experienced fundraiser with a proven track record of success;
2. Excellent with one-on-one skills;
3. Personally disciplined;
4. Encouraging, enthusiastic, and motivating
5. Highly focused and skillful at holding you accountable;
6. A good listener who believes the best in you;
7. A creative problem solver;
8. A prayer warrior who really prays for you regularly;
9. A strategist, counselor and pastor who speaks the truth in love with you even if it is hard and when truth hurts;
10. A detective, teacher, mentor, manager and role model who is available.

Good and Bad Habits in Fundraising as People Raising

According to the famous motivational expert on success, Mr. Napoleon Hill, all of us are creatures with good and bad habits that can make us or break us depending on what they are. A habit, according to Webster dictionary online, is simply "an acquired mode of behavior that has become nearly or completely involuntary." As our people raising techniques have become acquired and habitualized, fund raising becomes gradually our second nature. The following is a practice-proven and time-tested, and tried-and-true list of ten good habits for us to cultivate and four bad habits for us to avoid and get rid of (Dillion, P. 203-204):

1. Prioritize your contacts both old and new. This can be done through cataloguing them by high, medium, and low priority.
2. Focus always on your top ten. Review the top ten constantly as the list can be very fluid. These top ten makes the biggest difference for you through their giving. Cultivate these key donor relationships.
3. Keep adding names. Expand your new contacts.

4. Keep thanking the people. This reduces donor turnover. Remember this statistically proven fact that for every 100 donors who stop supporting you, 66% think you don't care about them. Remember also that happy donors who are appreciated are your prime candidates to be asked to upgrade their giving with increased amounts.
5. Start getting people to give immediately to provide funds for emergencies and special projects.
6. Keep asking, "What is the next step for this prospect or donor?" This helps to maximize your opportunity.
7. Always start with the ideal: securing an appointment to meet.
8. Keep gathering data on your prospects and donors.
9. Keep recording information for further reference and future referrals.
10. Keep raising people's vision. As the vision goes, the mission and the money will follow. No vision, no provision; and more vision more provision, as the provision follows the vision!

While one develops and strengthens his good positive habits, the fundraiser should simultaneously avoid and eliminate bad habits. Be ware of these four bad ones and steer clear of them:

1. Don't tell your whole story when you are only making the appointments, for this will make the prospect feel that there is no need to meet;
2. Avoid the group ask, because in a group setting, people tend to lowball their giving. People will give much more when they are approached individually and challenged personally.
3. Avoid asking too low. When you ask high, you have the chance to pull up the donor's vision and thus his giving.
4. Don't raise funds without complete training. This is the obvious truth and sad fact that people who have not been trained in how to secure an appointment will be unable to get the appointments. And if they don't get the appointment,

they can't personally go and ask people for their gifts. This will and has resulted in missionaries disappointed, discouraged, depressed and even readily given up with doubts about their call from God!

There are 3 fatal fundraising mistakes that we must be keenly aware of so that we will not waste precious time and limited energy spinning the wheels but going no where (Aug 13, 2017, www.peopleraising.com). Since fundraising is all about people raising, and people raising is all about building and growing trustworthy relationships, one must not fail by not falling into these mistakes. (1). Don't fail to ask for financial support when the relationship is build substantially; (2). Don't fail to follow up with progress and praise reports. Remember the three key words in property purchase: location, location and location? The 3 key words in people raising as fundraising are: follow up, follow up and follow up. (3). Don't fail to thank the people. Say thank you sincerely, immediately and with emphasis, verbally or in writing to let them know that you received the gift, needed the gift and truly appreciate the gift. This will encourage further giving to your ministries.

What Motivates People to Give Their Monies to Your Ministries?

Based on our long-term commitments and experiences first as fundraisers and then as fellow givers to the causes of Christ, we have carefully summarized 12 key and real reasons why people give to your ministries. We know that this will help you once you intentionally cultivate yourself in these areas to be more effective:

1. People give to you simply because they like you;
2. People know you and therefore they give you;
3. People trust you, and therefore they support you. They give because there is a trusted relationship. In order to build trust which is known in leadership and steward as "the law of the solid ground" and the cornerstone of all healthy relationships, the fundraiser must know, live by and apply

the five "T" factors: Truthfulness, Transparency, Tests, Track-records, and Time.
4. People care about you! Care and share always go together. If you care, you will usually share, and when you share you show how much you really care. And as the old cliché says it right, people don't care how much you know until they know how much you care. And this principle of human interaction goes both directions.
5. People give their monies to your ministries because of your enthusiastic passion and genuine compassion for souls;
6. People give to your ministries because you take the innovative initiatives to approach them with your solid character and great competence;
7. People give because of an emotional connection, but they give more when they reach the decision and form the conviction that they are strategic investors in His mission with you, and not just passive or reactive contributors to your ministry;
8. People give when the "ask" is clear, specific and reasonable;
9. People give when there is follow-up with prayer requests, and praise and progress reports;
10. People give when they see your dynamic missions and faith in actions
11. People give when you show much fruitful manifestation: results!
12. People give to your missions because of shared values and visions.

The Vital Role of Prayer in Fundraising

Matt 9:38 --- Therefore pray to the Lord of the harvest to send out laborers into His harvest.

Mk 14: 32, 35-36, 38-39 --- He said to His disciples, "Sit here while I pray." ... He went a little farther and fell down on the ground and prayed... "Abba, Father, all things are possible for You. Take this cup away from Me; nevertheless, not what I will but what You will." ... "Watch and pray, lest you enter into temptation. The spirit indeed is willing, but the flesh is weak." Again He went away and prayed.

Phil 4:6 --- Be anxious for nothing, but in everything by prayer and supplication, with thanksgiving, let your request be made known to God.

I Thess 5:16-17 --- Rejoice always, praying without ceasing.

We must talk with God about men before we talk to men about God (anonymous).

The level of our prayer life is in direct proportion to the level of our power life, in that more prayer, more power; little prayer, little power; no prayer, no prayer. As we spend more personal and quiet time with our loving Lord in the Word and through prayers, we will experience more of His power, more of His presence, more of His Vision, provision and protection, and more of His correction and direction, which are all so critical and crucial for the deputation ministry of raising the necessary resources so as to go and do His missions and ministries. As the biblically recorded long priestly prayer of the Lord Jesus teaches us in John 17, we must be like Jesus to pray for ourselves, for others and for the whole world. Jesus prayed to God in the chapter specifically with four power points in that he prayed for His own glorification even as He has glorified the Father (V.4), sanctification of the believers (V.17), unification of the body of Christ (VV. 22-23), and the eventual evangelization of the whole wide world (VV. 21, 25). We must go ahead and pray likewise that our life as fundraisers will be sanctified always with the truth of God's Word and saturated always by the power of God's Holy Spirit, so that we can become holy vessels pleasing and accepted to God. We pray for more anointing to be strategically useful for the Master and go all out enthusiastically and energetically to spread the Gospel of God's grace, to win more souls and make more disciples of all nations so as to fully glorify our Lord Jesus!

Not only are we to pray just for ourselves and for God's good and gracious hand of spiritual and financial favors to rest upon us, we are to sincerely pray for God to help us raise an army of prayer warriors for our mission. We are also to pray regularly and sincerely for our donors both current and prospective, for as much as we need to have financial supporters, we need also spiritual supports of intense intercession at times even more urgently required for our ministries in very dark, hostile and dangerous regions. Relational fundraisers should, with an attitude of gratitude for their sacrificial and generous giving that enables them to do God's work, earnestly for their donors in the following necessary areas: physical health and healing, emotional strength and stability, marital and familial harmony, salvation of unsaved and rebellious family members, church unity and growth, financial favors and spiritual stamina to walk daily in close intimacy with the Lord in the Word and in the Spirit.

Always remember that fundraising is a spiritual ministry, and as such, it must be carried up spiritually, for God's work must be done in God's way before we can expect to secure God's supplies and provisions. What we do and how are do it are indeed equally important. Nothing can replace a personal, spiritual and relational touch between the fundraising missionary and the missionary God, and the touch between the donors and the fundraiser. In spite of all the technological advances and organizational tools readily available at our disposal, they can "never substitute God's power, which comes alone in answer to our fervent and prevailing prayers... dependence upon God in prayer is the ultimate way for doing spiritual work ... God works beyond our strategies... So work your plan as if it all depends on you, but knowing that in reality it all depends on Him... Our prayer activates a powerful God. It unleashes His resources to accomplish His purpose." (Dillon, PP. 220-222). Nothing worthwhile and worth doing in the kingdom work can be done without the discipline of prayer. It is a most fatal weapon against the enemy of darkness; it is the voice of triumph over all the doubts, anxieties, worries and fears, it is a sweet smelling savor of praise and adoration to the Author and Finisher of our faith Jesus Christ the Lord (Heb 12:2). The overcoming and overwhelming power of prevailing prayers will activate and energize us with boldness and wisdom to raise the funds and to finish His work. We will not grow weary or lose heart if we consider Him and concentrate on Him and His promises made alive, afresh, anew and afire by our never-ending prayer!

The Prayer of the Fund Raiser: Psalms 121

1. I will lift up my eyes to the hills --- where does my help come from?
2. My help comes from the Lord, the Maker of heaven and earth.
3. He will not let your foot slip --- He Who watches Israel will not slumber;
4. Indeed He who watches over Israel will neither slumber nor sleep.
5. The Lord watches over you – the Lord is your shade at your right hand;
6. The sun will not harm you by day; nor the moon by night.
7. The Lord will keep you from all harm --- He will watch over your life;
8. The Lord will watch your coming and going, both now and forevermore.

Reflections and Applications

Once again, remember always that fundraising is people raising! When you have the people with you, their support both spiritual and financial will also be with you. We are not targeting people's pockets, we are directly aiming and shooting at people's heart with our contagious vision and passion and mission. Raising money is about you sharing passionately your ministries to others with your core values. Core values are the deepest convictions in our core belief system that direct our daily behaviors. If others share the same core values with us, they will gladly join the same cause. It is out of these shared core values that we can direct and cast out our visions and missions in the ministries of the Lord. When the vision and the missions are personalized and actualized, and shared with other people, they will join you for the ministries with the sincerity and conviction of their heart. When you as a fundraiser have touched and gotten hold of the hearts with your humility, faithfulness and passionate ministries, you have gotten their hands and pocket books for the same cause and the common goal, which is beyond you and them.

Questions for you to consider are:

1. What are the core values you hold for your life and ministry?
2. How effectively are you really sharing your core values with others?
3. How can you better engage and involve others in the cause you embody?

Chapter 13

7 Effective Faith Strategies for Your Financial Vision, Vigor, and Victory

Luke 10:18-20 --- I saw Satan fall like lightning from heaven. I have given you authority to trample on snakes and scorpions and to overcome all the power of the enemy. Nothing will harm you. However, do not rejoice that the spirits submit to you, but rejoice that your names are written in heaven – Jesus Christ

III John 2 --- Beloved, I pray that you may prosper in all things, and be in health, just as your soul prospers.

I John 4:4 & 5:5 --- You, dear children, are from God and have overcome them, because the One who is in you is greater than the one who is in the world... For everyone born of God overcomes the world. This is the victory that has overcome the world, even our faith.

I Cor 15:57-58 --- But thank be to God! He gives us the victory through our Lord Jesus Christ. Therefore, my dear brothers, stand firm. Let nothing move you. Always give yourself fully to the work of the Lord, because you know that your labor in the Lord is not in vain.

II Chron 24:20 --- This is what God says: "Why do you disobey the Lord's commands? You will not prosper. Because you have forsaken the Lord, He has forsaken you."

While disobedience to God causes disasters, human obedience brings abundance, divine guidance, personal confidence and eternal Kingdom significance!

Human setback against you is often a divine setup for you (Gen 50:20). Don't you break down before you break through!

Welcome and embrace human adversities, as they are your divine universities for growth and maturity (I Cor 16:9).

The word "breakthrough" has been widely and frequently used these days by many people to describe major wins and victories. According to the www.dictionary.com, the definition for "breakthrough" is a military movement or advance all the way through and beyond an enemy's front-line defense; an act or instance of removing or surpassing an obstruction or restriction; the overcoming of a stalemate. In this chapter of faith and finances, we are using this powerful and militant key word "breakthrough" to refer to the sudden outpouring, outburst or manifestation of a prophetic vision and spiritual strategic revelation to awaken the people of God to a revolutionary realization and an enthusiastic participation in the purpose and plan of God so that they can move above and beyond their current stalemates to a newer, brighter and higher level of victory, success and prosperity.

To achieve all this, however, it will definitely require a lifestyle of radical transformation, a renewed personal commitment and total obedience of faith that alone will please the Lord to bless you with financial abundance, divine guidance, strong confidence and eternal significance. And in order for this to occur, no one else but you, have to personally see the incentives and take the initiatives to get motivated and mobilized with consistent and bold actions. God only helps those who are willing, eager and ready to obediently apply themselves. No one, not even the devil and all his demons, can mess up the will of God (III John 2 above quoted) for your life, finance and ministry except yourself. You must catch and embrace this vision with faith for your finances by getting rid of unhealthy, ungodly and unproductive habits, self-imposed mental emotional and spiritual boundaries, societal inertia, the debilitating lies and the vicious attacks of the enemy. Satan has had you bound for far too long, but Jesus wants you to be set free, spiritually and financially. It is time to examine and get rid of all the useless excuses and foolish assumptions. It is time for each and every one of us to grow in grace and glow in glory by taking serious, daily, personal responsibilities with these seven specific strategies to achieve the faith victory promised in I John 5:4, and reach financial abundance promised in III John 2.

Here are seven successful faith strategies for your financial life and victories that have proven reliable and valid time and again in our own lives and ministries. We'd like to share with you in an attempt to challenge and inspire you and with the sincere hope and prayer that you will make them part of your life habits that will make you prosperous and successful in all your being, doing and going. Here we go:

1. Always stand firmly on the positive promises of the infallible Word of God, and be filled and refilled by the presence and power of the Holy Spirit.

Here lies the key to your most important foundation of a life of faith and finances and values, vision and victory: to develop the intimacy of relationship with the Lord and to receive the legitimacy of your kingdom authority for your daily walk with the Lord. You can lay such a foundation by these 7 steps:

A. Meditation --- Meditate on the Laws and Truths of God and the powerful principles from the Word of God! Like meat marination, you will be filled with spiritual saturation with you Word meditation (Ps 1, Phil 4:8).
B. Preparation --- If you desire to have bumper production, you must spend time in spiritual, physical, mental and emotional preparation. Before he ever could defeat the evil giant

Goliath in the valley of Elah, David showed us that he had seriously prepared himself from early morning down to the details of selecting the five smooth stones to fully load up his shepherd's pouch for battle (I Sam 17). One central key to prosperity and victory in life is adequate and thorough preparation, for the devil is in the details.

C. Motivation --- Some negative people say that motivation does not work because it is short lasting. Well, neither does bathing! That's why you need to have a bath and get motivated daily, just like we must take up His cross in our walk daily (Lk 9:23). This can be achieved through daily reading the Word, prayers, inspiration quotes and moving autobiographies.

D. Mobilization --- Only when a person is sufficiently inspired and motivated with the lofty incentives and visions of heaven, can she or he be powerfully mobilized to be a moving force for good and for God. John 4 gives an a beautiful example and model of Jesus motivation and the Samaritan's mobilization, as she went around sharing the good news of Jesus and brought many to salvation through their faith encounter. There are three ways to influence people: by example, by example and by example (Jh 13:15, II Thes 3:9, I Pet 5:3). I am convinced that the best way to motivate and mobilize people, just as the best way to lead others, is by example! Matthew 9:35-38 is an excellent Jesus of Jesus motivated and mobilized in mighty ministries as an example for us to follow.

E. Application --- "Go and do likewise." (Lk 10:37). The more He sees us apply ourselves diligently and obediently, the more the Lord will supply us sufficiently and abundantly. This law never fails (Mk 2:5).

F. Collaboration --- Actively and deeply listening to others with respect and empathy, and sincerely loving and serving other people bring the greatest joy and fulfillment to your own lives. More of your human collaboration will cause more wealth creation. One must get along with others in order top get ahead in life. Your future net worth really does depend on your current network (Lk 5:1-11).

G. Manifestation --- You are the light of the world; let your light so shine before men that they will see your good deeds and give glory and honor and praises to your heavenly Father and your Lord (Matt 5:14,16)

2. Examine and enhance yourself intensively and extensively in these five key areas:

A. Perspective of life — it is your world view based on your values; Vision, vigor, valley and victory.

B. Motive of the heart --- Be brutally honest with yourself and with God and others as to why you do what you do.

C. Attitude --- Be positive, active and passionately proactive and then you will be extremely productive.

D. Balance --- Balance is beautiful in life as it assures us with the peace of mind. Balance comes as a result of our clear sense of life purpose and life priority. A life of balance is a life of focus and integrity. A balanced life is an effective, successful and fruitful life. Blessed are the balanced, for they show outwit, outwork and outlast everyone else.

E. Habits --- We are all creatures of habits whether we know them or not. The habits you form will either help you, or hurt and hinder you, break you or make you, all depends on what they are. We are what we repeatedly do. Excellence is not a single act, but a good constructive and productive and daily habit. Therefore, intentionally cultivating good and healthy personal spiritual, relational and financial habits is both crucial and critical for your prosperity and ultimate successes.

Develop rigorous and habitual disciplines that will make you vigorous and victorious. Financial fitness and freedom are largely a result of our life long monetary habits. Researches consistently and conclusively prove that while our faith matters in our finances, the consistent practice of our constant faith in relation to finances matters even more. While 20% of our financial success depends on our knowledge and information, yet the other 80% of our financial abundance actually comes from our daily behaviors and habitual lifestyle. Dr Stephen R. Covey (2004) teaches these seven proven healthy habits from his life-long studies of numerous highly effective people the world over. Here is a summary of the seven crucial habits for any and all successes that can be easily applicable to your faith and finances, with the first three emphasizing personal victory and the last four emphasizing public victory:

A. Be proactive and not reactive, for proactivity propels productivity;
B. Begin with the end in mind – the power of vision and visualization;
C. Put first thing first --- Priority provides primary purpose and passionate power in money life and missions ministries;
D. Think win/win --- Interpersonal leadership realizes that interdependence is a higher virtue than independence or dependence;
E. Seek first to understand, then to be understood --- the power of empathetic communication as deposit to the emotional bank;
F. Synergize --- cooperate with people intentionally, creatively and energetically;
G. Sharpen the saw – constantly renew and update yourself to live with clarity and in balance. You are never too old to learn and it is never too late to learn. To do the job right, an effective tool is an absolute necessity.

According to Dr. Covey (pp. 70-72) who cited the famous psychologist Viktor Frankl that discovered the basic principle of the nature of man, that the first and the most basic habit of a highly effective person in any environment, is the habit of proactivity. It means that human behavior is a function of our conscious choices and careful decisions, not our conditions. Humans can be responsible to take initiative to subordinate feelings to their internalized values. We have the initiative and the responsibility as mature human beings to make things happen proactively and not reactively. The ability to subordinate an impulse to a much stronger value is the essence of a real proactive person.

I am what I am today because of the conscious choices I made yesterday. Based on my (HY) personal research and life experience, these are my simple seven-step, habitually-proven pattern in effectively reaching my objective:

- A. Develop a kingdom perspective which does not allow us to be passive or reactive;
- B. Be always positive, active, proactive, collective, and then you will be productive;
- C. Review the retrospective and preview the attractive prospective;
- D. Consider another innovative and creative alternative;
- E. Offer the relevant incentive;
- F. Always take the personal initiative;
- G. Be constantly reflective, to be more effective so as to reach your final objective.

3. Invest in yourself constantly and continuously: To live is to learn, and to learn is to earn! Your education level generally determines your economic level, and what's in your head ultimately decides what's going to be in your hand!

The best investment is self-investment and education as an investment is the solid foundation for financial victory and wealth creation. One must keep growing in the grace of God (II Pet 3:18) in order to keep glowing for the glory of God. Luke 2:52 provides us a compelling example of the growth of Christ our Lord. "Jesus grew in wisdom, in stature, in favor with God and men." This means that we must grow also holistically to be like Jesus in the four areas: physical, mental, social, and spiritual.   To get the job done effectively, it is of necessity that you develop and possess the right tools. Keep sharpening your saw by investing in yourself and by renewing of yourself in these four crucial areas (Covey, P. 288):

> A. Physically: Exercise, nutrition, rest, and do stress management;
> B. Mentally: Reading, visualizing, planning, journaling and writing;
> C. Emotionally/Socially: Fellowship, service, empathy, synergy and Intrinsic security;
> D. Spiritually: Study the Scriptures, prayers, meditations, value clarification, and core commitments.

4. The power of a vision

Set a specific and lofty goal for both your faith growth and financial abundance after much prayer. Jesus the Lord famously declares that the kingdom of God does not come visibly or by mere observation, because the kingdom of God is within you (Luke 17:20-21) when you worship Jesus as the King in your heart. Oliver Wendell Holmes was quoted as saying that, "What lies behind us and what lies before us are tiny matters, compared to what lies within us." Based on your core values, you should develop both a vision statement (what to accomplish) and a mission statement (how to go about and go out to actually accomplish it). The vision drives the mission, and the mission sharpens and strengthens the vision. No one can be a true missionary if she or he has not become a visionary. That is why the words of the Lord, the words of vision in Luke 10: 18-20 are so powerful as our central spiritual motivation and kingdom missions mobilization.

Before you are to go, you must have a goal; if you don't have a goal, you really don't have anywhere to go. And if you don't know where you are going, how then can you know how far you have gone? Therefore, sit down, pray and think and study in order to set a smart goal. Once you set your goal, you will discover your role. It is important that your goal is SMART, which can be an acronym for being Specific, Measurable, Attainable, Realistic, and Testable. In order to achieve that specifically set goal, one must constantly visualize it, vocalize it, verbalize it, and vitalize it and actualize it before you can realize it! You must practice faith declaration with your lips, accompanied with consistent actions of focus and discipline, and then financial demonstration in your lives, little by little, day after day, will become a wonderful manifestation to the glory and praises of the Lord. The blessing of the Lord brings wealth, without painful toil or sorrow for it (Prov 10:22). What a gracious and glorious God of generosity we have and we serve! Hallelujah to His holy name!

A careful study of Mark 11:22-24 reveals these 7 central points as spiritual principles for our daily practices. If the mind can conceive and the heart truly believe, then the person can achieve if she or he will consistently behave. They are 7 words I have chosen with the same ending for easy memorization and speedy application:

- A. Perceive — what the Lord is saying and where the Spirit is leading;
- B. Conceive --- become impregnated with the heavenly vision;
- C. Receive --- personalize it as your very own;
- D. Believe deeply in your heart and soul;
- E. Behave --- make consistent and disciplined efforts to run with it;
- F. Achieve --- you will be blessed if you will do them!
- G. Give --- you're blessed to bless. Then you will be more blessed (Lk 6:38)

5. Prioritize your life with essentialism and minimalism.

Remember to put first thing first, and always to keep the main thing the main thing. Focus on the vital few, and don't be disrupted or distracted by the trivial many! The wisdom of life consists in the elimination of all the nonessentials. Here is our simple list for you to consider and apply to your own stewardship life:

- A. Practice gratitude and contentment;
- B. Start depositing in the "Donate Box";

C. Focus on faith, family, friends, finances and freedom;
D. Clear the clutter with "less but better";
E. Encourage and compliment someone everyday;
F. Distinguish between a must-have and the nice-to-have;
G. Exercise daily spiritual, mental, financial and physical disciplines.

6. Develop a solid strategy and follow through with a plan for constant and consistent action and careful evaluation.
Be extremely industrious and diligent to make money and totally frugal and thrifty to save money so that you will accumulate much money with debt-free living and generous giving and profitable investing. All this of course will require you to be a highly disciplined with both rigor and vigor as a real disciplined disciple of Christ, for the first and most obvious attribute of a true disciple is discipline. And don't waste any money or time; especially don't squander the precious gift of God: your life. When a person carelessly and casually squanders his time, he is actually wasting his life, because time is the element that makes life. Read the famous little book (listed in the bibliographical reference at the end of this book) that I use often in my teaching ministries *Don't Waste Your Life* by Pastor John Piper to challenge and inspire, motivate and mobilize yourself for a greater and Godly purpose. Don't waste your life in the world for the devil; but be willing and ready to risk and even lose your life for the Lord! This is a critical and integral part of our spiritual and financial stewardship worthy of daily reminders and repeated emphasis.

7. Intentionally live and practice the interpersonal and relational stewardship as a personal lifestyle and leadership distinctive with strong emphasis on these five (5) characteristic concentrations: communication, connection, cooperation, creation and contribution.

A. Empathetic Communication – it is not defensive; it is not reactive it is not merely and superficially respectful and emotionally sympathetic. Communicating with empathy means being willing to put yourself in others' shoes and feel their pains, frustrations and struggle, and share their joy without any jealousy. Cry with those who cry; mourn with those who mourn, and rejoice with those who rejoice! Do not be proud or conceited, but be willing to associate yourself with people of low position (Rom 12:15-16). Thus you will deposit much into their emotional and relational bank account. Empathetic communication entails also active listening, listening not just with our head or ears, but with one's heart of tender receptivity. It is non-judgmental and non-interruptive. It is deeply personal.

B. Heart-to-heart Connection: be authentic and personal and compassionate in approaching people with care, and be willing and even eager to share. Always seek to touch and bless their heart before you ask for their hand. Remember to always give before you receive, sow the seeds of loving kindness and generosity first, and then you will reap a bumper harvest of good will and good relationships conducive to your growth, goal setting and go getting! Proactively seek out people of the same values and vision, and sincerely care for and share with, and then many unexpected doors of opportunities will be opened to you.

C. Creative Cooperation --- When we choose intentionally to work with certain people, passionate positive and proactive people, it will create a special force called synergy. Synergy is the combination and multiplication of individual energies. Working with people harmoniously further stretches and greatly strengthens you. In order to get ahead in life, faith life and finance life, we must learn the art and science of getting along with many others. No one alone can accomplish the mission, the Great Commissions; we must constantly enlist, encourage, equip and empower the workers for the Lord's ripe vineyard, as we see Him doing it in the famous parable of the vineyard in

Faith and Finances

Matt 20:1-16. Study it, discover the hidden treasures and apply and invest them in your own stewardship life. Then you will experience amazing growth and transformation. That we can sure promise you! And it is really infallible!

D. Wealth Creation --- Where there is a synergistic collaboration, there will inevitably be new creation: new ideas, new patterns, new paradigms, and many other innovative alternatives to provide better goods and services. All this will invariably lead to abundant prosperity with such creativities and commercial activities when the innovations are put into actions that will certainly lead to production with much profitability.

E. Generous Contribution --- This is the grace of giving and the gift of generosity that Bible strongly stresses and promotes. Budgeted and planned giving should be characteristic of our regular lifestyle as followers of Christ: blessed to be a blessing, and then much more blessings will come back to you. What a virtuous cycle this is! If we love profoundly, we must give generously; and if we really care, we will liberally share. And people normally share with those they know, like, trust and care for. The most beautiful thing about contribution and donation is this: the more we give, the more we have, because the more we pour out into others, the Lord will pour more back: double and triple portions, and many folds into our lives and ministries. His fountain of supply can never run dry! This is the principle in Luke 6:38 "Give and it will be give unto you". This timeless and universal truth can be applied physically, mentally, emotionally, financially and spiritually. We are personal witnesses and have many testimonies in this blessed virtuous cycle. It has never failed and it will not fail, as God is infallible.

Reflections and Applications

It is important and even easy to make plans, but one needs to realize that the plans may not be necessarily or automatically carried out in action. At times, It might be divine intervention for us to change course, and other times we lack the will to carry the plans out. The Holy Bible teaches in Proverbs 16:9 that in his heart a man plans his course, but the Lord determines his steps! In the American culture, so many people make New Year resolutions on all kinds of things out of the excitement of the moment for a new beginning, but most of us forget what we made a week or a month later only to wait and repeat the same old routines for the start of the next year. A Chinese proverb summarizes it well that the resolute makes resolutions once and for all, but the irresolute keeps making resolutions all the time.

When I (Hong) was in high school (1978-1980), I had a good friend and school mate who liked to make extensive and intensive plans with dates, subjects, goals and objectives on paper. He not only loved doing it for himself, but also went out of his way to eagerly offer his planning expertise and free service to help me do the same, so as to make it to the most competitive annual 3-day National College Entrance Exams. The only problem was that he changed the study plans often with various sets of strategies, and they were nothing more than paper warfares, which cost me several sleepless nights and many precious expensive notebooks. Although his intention was good, yet it was not my plan or goal and failed thus to fit my personal ambition, situation or condition. I learned a useful life lesson from the experience that in order to be productive and profitable, the plan has to be both personal and practical out of one's heart desire and according to the Word and the will of God.

You might ask yourself the following questions:

1. What will be my financial vision and plan for the future?
2. How much does the God Factor play in the fulfillment of my plan?
3. What kind of plans will be personable, practical, suitable and workable for my situation at such a time as this?

Chapter 14

Faith and Finances
A Personal Kingdom Theology
With A Powerful Financial Testimony

Proverbs 23:7 --- As a man thinks in his heart, so is he.

Your life is what your thoughts make it --- Marcus Aurelius

As the mind goes, the man follows; What's in your head will eventually determine what's in your hand.

Acts 10:38 how God anointed Jesus of Nazareth with the Holy Spirit and power, and how he went around doing good and healing all who were under the power of the devil, because God was with him.

Acts 1:8 But you will receive power when the Holy Spirit comes on you; and you will be my witnesses in Jerusalem, and in all Judea and Samaria, and to the ends of the earth."

II Peter 1:3 His divine power has given us EVERYTHING we need for life and godliness through our knowledge of him who called us by his own glory and goodness.

Ephesians 3:20 Now to him who is able to do immeasurably More than all we ask or imagine, according to his power that is at work within us.

Luke 17:20 Once, having been asked by the Pharisees when the kingdom of God would come, Jesus replied, "The kingdom of God does not come with your careful observation,17:21 nor will people say, 'Here it is,' or 'There it is,' because the kingdom of God is within you." — Jesus Christ.

It is our personal conviction and experience that if we will do what we can do naturally, then God will do what we can not do supernaturally! And if we will faithfully apply, the God will fruitfully supply — Drs. Hong & Esther Yang

Rejoice in the Lord always. Again I will say, rejoice! Be anxious for nothing, but in everything by prayer and supplication, with thanksgiving, let your request be made know to God; And the peace of God, which surpasses all understanding, will guard your hearts and minds in Christ Jesus. Finally, Brethren, whatever things are true ... noble...just... pure... lovely... of good report, if there is any virtue and if there is anything praiseworthy --- meditate on these things. The things which you learned and received and heard and saw in me, these do, and the God of peace will be with you. But I rejoice in the Lord greatly that now at least your care for me has flourished again; though you surely did care, but you lacked the opportunity (to share). Not that I speak in regard to need, for I have learned in whatever state I am, to be content: I know how to be abased and how to abound. Everywhere and in all things, I have learned both to be full and to be hungry, both to abound and to suffer need. I can do all things through Christ who strengthens me... And my God shall supply all your need according to His riches in glory by Christ Jesus. Now to our God and Father be glory forever and ever. Amen. (Phil 4: 4, 6-13, 19).

Essential Life Lessons

Wow, Wow, Wow! That's all I can say after reading this anointed, authentic and authoritative Pauline passage of passion, purpose and power with the simplicity of my faith and the sincerity of my heart! What a purpose-driven and passion-packed passage of profound Pauline theology and powerful Christian philosophy that I (HY) have long adopted and personally adapted to my life and ministries in faith and finances and in money matters for our mighty and multiplied missions over the past 30 plus years. Let me point out several essentials life lessons from the quote that have been really and truly time-tested and practice-proven in our marriage, family, kingdom connections and and worldwide ministries!

1. Be joyful in the Lord always! I am more convinced than ever before that the clearest visible evidence of His presence in the Christian life is JOY! In His presence, is there the fullness and abundance of joy and the joy of the Lord is our strength (Ps 16:11 & Neh 8:10)! The joy we have internally in the Lord as a result of our daily quiet times of intimacy and communion with the Lord, is truly joy unspeakable and full of glory, regardless of the external circumstances or situations. The more we are joyful in Him, the more we are faithful, fearless, forceful and fruitful for Him!

2. Be thankful to the Lord! One of the greatest of all attitudes is the human attitude of sincere gratitude that gives us present fortitude and future altitude. Feeling thankful and being grateful is the healthiest of all human emotions, as it has been psychologically proven. As Christians, we are to give thanks to our gracious and generous God with a grateful heart for Who He is in our lives and for what He has done for us. I thank God for His salvation of my soul, for His healing of my body, for His touching my mind with the mind of Christ, and for His transforming power in our lives and ministries over the past 30 plus years so that we can make a difference and cause impacts and influences for Jesus in countless lives al over the world. The Holy Bible in I Thessalonians 5:18 reminds and commands us to "give thanks in all circumstances, for this is the will of God in Christ Jesus concerning us." When we are thankful, we become more contented and joyful, thus also powerful, for the joy of the Lord is our strength (Neh 8:10).

3. Be content with His provision! One of the sure secrets of life is to learn to be content in all circumstances. The Bible instructs us never to be covetous or greedy, but on the contrary, we are to be content, for godliness with content is great gain (I Tim 6:6-8). We have brought nothing to this world when we were born, and certainly we cannot and will not be able to take anything out of it when we die!   One of the favorite programs on Fox Business is Strange Inheritance which always strikes me with The Last Word: Remember, you cannot take it with you! Therefore, having our basic necessities met, let us be content and grateful with that. A well-known Jewish proverb says it so well with both Q & A: Who is wise? The one who can learn from everyone; who is powerful? The one who can overcome his own ego! Who is honorable? The one who honors others; and who is rich? The one who is content with what he has! An ancient Chinese saying goes, "He who is content is the one who is happy." Puritan theologian Thomas Watson is quoted in the *NIV Stewardship Study Bible* as he points out the three characteristics of contentment in that, "1. Contentment is a divine thing; It becomes ours, not by acquisition, but infusion; It is planted by the Spirit of God in the soul; it is a fruit of heavenly birth. It is very observable that contentment is joined with godliness... 2. Contentment is an intrinsic thing; it lies within a man not in the bark but in the root. Contentment hath both its fountain and stream in the soul... 3. Contentment is a habitual thing; it shines with a fixed light in the firmament of the soul; it is settled temper of the heart... it is not casual but constant." (P. 328).

4. Be anxious for nothing! One cannot have the spirit of contentment and celebration until he or she has learned to be anxious for nothing. We will never have a carefree indifference to things until we totally trust God.... And when we trust God, we are free to rely entirely upon Him to get what we need (Richard J. Foster in the *NIV Stewardship Study Bible,* P. 327). Jesus teaches us so vividly with object lessons and historical references in Matt 6 why we should not live with worry. I have experientially learned over the many years of both local and global (thus "glocal") ministries that humans are prone to fear and worry, and that like anger, they do not accomplish the righteousness of God. As a matter of fact, worries in the final analysis are irreverent, irrelevant, and ultimately irresponsible on our part, as one of my real missions heroes, a spiritual master and financial mentor the late Bishop Dr. Lovell R. Cary taught me and modeled for me over the past 25 years both by precepts and example.

5. Be thoughtful on the positive virtues. The one thing we have learned in basic human psychology 101 is that one can change the ways of his life by changing the ways of his thoughts. Therefore our life is a by-product of our thoughts. As a man thinks in his heart, so is he. And as the mind goes, the man follows. We are to be responsible for our lives, and we must be also responsible for our thoughts first, as the latter directly influences the former! Focus on the promises of God, and you will be promisingly positive, and your life and ministry will be powerfully prophetic, passionate, persuasive, and potentially productive and prolific, for positivity propels productivity and even profitability (Matt 25, kingdom economics 101 for all to learn, with the famous Matthew Effect in verse 29).

6. Be active and proactive in doing the right thing in the right way for the right reason! Thoughts lead to action when there is a definite plan and a specific deadline! The Word of God in James 1:22 reminds us of the fact that we are what we do! Do not become mere passive hearers of the Word of God only, thus deceiving yourselves; but be ye active doers of the Word also! A wise man does at once what the foolish man does at last (Jewish Proverb with your reading of Matt 25:16)! Jesus the Lord both teaches and challenges us with these words at the conclusion of His Sermon on the Mount with authoritative admonitions for our immediate implementation and active application of His divine instructions. "Therefore, everyone who hears these words of mine and puts them into practice is like a wise man who build his house on the rock. The rain came down, the streams rose, and the wind blew and beat against that house; yet it did not fall, because it had its foundation on the rock. But everyone who hears these words of mine and does not put them into practice is like a foolish man who built his house on the sand." (Matt 7: 24-26). Wow how clear and convincing these words are!

7. Be confident in the unfailing promises of your God! As it has been our presupposition throughout this book that everything has two sides (like the bright and dark sides of money, sex and power), just like the two sides of the same coin. If you obediently carry out your part of the premises, then God will abundantly perform His part of the precious and powerful promises He has made for us. This is seen clearly in many verses in Deuteronomy 28 and Leviticus 26. This kingdom law of human premise and divine promise becomes especially succinct in the famous revival verse of all times in II Chronicles 7:14 and the missions verse in Matthew 24:14 with both the if and the then, for there is no then without if, just as there is no promise without the premise. We must cheerfully do our part before we can expect the Lord to do His part for us. We can rest assured once and for all that as we apply and heed, He will supply all our need. The One who has called, commanded and commissioned us is faithful and powerful, and He will do it (I Thess 5:24). And we can be confident of that truth!

Five Key Precepts

Of all the vital essentials of faith and finances, monies and ministries that we have been so privileged by His grace and for His glory to have learned over 30 years of practices and experiences around the world, the concepts, convictions and conducts across human cultures that we can easily and eagerly and exuberantly share with you, we have chosen, after much prayerful and careful considerations, five (5) key precepts with examples to emphasize here as they are fundamental from God's Holy Scriptures, and are absolutely foundational for our successes, victories and prosperity even as our soul prospers in the Lord our God, be it physical, mentally, volitional, marital, familial, relational, financial and spiritual. They are, namely: Perspective, Motive, Attitude, Balance and Habit in who we are and what we do! Let us heed these solid instructions, and be prepared and motivated for active daily practical applications, for knowledge is real power when it is properly and habitually applied.

1. The Right PERSPECTIVE Propels You to Purpose, Passion and Prosperity.

It is indeed the truth of life that everything in our lives comes from our particular life perspective. The foundation of our perspective is the core values we hold dear and near to our heart and soul that are the non-negotiable and the absolute essentials. Our faith in the Lord and in the powerful promises of the Word of the living God, more than anything else in this world and in this life, furnishes us a value system and a Christlike worldview that guide us every step of the way, and guard us every moment of the day. It forms and shapes our character and conducts in many ways, especially in how we view money and possession in light of eternity. We are what we sincerely and firmly believe at the center of our soul and the core of our heart. And our belief system forms our perspective and informs our lives, and transforms our role as spiritual stewards and Christian leaders in service to the King of kings. It is written: "I believe; therefore I have spoken." (Ps 116:10). "With the same spirit of faith, we also believe and therefore speak, because we know... All this is for your benefit so that His grace that is reaching more and more people may cause thanksgiving to overflow to the glory of God." (II Cor 4:13-15). What a refreshing and accurate declaration of the central truth of the Christian faith, with the renewed power from a spiritual perspective! Praise to His precious name! To Jesus be all the glory and He will give us the victory, especially financial victories!

We have always Beene challenged and inspired by a true saint of the faith over many years now. Here is the kingdom perspective of a spiritual and successful saint of all times Mother Teresa of Calcutta India (The world honors successes, but God honors faithfulness because it is the godly success — Mother Teresa) whose compelling lifetime testimony of the love of God for the world has been indisputably backed up by her lifelong serving, suffering and sacrificing with and among the poorest of the poor, with a cup of cold water in the name of Jesus:

Anyway
"People are often unreasonable, illogical and self-centered.
Forgive them anyway.
If you are successful, you will win some false friends and some true enemies; succeed anyway.
If you are kind, people may accuse you of selfish ulterior motives.
Be kind anyway.
If you are honest and frank, people may cheat you.
Be honest and frank anyway.
What you spend years building, someone could destroy overnight; build anyway.
If you find serenity and happiness, people may be jealous.
Be happy anyway.
The good you do today may be forgotten tomorrow.
Do good anyway.
Give the world the best you have and it may never be enough.
Give your best anyway.
For you see, in the final analysis, it is between you and God;
It was never between you and them anyway."

Have you ever seen a tombstone with a dollar $ sign on it? Of course not! Have you ever observed a U-haul truck accompanying a hearse? Neither have I. No matter how much a person makes or accumulates in life financially or materially, he cannot take it with him after he dies. No one wants a final judgment on himself or his life based on what he has got. "A man wants people to read in his obituary, not a balance sheet of his wealth, but a story of his service to humanity" (Russ, Crosson, P. 222).

2. The HEART MOTIVE Affects All That You Do.
To the Lord, the motive of the heart is much more essential and crucial than the moves of the hands. The Lord does not look at people as people look at people. Man will evaluate and judge you according to you external appearances of heights, weights, and strength and looks, degrees, pedigrees, economic stratus, and social

connections, But God looks only at the heart (I Sam 16:7). Above all things you must guard your heart, for it will affect everything you do (Prov 4:23)! Keep your heart with all diligence, for out of it springs the issues of life (NKJV). In other words, everything you and I do eventually and ultimately flow out of the hearts that reveal our true and real motives.

Spiritual Stewardship as Christian leadership must start from the examination of the true motive of the heart. We are commanded by the Lord in Matt 6:1-34 to have periodical motive check-ups so as to make sure that we will be doing things always with the three R's: the Right thing in the Right way for the Right reason. As fallen human beings in a sinful world of many seductions, temptations and distractions, we all can easily go astray, and get caught up with image making rather than kingdom building. Jesus in the great Sermon on the Mount severely warns us against hypocrisy and facades, doing good work only to be seen of men and to get the praises of people instead of wholeheartedly serving and pleasing the Lord. To Him, our character and conviction are much more crucial than our external appearances and reputation. While the law seems to regulate our behaviors with lots of "do's" and "don'ts", the Lord stresses the crucial importance of the purity of our heart motive. We are of the strong conviction that when the heart is fundamentally wrong, nothing can be eventually right; and when the heart is right in its motives and intentions, nothings will be eventually wrong! Everything in the end will work out all right. You are motivated and mobilized by your heart MOTIVE.

The great weeping prophet Jeremiah (17:9) points out that the heart of man is deceitful above all things and is desperately wicked. The Lord Jehovah God does not look at man as man looks at man, for He only looks at the heart (I Sam 16:7). He knows what's deep and hidden in our hearts as only He can see us through. No wonder He warns and rebukes the hypocrites, saying that they served Him with their lips, but their hearts were far away from God. In other words, their hearts was not in their service for and worship of God, just going through the motions with highly adulterated ulterior motivations. What a perfect definition of hypocrisy as in stage acting, trying to fake it to make it, as many do in life and unfortunately even in ministries and mission. But as the Word of God warns us that in the final divine judgment (Romans 14:12), So then, each of us will give an account of himself to God. No favoritism and no exceptions. The heart of all issues is the issue of the heart. At the heart of all human matters, even money matters, is the matter of the heart, first and foremost!

Lasting changes do not come just from mental conditioning or behavioral modification. They find their roots in a transformed and renewed heart. The Holy Bible repeatedly urges us to test ourselves and examine the state or the condition of the heart. With our hearts we think (Prov 23:7 – for as a man thinks in his heart, so is he!), we feel, we choose and commit, react and respond. The human heart is the storehouse of our core beliefs and the seat of our character; and it is from the heart that come thoughts, acts, habits and the real motivational forces. Psalms 78:70-72 informs us of the historical fact as to why God chose David from the sheep pens to be His servant and shepherd over the people of Israel. The Lord knew what was in David's heart, anointed David to lead the people first of all because of "the integrity of his heart", and then the skillfulness of his hand. The heart of humility and the motive of purity are what the Lord is looking for and looking at in all of us. This is essential and crucial, for who we really are and why we do what we do matter greatly to the Lord.

Much wisdom can be grasped and applied by checking on-line from the Ron Blue Institute that has helped lift millions of people out of their financial troubles by strong emphasizing these four essential Hs of financial wisdom: Heart, Health, Habits and Hope!

Heart. Behaviors follow belief. Your action needed is to assess your heart with the four beliefs in stewardship in Ps 24:1, contentment in Heb 13:5, faith in Heb 11:1,6 and wisdom in James 1:5.

Health. Take your reality check today. Your action needed is to complete your checklist to identify your current objective reality in terms of the accurate percentage ___% of your living, giving, debt owing, owning and investment growing. True Christ followers live by practicing enjoyment and contentment because money is a tool (I Tim 4:4, 5:8, 6:6-10). We are to give by opening our hands to release God's resources (Lk 16:13). We are to pay taxes with gratitude as they reflect God's provision (Matt 22:17-21). We are to eliminate debs because they always presume upon the future (Prov 22:7 , James 4:13-16). And finally we are to grow by demonstrating financial maturity: giving up today's desire for tomorrow's benefits.

Habits. Assess your strengths and weaknesses in light of these five biblical principles: spend less than you earn (Prov 10:4), give generously (II Cor 8:10-11), avoid the use of debt aggressively (Prov 22:7, Ps 37:21), set long term goals (Eph 2:10), and plan for financial margin (Prov 6:6-8).

Hope. "Changing habits to increase margin is the only way to meet long term goals and align our hearts and hope toward eternity. Without margin, it is difficult to respond to God's call on our lives and to meet the needs of those He has put in our lives." (Ron Blue). Instead of struggling to barely make the ends meet or merely surviving by living from from pay check to pay check, one becomes financially stable, secure and strong with surplus by developing an emergency fund, by saving for long term goals and by investing increasing and gradually growing with abundance! Thus living with the bright promises of God for a better tomorrow and a fabulous future of Jer 29:11!

3. ATTITUDE Is Everything

The single greatest discovery of all time is that a person can change his future by changing his attitude. Your attitude deeply affects your life; Your internal attitude literally determines your external altitude and spiritual longitude, personal latitude, and financial fortitude, because a victorious and abundant life in Christ Jesus is lived out daily from the inside out, even as the Lord surprisingly and convincingly taught the disciples both then and now that "The kingdom of God does not come visibly...because the kingdom of God is within you." (Lk 17: 20-21).

" I believe the single most important decision I can make on a day to day basis, is my choice of attitude. It is more important than my past, my education, my bankroll, my success or failure, fame or pain, what other people think of me, or say about me, my circumstances or my position... It alone fuels my fire or assaults my hope. When my attitude is right, there is no barrier too high, no valley too deep, no dream too extreme, no challenge too great for me." (Pastor Charles Swindoll).

"The longer I live, the more I realize the impact of attitude on life. Attitude to me is more important than facts. It is more important than the past, than education, than money, than the circumstances, than failures, than successes, than what other people think, say or do. It is more important than appearance, giftedness or skill. It will make or break a company, a church, a home. The remarkable thing is we have a choice every day regarding the attitude we embrace for that day. We cannot change the past. We cannot change the fact that people will act in a certain way. We cannot change the inevitable. The only thing we can do is to play on the one string we have, and that is our attitude. I'm convinced that life is 10% what happens to me, and 90% how I react to it. And so it is with you! We are in charge of our attitudes!" (Pastor Charles Swindoll).

Your attitude is your daily choice and your personal responsibility. The attitude you responsibly choose today will reflect your past, describe your present, and predict your future. My personal Hong Yang Acronym for the word ATTITUDE is as follows:

A --- Always
T --- Take
T --- The
I --- Initiative
T --- To
U --- Unselfishly
D --- Display
E --- Enthusiasm

Money has become the grand test of a person's virtue. "If a person gets his attitude toward money straight, it will help straighten out almost any other area of his life" (Billy Graham). According to Researcher Harold Myra (2005, PP. 107-121), one of the secrets of Dr. Billy Graham's extraordinary ministry successes was the area of finances. Here is a summary of some of the key policies and effective strategies from the marketing genius of Rev. Billy Graham:

A. There is nothing wrong with men possessing riches. The wrong comes when riches possess men, for the love of money is a root of all kinds of evil (I Tim 6:10). Live a life of simplicity, sincerity, authenticity and charity.
B. A spiritual leader must care about money as it is his responsibility for good stewardship. Take money seriously. But above all, don't be greedy or love money (Lk 12:15).
C. Be transparent, and be accountable to qualified others.
D. The sense of trust is essential and integrity is critical.
E. Clear Vision from God and diligent authentic communication with the board and employees and donors are indispensable to secure adequate resources.
F. Be conservative. Spend less than you raise. "Whatever God provides, we will live within the budget." (Billy Graham). No debts allowed.
G. Always listen to his God, his gut, and his advisors before making the final decision. Listen. Learn, live, love and lead!
H. Focus on the vision, be kept away from distraction, and never waste resources.
I. Be sensitive to needs, and be generous in giving away resources to help others fulfill the vision and the mission God gives them.
J. Missions won't succeed without sufficient cash flow and economic vitality. Leaders must be in close touch with reality.

Your attitude is a special secret to your survival and success. What is success? According to the famous British statesman and philosopher Sir Winston Churchill who truly lived it and experientially proved it, that success is "the ability to go from failure to failure without ever losing your enthusiasm". What a winning attitude with such an optimistic regard for life and success! As faithful followers of the Lord Jesus Christ, we must develop an attitude that is positive, proactive, passionate, productive so as to be prolific and persuasive in our impact and influence.

4. The Beauty of BALANCE.
Isaiah 11:1 & 37:31: A shoot will come up from the stump of Jesse; from his roots a branch will bear fruit... Once more a remnant of the house of Judah will take root below and bear fruit above.

We must learn to grow deep and strong roots in order to bear much rich and lasting fruit, for it is the root that determine the fruit. No root no fruit. No direction no destination.

Blessed are the balanced for they shall outwit, outwork, outrun, outlast and out give everyone else.

Avoid extreme excesses so that you may achieve real successes. And that takes good balance. Too much good is bad for you; too much light blinds the eyes; too much oil quenches the wick; and too much blessing will become a curse.

Benjamin Franklin's rule of life: Nothing brings more pain than too much pleasure; nothing brings more bondage than liberty.

Life is like riding a bicycle. To keep your balance, you must keep moving. --- Albert Einstein.

The compass and the clock: An analogy of a balanced life:

The clock measures time while the compass measures direction. The clock represents the incessant and unending busy human activities and speed, while the compass points to life's direction and destination. The life lesson we can draw from this analogy is quite obvious: while activities in our life are important, they are not the same as accomplishments. In order for one to be happy in life, tie it to a lofty goal, not a person or an object. And in order to be meaningful and fulfilling, life must have purpose and priority. Action without direction is like an octopus on a roller skate: there is plenty of motion and commotion, but there is no sense of purpose or direction. To achieve a well-balanced life of stability and strength, we (Yang, P. 213-214) offer these simple and practical suggestions for your consideration and application:

A. Define and identify your life purpose and priority by developing your core values based on your faith system;
B. Distinguish and determine between the important and the urgent, knowing well that what's urgent may not always be what's really important (the tyranny of the urgent);
C. Do what you can with what you have by focusing on What's Important Now (WIN), in terms of the essentiality and in light of eternity;
D. Reflect in order to create more effect. With the help of the Scripture, the Spirit, and mentors, be constantly reflective in order to obtain the right perspective to become more effective. Accurate assessments enhance future improvements.
E. Maximize your strengths and minimize your weaknesses.
F. Learn from those who exemplify and epitomize excellence to better yourself. In order to get ahead in life, you must learn to get along with others;
G. Relax and rejoice with a heart of gratitude and a spirit of contentment after giving your very best efforts. This way, you will live a life of balance and beauty and bountifulness in three directions and dimensions: upward with God, inward with the self, and outward with others (Isaiah 6:1-9), living a life with no regret, no reserve, no retreat and never retire.

The Success Insider: Seven Special Steps to your Success – Please read Psalm 1 and then internalize these success steps.

A. Spiritual Intimacy --- private, personal and daily quiet time with the Lord in the Word and pray in the Spirit (John 15:4-7).

B. **Personal Identity** --- You are what God says you are. You know who you are because you know whose you are (Acts 27: 23).
C. **Serious Industry** --- always be diligent to apply yourself. The more you are diligently obedient, the more you will be victoriously abundant (Lk 5:1-11).
D. **Christian Liberty** --- You know the truth and the truth has set you free. You are free in the Son and you are free indeed (Jh 8:31—32, II Cor 3:17).
E **Kingdom Authority** --- "I have given you authority…" (Lk 10:19).
F. **Abundant Victory** --- Anyone born of God will overcome the world, and this is the victory that has already overcome the world, even by faith in Christ Jesus the Lord (I Jh 5:4).
G. **Prosperity, Glory and Eternity** --- You shall prosper in all things as you trust and obey all His commandments (III Jh 2), and you will certainly hear the gracious loving Father say to you, "Well done, my good and faithful servant! Enter into the joy of your Lord." (Matt 25: 21).

5. The Law of Habit: We Are What We Repeatedly Do!

The success of your life depends on your daily routines. You are what you repeatedly and habitually do. Excellence is an art won by training and habituation. We do not act rightly because we have virtues or excellence, but rather we have those because we have acted rightly and consistently. Excellence, therefore, is not an act; it is a habit. (Aristotle). The only way you can have good habits is by constant learning and seriously practicing on a regular basis until it becomes your second nature, so to speak. Every once in a while, all of us must be reminded of the fundamental principle and successive sequence of sowing and reaping. We all know that we reap what we sow, the kingdom law emphatically instructed and illustrated in many biblical passages. Sow thoughts, we will reap actions; sow actions, we will reap habits; sow habits, we will reap our character; sow character we will reap our destiny. Good habits develop good character that will guide us to great destiny! There are 7 major goal-oriented habits of successful people (www.briantracy.com) that are quite helpful for us all:

A. They are goal oriented, goal setters and go-getters.
B. They are results driven through continuous learning and effective time management.
C. They are action oriented. You have the power within you to push aside your fears and overcome procrastination, and to take bold actions.
D. They are people oriented. Focus on being more pleasant with people in life is a great way to promote a positive and productive thinking lifestyle.
E. They are health conscious, knowing that their health is the single most important thing they have.
F. They are honest people of integrity who practice the "reality principle" of complete objectivity.
G. They are self-disciplined. The ability to master and control yourself is the single most important quality to develop and it guarantees all the other habits to work out smoothly and successfully.

The Yang Spiritual Strategies for Successful Stewardship:

A. Knowing that God is always the sovereign owner of all things, and that He is at work most assuredly with creative energies;
B. As a faithful steward for the Lord, functioning by faith and with fruit at managing God's businesses;
C. Working diligently and intelligently, honor the Lord with your labor;
D. Saving rigorously to build up liquidity for emergency and lay down a firm foundation for prosperity;
E. Budgeting strictly to spend wisely --- The best one to reach prosperity is to increase your income and to decrease your outgo, thus creating a good healthy margin; for if your outgo becomes bigger than your income, then your upkeep will be your downfall!

F. Preventing and demolish any debt occurrence aggressively and mercilessly;
G. Training up your children and others responsibly by both of your precepts and your visible example;
H. Investing wisely and consistently with a long-term view;
I. Giving purposefully and generously;
J. Enjoying life as a gift of God with family and friends joyfully and gratefully. Here is one of our fundamental philosophy of life: Endure the hardships of life without complaints; and enjoy the blessings of life without guilt.

A Personal Financial Testimony

Deuteronomy 28:1 If you fully obey the LORD your God and carefully follow all his commands I give you today, the LORD your God will set you high above all the nations on earth.28:2 All these blessings will come upon you and accompany you if you obey the LORD your God:28:9 The LORD will establish you as his holy people, as he promised you on oath, if you keep the commands of the LORD your God and walk in his ways.28:10 Then all the peoples on earth will see that you are called by the name of the LORD , and they will fear you.28:12 The LORD will open the heavens, the storehouse of his bounty, to send rain on your land in season and to bless all the work of your hands. You will lend to many nations but will borrow from none.28:13 The LORD will make you the head, not the tail. If you pay attention to the commands of the LORD your God that I give you this day and carefully follow them, you will always be at the top, never at the bottom.

III John 2 — Beloved, I wish above all things that thou mayest prosper and be in health, even as thy soul prospereth.

The Threefold Blessings (salvation, health and prosperity) in the great gracious and glorious Gospel of Christ can be clearly observed in the Biblical verse above and amply verified throughout the entire Scripture and validated in our life experiences of following and serving the Lord heart and sou. For much more details as to how to apply them to your life and ministries, do please read the book by Pastor David Cho listed in the bibliography at the end of the book. We firmly believe these as part and parcel of the whole counsel of God for His children as that we can be credible and powerful testimonies in this increasingly dark and desperate world of dubious ambiguity, confusion and suspicion. No wonder the Lord God both verbally declared and actually demonstrated in Deuteronomy chapters 8 and 28, that it is He who has given us the abilities and the power to acquire wealth so as to establish His covenant with us, and so that we in turn will be blessed abundantly to bless others generously! This indeed is promise made and promise kept especially in the cases of the most outstanding and peculiar of all people's, the Jewish people, and the God-fearing Christians. We must likewise spiritually conceive, firmly believe, and consistently and constantly behave before we can abundantly receive and achieve! When God sees your faith in action as you sow the seeds (Mk 2:5), He will make miracles happen to meet the needs, increase our faith, validate our testimony and manifest His power and glory so that other peoples and nations can see and know our faith in the Jehovah Jireh Jesus!

   I (Hong) was born literally in a little mud house in a poverty-stricken rural village outside Anyang, Henan Province in central China. And so was Esther, my wife of 33 years now who was my childhood sweetheart from the same dusty impoverished village. Like every poor villager and struggling peasant I knew in that oppressive atheistic communist Maoist system, we learned through daily experiences the reality of fear, hunger and starvation, with tales of even cannibalism in the early 1960's. In order to survive physically, along with other little boys, I often had to dig grass roots, peel barks off elm trees and collect willow leaves to cook and eat. For literally two years, my family of 4 did not even have one single meal with any meat whatsoever as it was a huge luxury, even as rice was in China then. We barely had enough sorghum or corn to eat and survive, and corn has been culturally considered "food" fit only to feed pigs and cows. Simple wheat would be a huge luxury for us peasants as the lowest echelon of the Chinese society.

No one was allowed to own even one inch of land then and it's still the same today. Everyone had to work in the so-called "People's Commune" and lived strictly with daily rationing quotas which left us starving all the time, so hungry with grumbling stomach pains that I could not fall a sleep many a night. Even as a teenager, I literally begged for the communist brigade leaders to assign me as much work as possible to make a little extra money. In order to make a few more extra "points of merit", which meant a few more pennies or dollars to be earned at the end of the year, I tried to sell sesame candies on foot, clean chicken houses, and collect donkey and cow droppings (for sale as fertilizers) along the dirty roads from village to village on an old bicycle borrowed from my dad. I tried my very best with a strong sense of responsibility and personal discipline as the first-born to help my dad provide for the family. In the face of extreme and abject societal poverty and my mother's frequent illnesses, I was determined to better my situation and improve myself and my family financially with diligence, intelligence, sheer will power and creativity. And as a result, I was a lot better off than all my teenage playmates and peers of my village, most of whom had neither clue to life nor ambition for anything lofty in life.

In addition to all the odd jobs I could find and do during the weekends and the summers, I studies very hard as I always believed intuitively that education would improve my economy as it led to imagination and innovation. For a village boy like me, making it to college to study then was about the only way to move out of boring and humiliating peasantry and poverty, and move up in society. No one in the entire Yang clan had even finished high school at the time. Thankfully I was both fond of and good at studies. Fortunately I was admitted into Henan University in the summer 1981 with a full scholarship through the cut-throat national examinations and competitions, as the only student who made it out of the 150 high school graduates in my hometown. Needless to say, I was surely flabbergasted and highly elated beyond words, knowing that the new direction would determine my future destiny!

In Kaifeng the famous beautiful and ancient city famed for eight Chinese dynasties where Henan University has been located for over 100 years now, I again believed in myself and actively pursued academics. I applied myself daily till mid night studying as an English major and a Japanese minor. There were many scholars I admired and thus perspired to aspire to be one like them. No gains no gains as the saying goes. Well, hard work with determination and discipline really paid off. New knowledge and skills and connections were acquired to open new doors for further growth and greater prosperity. Besides being a top student with academic excellence, I worked as a family tutor and summer middle school teacher and make "a lot" of money for myself and my family. Not only did I proactively made money with every opportunity I got, I wasted none of it and saved most of it, and gave some to my family In need. Dad was surprised when I presented him was a few hundred dollars, when the average pay was only $20-30 a month as a coal minor or teacher! My savings account began to accumulate substantially in the local bank when most of the students had no money at all. I felt like living in financial prosperity like my father never had experienced. I was determined, disciplined and decisive with the belief to this day that opportunity of a life time must be grasped hold of during the life time of that opportunity for time and tide wait for no one. I was both hungry and eager to move up! Yet in spite of whatever little successes I accumulated materially and academically, deep down in ,y soul, I was lonely lost and miserable for more: meaning, purpose and truth in the midst of all the obvious lies going around. I was searching for spiritual significance and personal worth. I faced several personal and family issues as well. When I was very disappointed and deeply depressed, I got into drinking and smoking and did not even want to live any longer.

 Then, by the grace of God and to be glory of God, I finally heard of the Gospel of Christ for the first time ever in the fall of 1983 when I was already 20 years old while studying English and American literature which contained lots of Bible references and quotations. I was totally clueless as to what the authors were talking about, as we had always been, to this day, taught in China that religion is superstition and that there is no God of any kind. Providentially,

Faith and Finances

however, a Bible was made available to me soon afterwards. Jesus miraculously saved me by the power of His Word and by the conviction of His Holy Spirit in my soul as I read that rare KJV Bible (which was classified and condemned as spiritual pollution and western pornography) from cover to cover in two weeks with great hunger and eagerness. I had never felt such compassionate love, unspeakable joy, glorious hope, and the peace from the Prince which surpasses all knowledge and understanding, the peace and the purpose that I never had in twenty long years as an atheist and communist youth leader. Under the compelling conviction of the Holy Spirit and by the peerless power of the Word of God, I joyfully and gratefully followed Rom 10:9-10 and surrendered my heart and life to Jesus! I was gloriously and miraculously saved without even knowing a believer or heRing an evangelist! To God and Christ alone be all the praises and glory as He continues to empower me with victory!

Furthermore, the wise Jewish proverbs of the Old Testament and the fascinating powerful parables of Jesus in the New Testament made an indelible impact on my life, my faith and my finances as 80% of these proverbs and along with well over 2000 Bible verses have to do with money and wealth from the historical, Jewish, spiritual and eternal perspective. To say the least, I was greatly intrigued, interested and inspired to apply all these principles of wisdom to my life with actual practices and personal experiences. And over the past 30 years, they have worked wonderfully in our lives and ministries all over the world as infallible and universal Gospel truths. The results speak eloquently for themselves.

A fabulous funnel of God's favors came to my life as I earnestly and sincerely followed and practiced the Biblical principles of faith and finances with much fervor and force! God touched the hearts of two American Christian professors teaching English in China to help me with an open door and a handshake money of $20. The gracious Lord additionally moved miraculously my university authority to assist me, without me applying for or or asking them, and with them not knowing my financial situation, they decided to give me the urgently needed $2700 to cover all my travel expenses for my graduate study in the "School of Technology" for His global ministries in Cleveland, Tn, USA! My soul He indeed graciously saved and satisfied, and all my needs He more than supplied! What a great and marvelous God we serve! Praise the Lord Jesus for His powerful Word, divine wisdom, supernatural power, for our health, healing and the glorious hope we have in Him, as Colossians1:27 definitively declares that God has chosen to make known among the Gentiles the glorious riches of this mystery, which is Christ in you, the hope of glory!

Thanks be unto God who has provided us with more than enough so that we can live, move and serve as more than conquerors ((ROM 8:37) through Jesus our Lord who loves and strengthens us daily as a couple (known to others as the Dynamic Duo!) throughout the past 33 years in these good ole United States of America, the land of the free, and the home of the brave! Praise God for the church and God bless the USA! With the $20 seed money from Prof. Murl Dirksen in my pocket and by the sufficient gracious favors of God, I came to the USA and started my American sojourn on Sept 3, 1985! I was able to successfully finish 3 masters and 2 doctorates from 4 fully-accredited, wonderful institutions of higher learnings, all in 7 years and all with full scholarships, often working on two degrees simultaneously, serving as teaching assistant and research fellow, always doing part-time jobs on the side, making, saving, giving and investing money little by little and step by step. Praises be unto the Lord that Dr. Esther Yang finally joined me in the USA after our 8 days of marriage in China and almost 3 long years away from each other. Because of active diligence and special

God-given intelligence, she was divinely favored as well with more blessed results spiritually, academically and financially, just as the Proverbs 31 woman, a woman of authentic spirituality, realistic practicality, affluence, influence, prosperity and generosity. We were able to buy our first home in cash from hard work and scholarship savings as foreign students. Furthermore, God blessed us with two exceptional and beautiful daughters, medical Dr. Christina (29) and soon-to-be Theological Dr Lucinda (26) who are both very spiritual and successful and distinguished in their respective fields. With consistent diligence and God-given intelligence, along with good healthy habits of life, they have both greatly excelled at a young age with many achievements, rewards, and distinctions beyond our wild imaginations too. Hallelujah!

    1989 was a very special year for us as a couple and a family in Johnson City TN. I passed my oral and written exams as a licensed minister with the Church of God (Cleveland Tn USA); our first daughter Christina was born; we became permanent residents in America, and I earned my Ed.D from East Tn State University. Wow, so many great happenings! In the fall of 1989 as I was fully accepted by Harvard University to go for my post-doctorate, Church of God World Missions General Director Dr. Lovell Cary personally called us and invited us to join the department as Missionary Educators as he told us we were really needed in Asia and Latin America. After much thoughts and prayers together with Esther, I decided to give up Harvard and go for Missions! We moved to Cleveland TN at once, and we were to be paid $1000 monthly for a family of three from the fund we'd raise for our Hong & Esther Yang Ministries. We gladly accepted the offer, without reservation, question or hesitation, knowing it was God who touched Lovell to call us to serve Him. We started out by borrowing the first $1000 from Missions General Account so as to rent a cheap apartment with donated old furniture and buy grocery since we had nothing in our missions project number to start with. We were nevertheless, so excited, blessed and grateful to serve the Lord gladly wherever we could be used to win souls and make disciples!

    Hallelujah to the Jehovah Jireh who is our gracious and generous Provider! My God shall supply all your needs according to the riches of His glory in Christ so that we can do all things through Christ who strengthens us (Phil 4:13,19) with more than enough and who empowers us to live and lead as more than conquerors! For instance, on the very first Sunday for our deputation for missions in one church (not even a mega church) in Charlotte NC, the Lord provided us with an amazing amount, $45,000 in cash along with powerful prophetic utterances in tongues and with interpretations to edify us, affirm us and confirm with both premises and promises as this: "My child, My child, if you will stay pure and humble in Me and remain faithful to Me, then I will help you; I will strengthen you; I will bless and uplift you to do my will and finish my work! And for my glory and honor, you shall live and serve!" To this very day 29 years later, my wife and I still remember it well as if it were only yesterday! How amazing is our God!

Upon paying back the borrowed $1000 to the missions department's General Account, our personal missions account under Yang Ministries project number still had $44,000 as the remaining balance, and to this very day after almost 30 long years, it has never gone down below that number. On the contrary, the account has greatly increased and multiplied to millions upon millions of dollars to support and bless many special missions projects in dozens of nations and meet many missions needs around the world. Numerous international and missional leaders have been granted scholarships for their training so they can, and now are training actively many more. This is a Mission of Multiplication as the Lord demonstrated with the five loaves and two fish. Praise the Lord Jesus for allowing me to minister in a hundred some nations, and for using Dr Esther and me together as a team as His faithful, fervent, forceful, and fruitful conduits for His purpose, and as passionate, dynamic, pure and proven vessels for His glory and for the glorious global cause of Christ!

Indeed we are so abundantly blessed, and we are blessed to be a blessing to others in both faith and finances, both spiritually and materially, beyond measure, for no one can give what he or she does not have! And as we give, much more will be given to us, as Jesus emphatically teaches and practices in Luke 6:38, along with the productive and prolific and very profitable Matthew Effect (Matt 25:29). The mission of the Lord as stated succinctly is to give us life and that we might have His life More abundantly. So must we live out our lives and carry out our missions for Jesus with More abundance of faith and finances to increase and grow and bear much more lasting fruit (Jh 15:2) for Jesus greater glory and more praises to His holy and worthy name!

As we review the past with gratitude and joy, we also live the present with passion and purpose and power. We boldly embrace the future with the Jeremiah 29:11 promise and with confidence and hope (Rom 15:4,13) as Christ in us is the hope of glory. Since our future will be as victorious and bright as the powerful promises of our God, let us learn life lessons from all the heroes of faith, and live and lead by examples so as to inform, inspire others and invest in them. Let us invite them and involve them in faith and finances so that they also can increase and influence many others. In order to accomplish this aim, let us become more active and not passive, more optimistic and not pessimistic, more positive and not negative, more grateful and not greedy, more content and not covetous, in our humble and faithful services for the King of kings and the Lord of lords, the Author and the Perfecter of our most holy faith, Jesus Christ, who alone is able to do in us and through us exceedingly, abundantly, and immeasurably more than all that we can even think, ask or imagine, according to the power that is at work within us (Eph 3:20). To Him be all the glory, all the honors, and all the praises both now and forevermore, Amen!

Reflections and Applications

Theology is the study of the things of God, and a personal theology is the formation of your own personal convictions and beliefs concerning the things divine. It is through our personal theology that we form our strong beliefs regarding the way God works in every aspect of our daily life. How we believe in God and how we see Him at work will influence and affect how we behave and what we do. And what we do will produce the results which further impact our beliefs.

Hong has developed a personal theology that can be summarized in ten words: Trust Deep, AIM High, Work Hard, Live Well, and Die Laughing. This comes out of a deep conviction in the heart, and out of it is the formation of the goals of our life. Of the many goals in life, the highest one has to be the preparation of eternity in heaven to meet with our Maker. The lowest goal is to go to the bottomless pit of everlasting flames of torments in hell. Therefore, it is always better to set your goal high and heavenwards. With specific goals in various areas of our lives, we begin to work diligently and consistently towards their achievements. Goals becomes vain and faith become futile when we do not apply ourselves. Life becomes nothing and it's going no where without lofty goals and the corresponding efforts required.

As we work hard to achieve goals, we will have a sense of achievements and fulfillments and develop a sense of worth and importance as our faith also gets stronger through the things we do. As a results of the accomplishments, we need to learn to enjoy the fruit of our labor as the simple pleasures of life, the gifts of God for us. . As the Jewish proverbs goes, Enjoy your life now for it is not a rehearsal! We need to be heavenly minded, but at the same time we get to enjoy the things that God has graciously created for us on earth, thus living a life with no remorse, and no regret, as we get ready to meet the Maker!

Here are a few questions for you to ask yourselves and apply to your life:

1. What are the three most important goals you'd like to accomplish in this life on earth? And why are they so important to you?
2. What are the specific ways you have developed to effectively achieve your goals?
3. What are some of the simple pleasures of life that you really enjoy?

Chapter 15

Living a Life that Really Matters
A Passion for the Kingdom

Rom 12:1-2 --- I beseech you therefore, brethren, by the mercies of God, that you present your bodies a living sacrifice, holy, acceptable to God, which is your reasonable service. And do not be conformed to this world, but be transformed by the renewing of your mind, that you may prove what is that good and acceptable and perfect will of God.

Rom 12: 11-12. Never be lacking in zeal, but keep your spiritual fervor (fire, passion, enthusiasm), serving the Lord. Be joyful in hope, be patient in affliction, and be faithful in prayer.

Ephesians 5:15-18 --- Be very careful, then, how you live --- not as unwise but as wise, making the most of every opportunity, because the days are evil. Therefore, do not be foolish, but understand what the Lord's will is. Do not get drunk on wine, which leads to debauchery. Instead, be filled with the Holy Spirit.

Matt 6:33 --- But seek first the kingdom of God and His righteousness, and all that you need will be added unto you.

Matt 11:12 --- From the days of John the Baptist until now, the kingdom of heaven has been forcefully advancing, and forceful men lay hold of it.

Matt 13: 11, 31, 33, 44, 47 --- The knowledge of the secrets of the kingdom of heaven has been given to you... The kingdom of heaven is like a mustard seed... The kingdom of heaven is like yeast... The kingdom of heaven is like a treasure hidden in the field... Once again the kingdom of heaven is like a net that was let down into the lake and caught all kinds of fish.

Matt 16:18-19 --- And I tell that you are Peter, and on this rock I will build my church, and the gates of Hades will not overcome it. I will give you the keys of the kingdom of heaven

Mk 3:24-25 --- If a kingdom is divided against itself, that kingdom cannot stand. If a house is divided against itself, that house cannot stand.

Lk 9:62 --- No one who puts his hand to the plow and looks back is fit for service in the kingdom of God.

Lk 17:20-21 --- The kingdom of God does not come visibly... because the kingdom of God is within you.

Jh 3:3, 5 --- I tell you the truth, unless a man is born again, he cannot see the kingdom of God... Unless a man is born of water and of the Spirit, he cannot enter the kingdom of God.

Jh 18:36 --- Jesus said, "My kingdom is not of this world."

Matt 24:14 --- And this gospel of the kingdom will be preached in the whole world as a testimony to all nations, and then the end will come.

The central message of the Sermon on the Mount (Matt 5-7) is this: Orient yourself properly and aim for paradise. Then and only then — concentrate on today. Set your sights at the Good, the Beautiful, and the True, and then you focus pointedly and carefully on the concerns of each moment. Aim continually at Heaven while you work diligently on Earth. Attend fully to the future, in that manner, while attending fully to the present. Then you will have the best chance of perfecting both — Peterson, P. 359

Without any doubt whatsoever, the Lord Jesus taught and preached more on the Kingdom of God and the Kingdom of Heaven than any other topics in the whole Bible. He spoke on the Kingdom over 200 times. This is because what is frequent is important and what is important is frequent. What is important has to be made clear and what is clear is important! For the followers and disciples of the Lord Jesus Christ who truly desire to live their lives that really matter eternally, lives that impact and influence people for His purpose, His cause and His mission both locally and globally, we must first of all understand the will of God by our disciplined daily deep devotions to the Word of God, for no one can understand His perfect Will apart from His powerful Word. The Word of God not only contains the will of God for us, it is the will of God, just as Jesus who comes not just to give us peace, but He Himself is our shalom, our peace, and the true source of our prosperity. He does not just show us the light and the way, Jesus the Lord is the light and the way (John 8:12, 14:6)! It is through the precious, powerful, piercing and peerless Word of God that we know the will of God, obtain the wisdom of God, see and know the way of God in operation, develop the resolve to daily walk with God, receive the special encouragement to go and do the work of God! And since we can not get the job done alone by ourselves, in the bodily strength, therefore it is expedient that we must be filled and refilled by the anointing, the authority and the power of the Holy Spirit of God, endued with power to witness to and to disciple others for Jesus faithfully, fearlessly, forcefully and fruitfully all over the world! The Great Commission is not a great suggestion for us to consider; It is a command for us to obediently carry out. This is a no negotiable must for us all as authentic Christ followers!!

The Holy Spirit has indeed clearly revealed to us the mind of Christ (I Cor 2:9-16) and the will of God for us in the Holy Scriptures, including fifteen major aspects of the will of God in Christ Jesus concerning the children of God. This can be summed up in one of my all-time favorite biblical portions found in I Thessalonians 5:16-24 with the brief following outline. Let us read the passage now, as you will note in Verse 18 emphatically stating, "For this is God's will for you in Christ Jesus".

I Thess 5:16 Be joyful always;5:17 pray continually;5:18 give thanks in all circumstances, for this is God's will for you in Christ Jesus.5:19 Do not put out the Spirit's fire;5:20 do not treat prophecies with contempt.5:21 Test everything. Hold on to the good.5:22 Avoid every kind of evil.5:23 May God himself, the God of peace, sanctify you through and through. May your whole spirit, soul and body be kept blameless at the coming of our Lord Jesus Christ.5:24 The one who calls you is faithful and he will do it.

1. God wants His children to Be Joyful always (V. 16);
2. God wants His children to Be Prayerful incessantly (V. 17);
3. God wants His children to Be Thankful in all circumstances (V.18);
4. God wants His children to Be Fiery in the Holy Spirit (V. 19);
5. God wants His children to Be Prophetic (V. 20);
6. God wants His children to Be Discreet and Discernible in all spiritual matters (V. 21);
7. God wants His children to Be Careful in avoiding all kinds of evil (V. 22), including excessive indebtedness;
8. God wants His children to Be Peaceful (V. 23) as peace makers;
9. God wants His children to Be Holy (V. 23); as the Lord God Himself is holy;
10. God wants His children to Be Holistic and complete in our spirit, soul and body (V. 23);
11. God wants His children to Be Blameless at the coming of the Lord (V. 23);
12. God wants His children to Be Prepared and Ready for Him (V. 23), like the wise virgins in Matt 25, and not as the five foolish ones;

13. God wants His children to be Focused on His call in our lives (V. 24), not getting sidetracked by all the temptations, distractions and by our own human tendency of procrastination;
14. God wants His children to Be Faithful stewards and soldiers for His cause as He who has called us is always faithful (V. 24);
15. God wants His children to Be Confident and Courageous, as He will do it (V. 24) in us, for us, and through us, and ultimately for the good of man and the glory of God!

Seven More Steps To Achieve Your Kingdom Objectives

1. Develop a Scriptural, spiritual and eternal Kingdom perspective.
2. Be always positive and proactive and then you will be very productive.
3. See clearly the prospective.
4. Consider always another alternative.
5. Offer sufficient incentive. By the very human nature of fallenness, most of the people most of the time are motivated by the "self" as it is clearly stated in Luke 9:23 by Jesus and by His faithful and wise apostle James (4:1-3). People are often much too occupied and even obsessed with their self-image for self-serving and self-preserving in an attempt to achieve self-confidence, self-esteem, self-fulfillment, and self-actualization, as Dr. Abraham Maslow pointed out long ago along in his famous hierarchy of human needs. Based on this accurate understanding of humanity, the spiritual steward must learn to be an effective motivator and mobilizer of people according to the level of their real and legitimate needs and try to meet the needs with relevant deeds for a higher Kingdom purposes. Sow a seed to meet a need so that you will earn your right to feed and thus to lead! This is an integral and indeed vital part of Christian discipleship and leadership which extend to stewardship.

6. Take bold and personal initiative.
7. Be constantly reflective and active, and you will be effective to reach your God-ordained Kingdom objective.

Foundational Principles and Fundamental Practices for Kingdom Advances: What, How and Why

What: Live Biblically; Think Theologically; Engage Locally, and Reach Globally

Live Biblically --- The Holy Bible, the inspired inerrant and authoritative Word of God, is our absolute standard for victorious, abundant and prosperous living (Deut 28). If we obey its instructions, we will be blessed with correction, protection and direction for peace purpose and prosperity with Kingdom passion!

Think Theologically --- Come and let us reason together (Isaiah 1:18). The mind is a terribly thing to waste! God has endowed us with mental capacities for His glory! Let my people think according to the mind of Christ! And as we think spiritually and theologically, we will live prophetically, persuasively and prolifically. As a man thinks in his heart, so is he (Prov 23:7). We are what we think. And as the mind goes, the man and the money follow, because what is in your head will eventually determine what will be in your hand!

Engage Locally --- Engage yourself in your local church and community to train and teach by both of your authoritative precepts and your authentic example, living consistently and leading constantly with His indispensable principles and practices and with an indisputable pattern of Godliness with contentment which is great gain (I Tim 6:6).

Reach Globally --- Once we have established local influence, Christ followers must extent and expand its impact globally. This is the "glocalization" of the Great Commandment and the Great Commission! Go ye into all the world and preach the Gospel to all creation. Since world missions is the heart of God, it must be the motor of the healthy and vibrant church of Christ! Go quickly and tell, and until all have heard! This commission must become our passion to be carried out forcefully with great concoction and compassion!

How — Luke 14:25-35 --- The costs of discipleship, stewardship and leadership

1. Make up the mind --- No hesitation, no reservation, for genuine faith is No doubt, as genuine hope is No disappointment, and genuine love is No fear!

2. Count the cost --- Always look before you leap. Always pray before you proceed. Always analyze before you finalize or you will agonize! Always discern before you decide with the help of a reliable guide. Sit down and consider all the expenses, and calculate all that's needed with the development of a wise, realistic written budget to be strictly followed and reinforced.

3. Take the necessary risk --- All aspects of worthwhile human endeavors have certain amount and level of risks associated with them. No one can "play it safe" all the time. Don't waste your life trying to "play safe" and thus subtly being played by the devil of fears and mediocrity without your awareness; rather dare to take calculated risks physically, spiritually and materially for a higher cause and the higher calling of Christ. Be willing and be prepared to risk your life for Jesus, and even lose your life for Him, and then you will find it maximized and multiplied with joyful fulfillments and bountiful rewards (John 12:24). This is an infallible Kingdom law of the harvest concerning sowing generously and reaping abundantly.

4. Accept the responsibility --- Remember this fabulous formula as follows: Responsibility + Intentionality = Maturity, just as in: Industry + Frugality = Prosperity. Living the Kingdom life responsively and responsibly will mature and strengthen us spiritually and expand us exponentially!

5. Pay the price --- As we study Acts 1:8 in relation to Acts 8:1, a clear pattern emerges about paying the price of persecution and procuring the prize of power for the growth and expansion of the Kingdom of God. Revelations 2:10 reinforces this connection and principle by admonishing us not to be fearful, but to be faithful in the presence of evil and hardships of life, "Be Thou faithful unto

death (the cross), and I will give thee the crown of life." If we will be willing to do our part, our Lord is always ready to do His part. And this is true again in all areas and aspects of our lives, be it physical, relational, psychological, spiritual and financial (Lev 26 & Deut 28). No premise, No promise; No pains, No gains; No endurance, No enjoyment; No tears of sowing, No joy of reaping. No sacrifices, No successes; and no cross of death, then there would be no crown of life.

Why — Of all the journalistic questions of who, what, when, where and how, the most important and the most penetrating of all life's perplexities and complexities is the question "why", for it seeks the root cause of true intention and heart motive! Why am I here on earth, and why am I doing what I am doing? Life must have meaning, and the wise learns the art and the science of meaning making. Everything in life has a purpose. When we fully understand and are profoundly convicted of the purpose of life, we become bold, active, persistent and profitable. The well-known literary giant in American literature, Mark Twain once declared that "there are only two dates one needs to remember for his life to have meaning and fulfillment: the day when you were born, and the day when you discovered why! The more we know the why of life, the more we will experience the wow of it. As a couple, we are now more convinced by our experiences of living and ministering for the Lord (he who has experienced God has no need to explain God; and he who insists on explaining God shows clearly that he has not been really experiencing God!) that the deeper our faith in Him, the greater will be our favors and finances from Him as faith does increase finances and finances do increase faith. And the more we are blessed with His special favor, the less will be our toilsome labor!

Here is the passionate purpose Jesus the Lord coming down on earth, which serves as a model of motivation for us all His followers:

Mark 1:37 and when they found him, they exclaimed: "Everyone is looking for you!" 1:38 Jesus replied, "Let us go somewhere else--

to the nearby villages--so I can preach there also. That is why I have come."

John4:34 "My food," said Jesus, "is to do the will of him who sent me and to finish his work.

John12:27 "Now my heart is troubled, and what shall I say? 'Father, save me from this hour'? No, it was for this very reason I came to this hour.

We (Esther and Hong, as many have called us :the Dynamic Duo") have, by the grace of God, taught and preached the Word many times in many places all over the world. It is our conviction that in order to live a happy and blessed life of joyful satisfaction and fulfillment with the proper balance, we must deal with four life essentials, as the Lord Jesus clearly declared to us and convincingly demonstrated to us: (1). Our origin: where we came from; (2). Our identity: who we are, or whose we are (Acts 27:23, Ps 100); (3). Our purpose: why we are here on earth for such a time as this; and finally (4). Our destiny: Is this all there is to this thing called "life"? If not, then where will I be going after all this? The legendary founder of the school of Logo-Therapy Viktor Frankl who survived Hitler's Nazi concentration camp once concluded by saying that those who have a 'why' to live can bear with almost any 'how'. The search for meaning of life has been the central quest for humanity from the beginning. Life meaning enables us to make sense of our existence in spite of guilt, shame, injustices, suffering, chaos, and the inevitability of death. It also gives us a new perspective for our times in which the cults of success with no significance and hedonism dominate. Meaning analysis focuses our attention on the human spirit as the key source for recapturing health, wholeness and the caring of the holistic human person. It emphasizes the importance of us "human beings as value-bearers who are able to learn from the past, to live responsibly in the present, and to plan hopefully for the future." (Gould, 1993, P. xii). Dr. William Gould succinctly pinpoints the central affirmations of Frankl's logo-therapy:

1. Life has meaning;
2. Life with meaning is our central motivation for living;
3. We have the will and freedom to find meaning in how we think and in what we do;
4. We are mind, body and spirit, and they are interdependent with each other;
5. The human spirit is the key to enable us to exercise our will to meaning, to envisage our goals, and to move beyond our instinctual and impulsive needs to self-transcendence.

Scripturally speaking, we have been entrusted as spiritual and responsible stewards with four major reasons as to why we must embrace and extend the missional mandate of the Kingdom of God on earth before the second coming of the King of kings and the Lord of lords. Please open your Bible and prayerfully study these passages as they will challenge and inspire you to aim higher as your goal, go deeper in your thinking, and act bolder for the cause of Christ!

1. A Command from above – Matt 28:18-20.
2. A cry from beneath --- Luke 16: 19-31.
3. A call from without --- Acts 16:6-10.
4. A conviction from within --- I Cor 9:19-23.

A Kingdom Passion in 8 Dynamic Dimensions: MORE!

Jesus Christ: The thief cometh not, but for to steal, to kill and to destroy: I am come that they might have life, and that they might have it More abundantly! (Jh 10:10).

Jesus Christ: I am the true vine and my father is the Gardener, He cuts off every branch in me that bears no fruit, while every branch that does bear fruit he trims clean so that it will be More fruitful (Jh 15:2).

Jesus Christ: If you then, though you are evil, know how to give good gifts to your children, how much More will your Father in heaven give the Holy Spirit to those who ask him! (Lk 11:13).

Jesus Christ: For everyone who has, will be given More, that he might have abundance (Matt 25:29).

1. A passion to know King Jesus more intimately (Eph 1:17).
2. A Passion to love King Jesus more intensely (Jh 13:34-35).
3. A passion to trust King Jesus more profoundly (Is 26:3-4).
4. A passion to obey King Jesus more completely (Acts 5:29, I Sam 15:22).
5. A passion to serve King Jesus more gladly (Ps 100:2).
6. A passion to follow King Jesus more faithfully (I Cor 11:1).
7. A passion to please King Jesus more purposefully (II Cor 5:9).
8. A passion to proclaim King Jesus more boldly (Acts 4:31).

In order to do so, one must be both willing and able to serve as a vulnerable and faithful vessel, pure and clean, tried and true for the Master. Here is a anonymous and famous Christian poem I love, The Chosen Vessel which captures the essence of joyful and passionate Kingdom service, as the Lord Jesus decides and determines the right kind of earthen vessel and clay instrument to sovereignly empower and specially employ for His divine aim and eternal purpose:

The Chosen Vessel — Author Anonymous

The Master was searching for a vessel to use.
Before Him were many, which one would he choose?
"Take me," cried the golden one. "I'm shiny and bright.
I'm of great value and I do things just right.
My beauty and lust will outshine the rest.
For someone like you, Master, gold would be the best."

Faith and Finances

The Master passed on with no words at all.
And looked at a silver urn, grand and tall.
"I'll serve you Master, I'll pour out your wine.
I'll be on your table whenever you dine.
My lines are so graceful and my carving so true.
And silver will always compliment you."

Unheeding, the Master passed onto the brass,
Wide-mouthed and shallow and polished like glass.
"Here, here's!" Cried the vessel, "I know I will do,
Place me on your table for all men to view."

"Look at me," called the goblet of Crystal so clear,
"My transparency shows my content so clear.
Though fragile am I, I will serve you with pride,
And I will be happy in your house to abide."

Then the Master came next to a vessel of wood,
Polished and carved, it very solidly stood.
"You May use me, dearest Master," the wooden bowl said,
"But I'd rather you used me for fruit, not for bread."

The the Master looked down and saw a vessel of clay,
Empty and broken, it helplessly lay.
No hope had the vessel that the Master might choose,
To cleanse and to make whole, to fill and to use.

"Ah! Now this is the vessel I've been hoping to find.
I'll mend it and use it and make it mine.
I need not the vessel with pride of itself,
Nor one that is narrow to sit on the shelf,
Nor one that is big-mouthed and shallow and loud,
Nor one that displays its content so proud,
Nor the one who thinks he can do things just right.
But this plain vessel filled with power and might."

> Then gently He "Lifted up" the clay,
> Mended and cleansed it and filled it that day:
> He let the Vessel know — "There is much work to do....
> You are to pour out to others as I pour into you."

In order for us to bring the passion into fruition, the Christ followers must be better empowered and equipped with the following seven areas of emphasis:

1. Trust Deeper --- Let us trust the Lord with all of our heart and lean not on our own human understanding or carnal ingenuities! Jesus promises us perfect peace and prolific power when we are mentally and spiritually focused and stayed on Him as our source and strength (Isaiah 26:3-4)!
2. Aim Higher --- Since we have been raised with Christ, let us set our heart's affection on the things above where Christ is seated at the right hand of God. Let us set our minds on the things above and not the earthly things below (Col 3:1-2). Our aim on earth is to please Christ in every thing and in every way (II Cor 5:9) and to prepare ourselves ready for eternity.
3. Think Bigger --- Let this mind be in you which is also in Christ Jesus (Phil 2:5). Our God is a big God and let us think big as we serve a big God who loves us and empowers us to be able to do all things and to be more than conquerors (Phil 4:13, Rom 8:37). All things are possible with God and to him or her who believes, and nothing shall be impossible for God who is for us (Rom 8:31, Ps 56:9).
4. Act Bolder --- Like the early disciples of Jesus in the book of Acts, let us be filled and refilled with the outpouring of the Holy Spirit and mighty power so that we can preach Jesus and witness for Him with extraordinary boldness (Acts 4:13, 31). Courage is the mother of all virtues, and without courage there is no virtue! Cowardice counts for absolutely nothing. It is the courage to continue carrying on the cause of Christ that ultimately counts!

5. Work Harder and Smarter --- Divine Direction with human diligence and discipline determines the eternal destiny. Let us study Matthew 20 and 25, and learn lessons both positive and negative from the workers of the vineyard and the ones with 5 and 2 talents that the Lord commended as models. No hesitation, no reservation, no accusation, and no procrastination. Matthew 25:16-17 inform us that when they received the talents, these two went at once to put the money to work so as to gain more in ROI. No wonder the Jewish proverb declares to us accurately and emphatically "the wise does at once what the fool does at last!"
6. Do Better --- As we learn to work smarter and work harder, we will naturally do better! One of the Kingdom laws affirms that if we will do naturally what we can, faithfully, our Lord will do supernaturally what we can not, fruitfully, with more abundance. And if we will diligently and consistently apply our best, our God will bountifully supply all the rest with more than enough to accomplish His will and finish His work! The more we apply, the more He will supply! And this law is universal in all areas and aspects of our lives and ministries spiritually, relationally intellectually, inter-culturally and even and especially financially!
7. Achieve More --- With more and more resources achieved and accomplished, we will be able to go and win more souls and make more disciples in more. nations around the world Until All Have Heard for the glory, honor and praises of the Lord of lords and the King of king Jesus Christ! In I Thess 4:1 we learn that God desires for us to receive more and more revelation, wisdom and power so that the purpose will be that we will be able to accomplish and achieve more and more results for Jesus and His kingdom.

Reflections and Applications

The theme of the Kingdom of God or Kingdom of Heaven is an absolutely essential and vital one for us as followers of Christ. Even in the Lord's Prayer, He asked for the Kingdom of God to come on earth as it is in heaven. Throughout the Scriptures, Jesus commands it to prioritize our life by seeking first the Kingdom of God and His righteousness, and then all that you need shall be added u to us. He even likens the kingdom as a precious pearl of great price which demands our all, costs our all, and is worth our all to acquire and obtain it! Here we sees the desire of God for us to seek the kingdom, enter the kingdom, expand the kingdom of God on earth so as to be richly rewarded in heaven Because of all of our efforts for the advancement of His Kingdom. One can unmistakably see this emphasis throughout the teachings of the great Gospel especially personified in lives and ministries of the Lord Jesus and His faithful disciples such as Peter and Paul. May the kingdom of God become a personal priority and a daily reality in your own life so that you can also obtain and expand it and be greatly blessed and rewarded both on earth and in heaven!

Questions to ask yourself are:

1. What percentage of your life now is really involved in the work of the Kingdom of God?
2. How does your eternal kingdom vision affect you daily financial situation?
3. What rewards are you anticipating and expecting on earth in this life, and in heaven in eternity?

Conclusion

The final batter for Christian discipleship will be over the money problem: till this is solved, there can be no universal application of Christianity --- Balzac.

God gets our attention with our money issues, speaks to us through our financial circumstances, and teaches us useful and profitable lessons on faith and finances. No one can deny the reality that money indeed plays an enormous part in all of our lives, families, local ministries and global missions. No wonder the Holy Scriptures talk much more about this money thing with over 2350 verses than any other single topic of great importance. Fundamentally, there are always the four basic and central purposes that our Lord wants to achieve in and through us in regards to money matters we need to keep in mind and put them into practices in order to be fruitful and productive for Him and His global causes (Hughes & Kinkade, PP. 294-299):

1. The first purpose of money is to provide basic needs. To sustain the basic needs of life, we need the bare necessities of food in our stomach, clothing on our body and shelter over our head. We are to live with contentment and gratitude and thus joy, not fears, anxieties, or worries (Phil 4:6-7), as we trust the Lord for our daily needs. Give us this day our daily bread. The Lord knows that the recognition of our daily needs will help produce our daily dependence on God the Jehovah Jireh our wonderful Provider (Mt 6: 28-30). We are to seek first the Kingdom of God and His righteousness, and then the Lord will supply all our needs and necessities without fail.
2. The second purpose of money is to confirm His loving direction for our lives. One of the biggest life lessons for us

to learn in the Christian walk and work is that of discerning God's guidance through His giving or His withholding of money. God's work done in God's way will not lack God's supply; and if it is God's will, then it is God's bill. Vice versa. What is the difference between mere presumption and real faith? Faith is trusting God to achieve His purpose through us, while presumption is deciding first what we want to accomplish and then trying to get God to do it for us. God does not work that way!

3. The third purpose of money is to bless and enrich others in needs through the gift of our generosity. Acts 11:27-30 illustrates for us the mostly Gentile church of Antioch actively raising money and generously giving an offering to the needs of their fellow Jewish Christians suffering famine in Jerusalem. This act of generosity breaks down national, racial and cultural barriers, and builds bonds of genuine love in the body of Christ. This is the principle of sowing and reaping in II Cor. 9:6. The greatest of all benefits of giving is not for us the givers and them the receivers alone, but for the glory of God as it results in many overflowing and overwhelming "thanksgivings to God" (V. 12). God has blessed us to give with liberality to bless others in needs so that He Himself can be praised and glorified as all is said and done in His holy name by His own people! And as we give Him all the glory, He will empower us with more financial victory!

4. The fourth divine purpose of money is to show God's supernatural power through His miraculous provision. This demonstration of His divine provision has been recorded in many passages throughout the Word of God from Abraham to Elijah, from Jesus to all the apostles, and has been experienced by numerous people like us today in our lives and ministries. In this unique way, God declares and demonstrates once and for all that He is our Provider and Master worthy of all our adoration and obedience. Glory to God. Praise His Holy name!

Conclusion

Life Lessons from Aesop's Fable

The goose that laid the golden egg

There once was a man who owned a wonderful goose. Every morning the goose laid him a big, beautiful egg – an egg made of pure shiny, solid gold. This poor man could not believe his sudden good fortune. Every morning, the man collected the golden egg. And little by little, egg by egg, he began to grow fabulously wealthy and ridiculously rich. But the man wanted more, as his increasing wealth also increased his impatience for greed. "My goose has all those golden eggs inside her," he kept thinking. "Why not get them all at once?" One day he couldn't wait any longer. He grabbed the goose and killed her to get all the eggs inside. But there were no eggs insider her! "Why did I do that?" the man cried! "Now there is no more golden egg."

Implications and Applications

Here are the powerful and practical life lessons for us all to learn and to apply about God, gold and the goose:

Don't kill the goose that lays the golden egg. Don't cut the hands that feed you.

A short-sighted actions often destroys the long-term profitability of an asset.

Be patient, and disciplined in caring for and waiting on the goose. Short cuts never pay off in a long run!

Be grateful and responsible in taking care of the gift of God. This goose is trusted asset, representing your treasured relationships. If we care more for the blessings (eggs) than we do for the source of the blessings, the blesser (goose), we will become greedy, impatient and eventually lose both the blessings and the blesser.

As the famous old says reminds us, if a people care more for their rights than for their responsibilities, they will soon lose both!

The principle of abundance: always protect your investment and never lose your assets!

Don't be greedy. – Greed loses all by striving to gain all...Greed often over reaches itself. Greed always wants more but often loses all. The get-rich-quick schemes must be exposed and avoided. Remember it takes time for a fruit tree to grow, ripen and bear fruit. Likewise, spiritually It takes time to be holy. You can't be holy in a hurry.

Set certain boundaries and limits on our desires. Who is rich? The one who is content with what he or she has. Let us heed the Pauline admonition in I Tim 6:6 That godliness with contentment is great gain, and in 6:10 for the love of money is a root of all kinds of evil. Some people, eager for money, have wandered from the faith and pierced themselves with many griefs. What a prophetic warning against this greedy farmer!

A farmer, bent on doubling the profits from his land,
Proceeds to set his soil a two-harvest demand.
Too intent thus on profit, harm himself he must needs:
Instead of corn, he now reaps corn-cockle ad weeds.
(Ignacy Krasicki, The Farmer in www.en.m.wikipedia.org)

Be grateful and content, spiritual and realistic for His daily provision!

Be wise and frugal as a shrewd steward in its utilization!

Be faithful to endure to the end and God will make you fruitful!

Hebrews 13:5 Keep your lives free from covetousness (the love of money), and be content with what you have, because God has said, "Never will I leave you; never will I forsake you."13:6 So we say with confidence, "The Lord is my helper; I will not be afraid. What can man do to me?"

As a final summary, please make a special effort to seriously remember and personally practice these Seven Sacred Steps so that you will live with spectacular successes in your faith and finances:

1. God is the owner of everything we are and everything we have;
2. We as His stewards are to be always faithful and fruitful for Him;
3. Working hard by always acting your wage and living within and even intentionally below your means! Industry > Frugality > Prosperity > Generosity!
4. Avoiding and demolishing any debts in Your life;
5. Saving as much as possible for liquidity;
6. Investing to grow and increase for the future;
7. Giving with liberality wisely and joyfully with a plan and purpose (II Cor 9:6-7).

At the very conclusion of this book, we'd like to once again repeat the five key foundations for all critical areas and vital aspects of life, certainly not for redundancy, instead, for stronger and heavier emphases as we come to the end. These are infallible spiritual success strategies for your financial freedom, financial fitness and financial force, living a life that really matters eternally with purpose, power, passion and the indispensable process of perseverance. May these five key elements empower and equip you, as they did us, with the help of God, in your dynamic progress in both your faith and your finances:

1. Perspective --- See ye first the Kingdom of God and His righteousness; and then all that you need shall be added

unto us (Matt 6:33). Explore and examine all things and treat all peoples from His spiritual eternal Kingdom perspective. It is no secret that our perspective predicts precisely our prospect.

2. Motive --- The Lord looks only at the heart (I Sam 16:7) because it is deceitful above all things and can be desperately wicked beyond human cure (Jer 17:9). (Whatever you do, work at it with all your heart, as working for the Lord and not for men, since you know that it is from the Lord that you will receive an inheritance as a blessed eternal reward. It is the Lord Jesus Christ we trust, obey and serve!

3. Attitude --- Let this attitude be in you which is also found in Christ Jesus (Phil 2:5): the resurrection attitude of humility, purity, sensitivity, trust, obedience and sacrifices with sincere services. Then God will succinctly see your sincere faith at work and grant you with extraordinary successes!

4. Balance --- Let your moderation be known unto all men (Phil 4:5 kjv), for the Lord is at hand. When we are spiritually physically and financially balanced, we are stable, steady, stout and strong to encourage and empower many others in needs! Blessed are the balanced for they will outwit, outwork, outgive and outlast everyone else! Let us follow the rule of life given by the wise man whose image is on the largest U.S. $100 bill, Benjamin Franklin: Nothing brings more pain than too much pleasure, and nothing brings more bondage than too much liberty. Even what's seemingly a curse can turn out to be a divine blessing when viewed in a spiritual eternal perspective, and too many blessings have proven to become a terrible curse as they often and easily lead to indulgence, ingratitude, indolence and insolence!

5. Habit — If anyone would come after me, he must deny himself and take up his cross daily and follow me (Luke 9:23). One thing we know for sure is that we are what we repeatedly do. Excellence therefore is not a single act, but a consistent and constant habit. Our habits can either make us or break

us depending on what they are. So is it financially, as only 20% of one's economic strength comes from his financial information and knowledge, while 80% of his prosperity and successes really depend on his daily habitual life style. Let us be keenly aware of the good and Godly habits, and let us become more diligent and disciplined to cultivate and develop them so that we as Christ followers can become a credible, compelling, indisputably forceful and shining testimony for all to see and know, not for ourselves at all, but for the glory of God and for the good of man!

The Serenity Prayer --- Reinhold Niebuhr
God grant me the serenity to accept
the things I cannot change;
The courage to change the things I can;
and the wisdom to know the difference.
Living one day at a time;
Enjoying one moment at a time;
Accepting hardship as the path to peace;
Taking, as Jesus did, this sinful world
As it is, not as I would have it;
Trusting that He will make all things right
If I surrender to His will;
That I may be reasonably happy in this life and
supremely happy with him forever in the next.
Amen!

Bibliographic References

Alcorn, Randy (1989). *Money, Possessions and Eternity.* Wheaton IL: Tyndale House Publishers, Inc.

Alcorn, Randy (2008). *The Treasure Principle.* Colorado Springs, Co: Multnomah

Bentley, Chuck (2013). *The Worst Financial Mistakes in the Bible.* Atlanta Ga: Crown Financial Ministries, Inc.

Blue, Ron, and Michael Blue (2016). *Master Your Money.* Chicago: Moody Publishers.

Burkett, Larry (1975). *Your Finances in Changing Times.* Chicago: Moody Press.

Burkett, Larry (1987). *Answers To Your Family's Financial Questions.* Pomona, CA: Focus On The Family Publishing.

Burkett, Larry (1993). *The Complete Guide to Managing Your Money.* New York: Inspirational Press.

Cathy, S Truett (2011). *Wealth: Is It Worth It?* Decatur GA: Looking Glass Books.

Chapman, Gary (1995). *The 5 Love Languages: The secret to Love That Lasts.* Northfield Publishing House.

Charles, H.W (2016). *The Money Code: Becoming a Millionaire With the Ancient Jewish Code.* Middletown, DE.

Cho, David Yonggi (1987). *Salvation, Health & Prosperity.* Altamonte Springs, Fl: Creation House.

Clason, George S (1955), *The Richest Man In Babylon*. New York, NY: Penguin Book.

Clouse, Robert G (1984). *Wealth and Poverty: Four Christian Views of Economics*. Downers Grove, IL: Intervarsity Press.

Covey, Stephen R (2004). *The 7 Habits of Highly Effective People*. New York: Free Press.

Crosson, Russ, and Kelly Talamo (2012). *The Truth About Money Lies*. Eugene, OR: Harvest House Publishers.

Dayton, Howard L (1979). *Your Money: Frustration or Freedom?* Wheaton IL: Tyndale House Publishers, Inc.

Dayton, Howard (2011). *Your Money Counts*. Carol Stream, IL: Tyndale House Publishers, Inc.

Foster, Richard J (2009). *Money, Sex and Power: The Challenge of the Disciplined Life*. London: Holden & Stoughton Ltd.

Foster, Richard J (1988). *Celebration of Discipline*. San Francisco: Harper and Row.

Gladwell, Malcolm (2008). *Outliers: The Story of Success*. NY: Back Bay Books.

Gould, William Blair (1993). *Frankl: Life With Meaning*. Pacific Groce, Ca: Brooks/Cole Publishing Company.

Hill, Napoleon (2011). *The Law of Success*. Blacksburg, VA: Wilders Publications, Inc.

Hughes, Selwyn, and Thomas Kinkade (1997). *Every Day Light*. Nashville, TN: Broadman and Holman Publishers.

Bibliographic References

Hybels, Bill (2014), *Simplify: ten practices to unclutter your soul*. Carol Stream, IL: Tyndale House Pubishers.

Johnson, Dani (2011). *First Steps to Wealth*. Las Vegas, NV: Call to Freedom International.

Keesee, Gary (2011). *Money Mysteries from the Master: Time-Honored Financial Truths from Jesus Himself.* Shippensburg, PA: Destiny Image Publishers Inc.

Kiosaki, Robert T, and Sharon L. Lechter (1997). Rich Dad, Poor Dad. NY: Warner Business Books.

Klay, Robin K (1986). *Counting the Cost: The Economics of Christian Stewardship*. Grand Rapids, MI: William B Eerdmans Publishing Company.

Lapin, Daniel (2002). *Thou Shall Prosper: The Ten Commandments for Making Money*. Hoboken, NJ: John Wiley & Sons, Inc.

Lapin, Daniel (2014). *Business Secrets From The Bible*. Hoboken, NJ: John Wiley & Sons, Inc.

Malloch, Theodore R (2014). *Spiritual Enterprise: Doing Virtuous Business* (Chinese version translated by Fenggang Yang). Beijing: Enterprise Management Publishing House.

Martin, Jonathan (2008). *Giving Wisely*? Sisters, Or: Last Chapters Publishing.

Maxwell, John C, and Tim Elmore (Ed) (2007). *The Maxwell Leadership Bible* (Revised and Updated). Nashville: Thomas Nelson.

McCoy, Jonni (2009). *Miserly Moms: Living Well on Less in a Tough Economy*. Minneapolis, MN: Bethany House.

Munroe, Myles (2005). *The Spirit of Leadership*. New Kensington, PA: Whitaker House.

Munroe, Myles (2010). *Rediscovering the Kingdom: Ancient Hope for Our 21st Century World.* Shippensburg, PA: Destiny Image Publishers, Inc.

Myra, Harold, and Marshall Shelley (2005). *The Leadership Secrets of Billy Graham.* Grand Rapids MI: Zondervan.

NIV Stewardship Study Bible (2010). Grand Rapids, Mi: Stewardship Council.

Peterson, Jordan B (2018). *12 Rules For Life: An Antidote To Chaos.* Canada: Random House.

Piper, John (2007). *Don't Waste Your Life*. Wheaton IL: Crossway Books

Ramsey, Dave (1999). *MoreThan Enough.* New York: Viking Penguin.

Ramsey, Dave (2007). *The Total Money Makeover: A Proven Plan For Financial Fitness.* Nashville, TN: Thomas Nelson.

Richards, Jay W (2009). *Money, Greed and God.* NY: Harper Collins.

Rosten, Leo (1972). *Treasure of Jewish Quotations.* NY: McGraw Hill.

Djulman, Mard, Ed (2007). *The Wicked Wit of Benjamin Franklin.* NY: Gramercy Books.

Tawney, R.H (1926). *Religion and the Rise of Capitalism.* NY: Penguin Books Inc.

Weber, Max (1958). *Protestant Ethic and the Spirit of Capitalism.* NY: Charles Scribner's Sons.

Wilde, Paul and Carolyn (2006). *Seven principles of Financial Freedom and Peace of Mind*. Minneapolis, MN: River City Press, Inc.

www.success.com

Yang, Hong Y (1995). *A Passion for Christ: Personal Spiritual Revival in the Last Days*. Cleveland Tn: Pathway Press.

Yang, Hong Y (2000). *Authority to Overcome: Soaring High on Eagle's Wings.* Cleveland Tn: Pathway Press.

Yang, Hong Y (2013). *Life Lessons: Effective Strategies for Winning the Victories.* Cleveland TN: Derek Press.